'A
si
be

T
R
da
pe
so
cr
so

T
th
th

•
•
•

Li
in

M
ve
D
ar

European Culture and Society

General Editor: Jeremy Black

Published

European Culture and Society Series
Series Standing Order
ISBN 0–333–74440–3
(*outside North America only*)

You can receive future titles in this series as they are published by placing a standing order. Please contact your bookseller or, in case of difficulty, write to us at the address below with your name and address, the title of the series and the ISBN quoted above.

Customer Services Department, Macmillan Distribution Ltd
Houndmills, Basingstoke, Hampshire RG21 6XS, England

POLITICAL THOUGHT IN THE AGE OF REVOLUTION 1776–1848

BURKE TO MARX

Michael Levin

First published 2011 by
PALGRAVE MACMILLAN

Palgrave Macmillan in the UK is an imprint of Macmillan Publishers Limited, registered in England, company number 785998, of Houndmills, Basingstoke, Hampshire RG21 6XS.

Palgrave Macmillan in the US is a division of St Martin's Press LLC, 175 Fifth Avenue, New York, NY 10010.

Palgrave Macmillan is the global academic imprint of the above companies and has companies and representatives throughout the world.

Palgrave® and Macmillan® are registered trademarks in the United States, the United Kingdom, Europe and other countries.

ISBN 978–0–230–27210–1 hardback
ISBN 978–0–230–27211–8 paperback

This book is printed on paper suitable for recycling and made from fully managed and sustained forest sources. Logging, pulping and manufacturing processes are expected to conform to the environmental regulations of the country of origin.

A catalogue record for this book is available from the British Library.

A catalog record for this book is available from the Library of Congress.

10   9   8   7   6   5   4   3   2   1
20 19 18 17 16 15 14 13 12 11

Printed in China

It is an age of Revolutions, in which everything may be looked for.

Thomas Paine.

Whatever happens, every individual is the child of his time: so philosophy too is its own time apprehended in thoughts.

G.W.F. Hegel.

Contents

Preface

The years from 1776 to 1848 saw fundamental shifts from the politics of the court to that of the masses and from autocracy to emerging democracy. It is a key period in what may be termed 'modernity', the main components of which we shall discuss in Chapter 2. Unsurprisingly, these years of revolution, stress and transition produced some fundamental reflections on politics and society. In this relatively brief period, we have an extremely rich cluster of some of the most significant thinkers in the whole long history of social and political thought. It is their ideas that we shall be examining in this book. These thinkers all engaged theoretically and, in some instances, practically with the great revolutionary events of their time, and produced some of the classic accounts of revolution and social change[1]. We start with Edmund Burke who was one of the main defenders of the American colonies in their dispute with the British Crown and also the most influential critic of the French Revolution. As a British Member of Parliament, he did his utmost to influence government policy on these events. He also, like Jeremy Bentham, gave practical help to refugees fleeing revolutionary France. Thomas Paine was the most significant advocate of American independence, took part in the revolutionary struggle there and later both defended the French Revolution from Burke's attacks and became a deputy in the French parliament, where, at great risk to himself, he pleaded, in vain, for the life of King Louis XVI. Jeremy Bentham was a critic of traditional law and wanted legal systems rationalised. The revolutions seemed to provide just the opportunities that he wanted, though, to his great regret, his recommendations were not followed. Bentham was, though, made an honorary citizen of revolutionary France, as was Thomas Paine. Georg Hegel recognised that the French Revolution was the outcome of recent developments in thinking but rejected the ways in which such ideas were implemented, for liberal individualism seemed to neglect the need for community and social coherence. Alexis de Tocqueville came from a family of victims of the French Revolution. He studied the American political system to discern the extent to which democracy could be kept compatible with freedom. He also wrote a classic eyewitness account of the 1848 French Revolution, after which, for a short period, he became French foreign minister. Karl Marx and Friedrich Engels did not write in any detail on the 1789 revolution, yet it was a fundamental influence on their thinking, for it provided their model of how one class overthrows and succeeds another, in consequence of which one socio-economic structure is replaced by another. Engels played a minor military role in the German revolution of 1848–9, the failures of which he and Marx eventually attributed to the relatively undeveloped state of the industrial proletariat.

With Burke, Hegel and Tocqueville, we find a critical attitude to modernity, perhaps centrally on account of its destruction of community. Our four radical critics of the old order do so on quite different bases: Paine on lack of rights; Bentham on lack of happiness; and Marx and Engels on class exploitation. However, too simple and apparently clear-cut divisions between conservatives and radicals neglect their significant affinities. For example, Burke noted the rise of a new class to power, Hegel criticised the irrationality of many traditional procedures, and Tocqueville outlined the injustices of the old regime in France.

Though this work draws on some of my previous writings, it has principally been a product of my retirement. This has made it a great pleasure as it has been completed away from the pressures of recent academic life. I worked on it merely when I felt so inclined. Since ending my teaching career, my main official link with the university world has been as a convenor of the Seminar in the History of Political Ideas at the Institute of Historical Research, London University. I'm grateful to my fellow convenors and other members of the seminar for providing such a congenial and stimulating forum for the discussion of political ideas. Fellow Convenor Gregory Claeys read the Burke and Paine chapters and kept me writing by the simple expedient of frequently asking how I was getting on with it. I am very grateful to him, and also to David McLellan for helpful comments on the Marx and Engels chapter.

Thanks also to Sonya Barker, my editor at Palgrave Macmillan, for always being positive. Finally I'd like to say that my basic intention has been to write an introductory account that is intelligible to undergraduate students taking courses in the history of political thought.

Chronology

1780.	Burke becomes MP for Malton.
1781.	Kant, *Critique of Pure Reason*.
	October. British surrender at Yorktown.
1782.	March. Burke becomes Paymaster-General.
	June. Burke resigns from Shelburne administration.
1783.	Feb.–Dec. Burke became Paymaster-General again.
1787.	United States Constitution ratified.
1788.	Attempted impeachment of Warren Hastings begins in the House of Lords.
	Kant, *Critique of Practical Reason*.
	Paine returns to England.
1788–93.	Hegel studies theology at the University of Tübingen.
1789.	May. States-General meets.
	June. French National Assembly established.
	July 14. Fall of the Bastille.
	Aug. 4–11. French decrees abolishing feudal rights.
	Nov. Richard Price defends French Revolution.
	Bentham, *Introduction to the Principles of Morals and Legislation*.
1789–90.	Paine in France.
1790.	Nov. Burke, *Reflections on the Revolution in France*.
1791.	Feb. Paine, *Rights of Man*, part one.
	June. Flight to Varennes of French royal family.
	Aug. Burke, 'Appeal from the New to the Old Whigs'.
1792.	Feb. Paine, *Rights of Man*, part two.
	June. Paine charged with sedition in London.
	Aug. Louis XIV deposed.
	September. French monarchy abolished.
	Paine escapes to France and represents Calais in the French Convention.
	Bentham made an honorary citizen of France.
	Dec. Paine's trial *in absentia* for seditious libel.
1793.	Jan. Execution of Louis XVI.
	Dec. Paine arrested and held in Luxemburg prison, Paris.
1793–1800.	Hegel employed as a tutor in Berne and then in Frankfurt.

1794.	Jan. Paine, *Age of Reason*, part one.
	July. Fall of Robespierre.
	Nov. Paine released from prison.
1795.	Kant, *Eternal Peace*.
	Paine readmitted to French Convention.
1796.	Paine, *Age of Reason*, part two.
1797.	July 9. Death of Burke.
	Paine, *Agrarian Justice*.
1801–7.	Hegel teaches Philosophy at the University of Jena.
1802.	Oct. Paine returns to the United States.
1804.	Napoleon crowned Emperor of France.
1805.	July 29. Birth of Alexis de Tocqueville.
1807.	British slave trade abolished.
	Hegel edits a newspaper in Bamberg.
1808.	Fichte, *Addresses to the German Nation*.
	Hegel becomes principal of a secondary school in Nürnberg.
1809.	Bentham met James Mill.
	June 8. Death of Paine.
1813.	Robert Owen, *A New View of Society*.
1815.	June 18. Battle of Waterloo.
1816–18.	Hegel teaches philosophy at the University of Heidelberg.
1818.	May 5. Birth of Karl Marx.
1818–31.	Hegel teaches philosophy at the University of Berlin.
1819.	Bentham's 'Radical Reform Bill' published.
1820.	Nov. 28. Birth of Friedrich Engels.
1821.	Hegel, *Philosophy of Right*.
1822–3.	Hegel first gave his lectures on what became *The Philosophy of History*.
1830.	July 26–30. Revolution in France.
	Riots in Germany.
	Belgium won independence from Holland.
	Polish uprising suppressed.
1831.	Nov. 14. Hegel dies of cholera.
	May 1831–Feb. 1832. Tocqueville travels to the United States of America with Gustave de Beaumont.
1832.	British first parliamentary Reform Act.
	Death of Bentham.

1833.	Slavery abolished in British colonial possessions.
1835.	Tocqueville, *Democracy in America*, vol. 1.
1835–7.	Engels in high school in Elberfeld.
1838.	July. Engels's first visit to England.
1839.	Feb. First Chartist Convention met in London.
	Tocqueville elected to French Chamber of Deputies.
1840.	Feb. German Workers' Educational Society founded in London.
	Tocqueville, *Democracy in America*, vol. 2.
1841.	Tocqueville elected to the French Academy
1841–2.	Engels's military service in Berlin.
1842.	Oct. Engels met Moses Hess and became a communist.
	Nov. First meeting between Marx and Engels.
1843.	Marx, 'Critique of Hegel's Philosophy of Right'.
	Marx, 'On the Jewish Question'.
1844.	Marx, *Economic and Philosophic Manuscripts*.
1845.	June. Engels, *The Condition of the Working Class in England*.
1846.	Marx and Engels, *The German Ideology*.
1848.	Feb. Marx and Engels, *Manifesto of the Communist Party*. Revolution in Paris.
	March. Revolution in Vienna, Budapest, Berlin, Milan, Venice.
	April. Chartist demonstration on Kennington Common.
	Tocqueville elected to the French Constituent Assembly.
	May. Frankfurt parliament opens.
	Dec. 10. Louis Napoleon elected President of the French Republic.
1849.	April–May. Collapse of Frankfurt parliament.
	May. Tocqueville elected to the Legislative Assembly.
	June–October. Tocqueville serves as French Minister of Foreign Affairs.
1850.	Marx, 'The Class Struggles in France 1848 to 1850'.
	Nov. Engels moves to Manchester to work for Ermen and Engels.
1851.	Dec. Tocqueville arrested after opposing coup d'état of Louis Napoleon. Imprisoned for 1 day.
1852.	Marx, 'The Eighteenth Brumaire of Louis Bonaparte'.
1856.	Tocqueville, *The Old Régime and the French Revolution*.

1

The Historical Context

In one of the best-known social history books of the last century, Eric Hobsbawm famously designated *The Age of Revolution*.[1] For him, it was the period between the French revolutions of 1789 and 1848, which he describes as witnessing 'the greatest transformation in human history since the remote times when men invented agriculture and metallurgy, writing, the city and the state'. His subject was not merely France, but 'the transformation of the world' caused by both the French Revolution and the 'contemporaneous [British] industrial revolution'.[2] In the same vein, Jay Winik has more recently described the late eighteenth century as 'the age that gave birth to the modern world. It is also arguably one of the most significant eras in all of human history.'[3]

The Atlantic Revolution 1776 and 1789

'The French Revolution has been regarded by subsequent generations as the emergence of the modern political world. It comprised a paradigm shift that irrevocably changed the way in which we think.'[4] To some, the revolution seemed like a thunderbolt that dropped unannounced out of a clear blue sky. Though it had no precedent in French history, it did have its antecedent causes. The state, for example, was in severe financial difficulties. The wealthiest citizens were exempt from taxation, and both state regulation and internal customs barriers curtailed the development of trade and industry. The Treasury was burdened both by its own cumbersome organisation and by a few decades of unsuccessful imperial competition with Great Britain, losing out to Robert Clive in India and General Wolfe in Quebec, though gaining some vicarious, though not financial, compensation through entering the War of American Independence on the rebel colonists' side.

In medieval Europe, it was common for monarchs only to summon councils or parliaments when they were in financial difficulties. Consequently, in August 1788 Louis XVI requested the Estates-General to meet the following year. It had last convened in 1614, so there was understandable uncertainty concerning some of the procedures. That it contained three houses – the clergy, the nobility and the Third Estate – was beyond dispute. What now proved contentious was whether to accept the old pattern of voting by Estate, in which case the two privileged orders of aristocracy and clergy could always outvote the Third Estate by two to one. The king had wanted the old traditions followed, but he gave way to pressure from the Third Estate in allowing them to double their traditional number of deputies to 600, leaving the other two Estates with 300 deputies each. So, unwittingly or otherwise, he conceded the principle that was soon to undermine the old regime that numbers were to be granted political weight.

The unresolved problem of whether the Estates should vote separately or together was pre-empted on 17 June 1789 when the Third Estate, by 491 votes to 89, proclaimed itself a National Assembly and called upon members of the other two Estates to join it in reforming France. The consequences of this decision were to seal the fate of the old regime, for in that change of terminology is encapsulated a key polarity between medieval and modern understandings of politics.

The transition from reform to revolution occurred less than a month later, when the old fortress of the Bastille was stormed on 14 July. This event, more symbolic than substantial, has remained the most iconic and famous moment of the revolution. Then on the night of 4–5 August, the aristocracy renounced most of their privileges. Feudal dues, noble status and even the system of Estates were all swept away. Massive and long-entrenched inequalities had been removed. The new presuppositions found expression in the Declaration of the Rights of Man and of the Citizen, decreed by the National Assembly on 26 August and 'modelled mainly on the manifestos set out by the Americans some years earlier'.[5] Among its pronouncements was the belief that 'Nature has made all men free and equal', that 'No man should suffer for his religious beliefs', and that 'Freedom of the press is the strongest support of public freedom.'

Until 1791, it had seemed that France might establish a constitutional monarchy on the British pattern. This hope evaporated with the King's flight to Varennes, his failed attempt to escape over France's eastern border. The Jacobin Republic with its 'reign of terror' followed in 1792–4. War was declared against Austria in 1792, the beginnings of the military export of the revolution to much of the European continent. This tendency was much strengthened when, in 1799, the head of the army became the ruler of the country. Napoleon Bonaparte soon made France the leading European power. In 1804, he crowned himself King of France. In the following years, he looked after his brothers, appointing Jerome as King of Westphalia, Louis as King of Holland, Joseph as King of Naples and Spain and keeping for himself the Kingdom of Italy. By 1812, the borders of France had extended enormously, to the north-east as far as Bremen and Hamburg and to the south-east to include Florence and Rome.

The year 1789, then, has its prominent placing because of the remarkable political events in France during that year and their consequences for large parts of the European continent. There is, however, more to it than that. It was also the year in which the American Constitution of 1787 was put into effect and in which George Washington became the country's first President. The US Constitution represented, just as much as the French Revolution, a sharp break with previously dominant political assumptions. It was an explicit documentation of the political system, quite novel then for a whole state, but the forerunner of what later became normal. Unlike everywhere else at the time, the Constitution allowed for no hereditary positions, claimed no theological basis and had no state religion or privileges for the church. The head of state, an elected President, was to be subject to law rather than, as under absolute monarchies, his (or, occasionally, her) word being law.

As the US Constitution was a consequence of their revolution of 1776, our age of revolution must begin a little earlier than Hobsbawm's. In 1776, the 13 North American colonies withdrew from the British Empire by asserting their independence. This seemed a lesser revolution than that in France 13 years later. The French overthrew an indigenous ruling class. Theirs was a truly social revolution that was then spread by conquest around much of the rest of Europe. The North Americans, by contrast, despatched their external rulers back to their home country. Theirs was the first major anti-colonial revolution, which produced what has been termed 'the first new nation',[6] but still the American Revolution had more modest aims than that of France. As Martin Malia has pointed out, the 'American colonists intended revolution according to the older sense of the word, that is a "restoration" of their historic rights as Englishmen', as had allegedly happened with England's so-called Glorious Revolution of 1688. However, 'when they got through, they had created a new nation and a republic, an outcome that was obviously "revolutionary" in the modern sense of post-Old Regime.'[7] It is also worth mentioning that the transfer of the Presidency from George Washington to John Adams in 1797 is the first example in modern times of an *elected* head of state peacefully transferring power to his successor. Already in 1776 Thomas Paine referred to the American colonies as 'This new world' which 'hath been the asylum for the persecuted lovers of civil and religious liberty from *every part* of Europe'.[8] The United States of America, then, from the beginning, achieved levels of freedom and equality of opportunity, key aspects of modernity, which contrasted substantially with the absolutist oppression from which parts of Europe were also gradually escaping. (Fuller presentation of the events of the American Revolution is given in Chapter 2, Section 2, on Edmund Burke and Chapter 3, Section 2, on Thomas Paine.)

The idea that these two separate and, in many ways, quite distinct revolutions were somehow linked was not uncommon at that time. Thomas Paine was among those who believed that the message of liberty was brought to France by those of her soldiers who had previously fought against the British in North America. When the American colonists' war with Britain ended, he believed that 'a vast reinforcement to the cause of Liberty spread itself over France, by the return of the French officers and soldiers. A knowledge of the practice was then joined to the theory; and all that was wanting to give it real existence, was opportunity.'[9] Paine's notion that France was previously acquainted with radical ideas was confirmed by one of the unlikely and remarkable survivors of the French Revolution, Bishop Talleyrand, who recalled that after 1776 'We talked of nothing but America.'[10] The Marquis de Condorcet, who was later to play a prominent role in the French Revolution, had for some years previously been closely following American affairs. In 1786, he declared it not sufficient that natural rights

> should be written in the books of philosophers and in the hearts of virtuous men; it is essential that the ignorant and weak should read them in the example of a great people. America has given us this example. The act by which she declared her independence is an exposition, simple and sublime, of rights that have been sacred, though long forgotten.[11]

Later the French aristocrat Alexis de Tocqueville noted that to 'the rest of Europe the American Revolution seemed merely a novel and remarkable historical event; whereas the French saw in it a brilliant confirmation of theories already familiar to them'.[12] The link, however, is more than ideological. It is also economic, in that French assistance to the American colonists' cause greatly exacerbated the financial crisis from which their own revolution emerged.

In twentieth-century scholarship, the idea of the Atlantic Revolution was most associated with the Frenchman Jacques Godechot and the American R.R. Palmer. In *France and the Atlantic Revolution of the Eighteenth Century*, Godechot asserted that the 'revolutionary movement began in 1768 in the republic of Geneva' and included uprisings in Russia, Ireland, Holland, Belgium as well as the 1780 Gordon Riots in London and, obviously, the American and French revolutions. In his view, all these disorders between 1770 and 1800 'actually belonged to a single great movement and formed a single Atlantic Revolution'.[13] R.R. Palmer agreed that 'All of these agitations, upheavals, intrigues, and conspiracies were part of one great movement ... There was one big revolutionary agitation.'[14]

These two revolutions indicated that the long age of court politics was coming to an end; that of mass politics was commencing. In the nineteenth century, the American and French revolutions were often regarded as contrasting examples of democracy in action; its controlled and constitutional face in North America and its violent, arbitrary aspect in France. By the twentieth century, such terminology needed modifying. Neither revolution had been democratic in terms of granting the vote to all men, let alone any or all women. Clearly, however, the revolutions had significantly moved their countries in a more democratic direction.

The Industrial Revolution

The other basic aspect of this transition was the Industrial Revolution. A still extant early marker of this is the world's first cast-iron bridge, built in Coalbrookdale in Staffordshire in 1779. This fact might be reasonably well known to children in the English Midlands, who enjoy school outings there, but on the whole, the bridge is less famous than it deserves to be. It survives as a monument to a process that transformed the globe and so should, at least, rank with Nelson's Column and the Houses of Parliament as a symbol of national achievement; that it doesn't indicates the relatively low status of science and technology in British culture. The iron bridge, then, represents a development that began in Britain and spread around the globe; among other things, it involved a fundamental shift from agriculture to industry and so from rural to urban life.

James Watt's crucial improvement of Thomas Newcomen's steam engine occurred just 10 years earlier, in 1769. Around the same time, the textile industry was transformed by the invention of James Hargreaves's spinning-jenny (1767), Richard Arkwright's spinning frame (1768) and Samuel Crompton's spinning-mule (1779). The cotton industry thus set the example in moving production from the home to the factory. It was 'the first industry to be revolutionized'.[15] These were more than just changes in the nature of production. Human life itself was transformed. The seemingly permanent old world of landed estates and small market towns cocooned in their own local affairs, largely self-governing and relatively self-sufficient, gave way to the enormous industrial conurbations created by the rise of textiles, coal mining and iron and steel production. The development of industry transformed the social structure of society. Rising commercial wealth challenged the preponderance of landed, aristocratic power. The new rich were complemented by a new poor. As the number of agricultural labourers declined, the number of a new urban working class increased.[16]

It is well-known that France had its surfeit of political changes; that Napoleon fell in 1815; that monarchy was restored under Louis XVIII; that Charles X abdicated after the revolution of 1830 and that Louis-Philippe abdicated after the February 1848 Revolution and was replaced by Louis Napoleon Bonaparte. Less attention has been given to its concurrent socio-economic changes, presumably because they were both less singular and less dramatic. They were, however, substantial. Between 1815 and 1850, French coal output went up from 0.9 to 4.4 million metric tons, while between 1835 and 1850, iron ore production more than doubled. In the public mind, Manchester was the symbolic city of the new industrial world. However, by the 1830s, Lyons was already a major textile centre, and according to one historian, 'Paris in 1848 was the world's greatest manufacturing city, with more than 400,000 industrial workers of all kinds.'[17]

We shall later witness the frustrations of both Hegel (Chapter 6) and Marx and Engels (Chapter 8) concerning German backwardness. Although there was large-scale textile manufacture at the beginning of the nineteenth century, general commercial development had long been hindered by the extraordinary mishmash of small, independent principalities, ecclesiastical states and 'free towns', each with their own customs barriers. Germany was helped into the modern world less by its own indigenous forces than as a result of Napoleonic conquest. French armies defeated both Austria (Austerlitz, 1805) and Prussia (Jena and Auerstädt, 1806), and the misnamed Holy Roman Empire collapsed in 1806. A year later Prussia abolished serfdom and also removed the traditional limitations on the sale of land. Then in 1811, the obligation of craftsmen to belong to a guild was abolished. A key factor for German economic development was the 1834 introduction of a customs union, the *Zollverein*, which by 1836 united 25 states with 26 million inhabitants. Within a few years, coal mining had begun in the Ruhr district, Krupp had installed the firm's first steam engine and Germany's first railway line was opened, a mere 7 kilometres between Nuremburg and Fürth. By 1850, this total had increased to 5856 kilometres. The railways were mostly state owned, a stark contrast to the situation in Britain. It was, of course, only some decades later that an eventually united Germany becoming a major industrial power, yet significant developments are already evident in our period. For example, between 1815 and 1850, German coal and iron ore output both increased over four times.

The development of commerce and industry everywhere occasioned a lively debate between rural and urban interests. In America, in 1787, Thomas Jefferson decided that 'our governments will remain virtuous for many centuries as long as they are chiefly agricultural.'[18] However the future lay more with Alexander

Hamilton, who in 1791 produced a Report on Manufactures which envisaged an industrial future for the country and called for government protection of emergent industries. This occurred in rather severe form when the Embargo of 1807 forbade all trade between the United States and any other country. Unsurprisingly, it was abandoned in 1809, though domestic manufacturing was stimulated by the British blockade during the war of 1812 and the protective tariffs that followed it. Early industrialism centred on the states of Massachusetts and New York, although it was Philadelphia in the 1820s which witnessed the emergence of trade unionism and a workers' political party. As with other countries, our period provided merely the early developments of a process that only achieved dominance decades later, yet enough had already occurred by 1840 for Alexis de Tocqueville to warn of an American 'manufacturing aristocracy'.[19] The 1840s were in fact a key decade of transition for the massive extension of the railways that provided the basic infrastructure on which the further development of trade and industry depended.

Throughout our period, a quite distinctive feature of the United States of America was that it contained two very different socio-economic forms: a developing capitalist economy in the north and a slave economy in the cotton-growing south. In terms of economics, Barrington Moore Jr. once argued that the two systems could in fact coexist: 'Plantation slavery in the South . . . was not an economic fetter upon industrial capitalism. If anything the reverse may have been true; it helped to promote American industrial growth in the earlier stages,'[20] for most of the cotton produced in the south was sold to the north and most of the cotton exports left from New York.

The 1830 Revolutions

The 1830 Revolution in Paris was triggered by the last, and fatal, attempt by a French monarch to act in the authoritarian manner of his forbears. In July of that year, King Charles X rejected the verdict of the electorate and dissolved the Chamber of Deputies that they had just established, this in a period of severe economic recession and disillusion with governments in which the increasing power of the church was widely resented. Three days of severe rioting ensued, in which around 2000 people were killed. This proved enough to force the abdication of France's last Bourbon monarch, and his replacement by Louis-Philippe, who turned out to be not only France's last Orleanist monarch but also France's last monarch as such.

These events were closely followed elsewhere and so, not for the last time, a French revolution stimulated uprisings in other countries. In Germany, riots in Brunswick, Saxony, Hannover and Hessen led to the writing of new constitutions. In the same year Belgium won its independence from Holland, there was civil war in Spain and Portugal, and an uprising was crushed in Russian Poland by the Russians aided by Austria and Prussia, precisely those powers that had partitioned Poland between them in 1795. Mike Rapport notes that 'In the retribution that followed, a staggering eighty-thousand Poles were dragged off in chains to Siberia.'[21]

We have outlined what Hobsbawm called the 'dual revolution',[22] political in France and industrial in the United Kingdom. These designations outline the most prominent aspect of the transformation in each country, but simplify in terms of the totality of change, for, over our period, Britain was strongly affected by the fear of political revolution and France by the reality of industrial change. In the eighteenth century, Britain had a reputation for being wild and insurrectionary. It had, in the previous century, executed its king. Then in the 1780 Gordon Riots, about a hundred London houses were destroyed in 'the largest, deadliest and most protracted urban riots in British history'.[23] Over our whole period, British politics was played out against a fear of political revolution. We shall see, for example, how seriously Edmund Burke (Chapter 3) in the 1790s took the threat from the small groupings who had welcomed the French Revolution, and how Friedrich Engels (Chapter 8) in the 1840s imagined and hoped that the Chartist movement would be part of a justly merited British revolution. In Britain, repression of free opinion continued not just during the revolutionary and Napoleonic wars but afterwards, most notably with the Six Acts of 1820 which followed the 'Peterloo' demonstration and massacre of the previous year.[24] Then in 1831, 1 year after another revolution in France, Lord Macaulay was clear that Britain had better legislate for moderate change lest something much worse prevail. His great speech to the House of Commons on the 2 March closed with the following warning: 'The danger is terrible. The time is short. If this [parliamentary reform] bill should be rejected, I pray to God that none of those who concur in rejecting it may ever remember their votes with unavailing remorse, amidst the wreck of laws, the confusion of ranks, the spoliation of property, and the dissolution of social order.'[25] Some later historians have concurred. E.P. Thompson, for example, believed that at that time Britain was 'within an ace of revolution'.[26]

The 1848 Revolutions

The revolutions of 1848 were the culmination of a decade of hardship and discontent in many European countries: of bad harvests, rising food prices, increased unemployment and commercial instability. Large industrial cities were growing with a rapidity unmatched by the development of welfare and health arrangements. Signs of discontent were there for all to see: bread riots in German cities, Chartism in England and beggars roaming the countryside in France. What of Paris, the acknowledged home of revolution? Isaiah Berlin once remarked that 'In the 1840s Paris is full of revolutionaries – Bakunin, Marx, Herzen, Louis Blanc, Proudhon, Dézamy, Blanqui, Leroux, George Sand's other socialist friends – Saint-Simonians, Fourierists, Socialists, Communists, anarchists.'[27] They did not have long to wait, though whether they would be happy with the outcome is quite another matter.

The most famous revolutionary tract of all is, of course, the *Communist Manifesto* by Karl Marx and Friedrich Engels. It so happened that it was published in an appropriately revolutionary month, February 1848, but the uprisings commenced not in Germany, where Marx had directed his attention, nor in England, which Engels had placed at the forefront of development. In the year of revolution, Italy, unmentioned in the *Manifesto*, was first off the mark with an insurrection in Palermo in January, followed by others in Turin, Tuscany and Lombardy in the following month. Rome declared itself an independent republic. In Venice, Austrian rule was overthrown and a republic proclaimed. Sicily and Naples rose up against the Bourbon monarch, Ferdinand II.

Of more significance for the continent was the Paris Revolution which commenced on 22 February and forced the abdication of King Louis Philippe. This was the event that scared monarchs the most throughout Europe, for 1789 was on the minds of reactionaries and radicals alike. The left-wing provisional French government gave the vote to all men over the age of 21, thus increasing the electorate from about a quarter of a million to nine million. Elections in April did not give the revolutionaries what they wanted, as a largely peasant electorate chose a conservative assembly. In June, over 1,500 people died when a workers' uprising was crushed by General Cavaignac's troops. In December, Louis Bonaparte was elected President for a 4-year term, which he overcame by a coup in December 1851. As before, a revolutionary period came to an end with a Napoleon in power.

In Germany, in 1848, there were riots in Berlin, Düsseldorf, Frankfurt, Aachen and Cologne. Much against his natural inclinations, Frederick William IV of Prussia was forced to appoint a liberal ministry. At the end of March, a preliminary parliament met in the Frankfurt *Paulskirche* to establish a German national assembly, but it was powerless without an army and soon collapsed. In Austria, Metternich was forced out of office and in Hungary the Habsburgs were dethroned and a republic was introduced. The Russian army put down the revolution in Hungary and played a major part in suppressing the Polish uprising in the Prussian Duchy of Posen.

The events of 1848 in France, as with 1789, raised the fear of imitation on the British side of the Channel, especially so given the context of Chartist agitation and a supposedly disaffected Irish minority in the major cities. Queen Victoria clearly lost confidence in the security of her position and implicitly, therefore, in the constitutional structure of the country, for in July 1848, she wrote to her uncle Leopold, the King of the Belgians, that 'Since the 24th of February I feel an uncertainty in everything existing, which ... one never felt before. When one thinks of one's children, their education, their future – and prays for them – I always think and say to myself "Let them grow up fit for *whatever station* they may be placed in – *high or low*." This one never thought of before, but I *do* always now.'[28] According to one influential historian of ideas: 'For all its solid and imposing strength, Victorian society, particularly in the period before 1850, was shot through, from top to bottom, with the dread of some wild outbreak of the masses that would overthrow the established order and confiscate property.'[29]

So, there was much fear of the revolutionary contagion and more indigenous riots and uprisings across the continent than at any time before or since. Yet, ultimately, it did not amount to as much as the most radical hoped and the most reactionary feared. In most cases, the oppositional forces were too divided to produce unanimous aims and too weak to achieve significant change. Lewis Namier entitled one of the best-known books on the subject as *1848: The Revolution of the Intellectuals*.[30] This designation applies most prominently to the Frankfurt parliament, which was one of his main interests, but also indicates the middle-class social base of those who tried to channel what were significantly working-class uprisings into middle-class constitutionalism. When it came to the crunch, the middle class preferred order to the threat of further chaos and so sought to compromise with the conservative forces that, not much earlier, had been their sworn enemy. So none of the new republics survived except that of France, and there, it was replaced by an authoritarian Emperor. This all seems like scant return for the radical impulse and effort, yet, according to Norman Davies:

> before long 1848 came to be seen as a watershed in Europe's affairs. The reactionary regimes had triumphed but only at such heavy cost that they could not bear a repeat performance. Constitutions that had been granted, imposed, and in some cases withdrawn were gradually reintroduced or widened... With some delay, monarchs realized that wise concessions to popular demands were preferable to endless repression. The basic liberal principle of government by consent steadily gained widespread acceptance.[31]

Mike Rapport has reminded us of another important aspect, the move towards equal citizenship rights: 'The events of 1848 gave millions of Europeans their first taste of politics: workers and peasants voted in elections and even stood for and entered parliament.' Of immense significance across vast swathes of eastern and central Europe was 'the abolition of serfdom, of the compulsory labour services and dues enforced against the peasantry'.[32]

There had, according to one estimate, been around 50 revolutions across Europe in 1848 and 1849.[33] The 1789 revolution had become European in scope because French revolutionary armies conquered much of the continent and tried to impose their favoured type of political and economic system; that of 1848, however, was European not through conquest but by ideological contagion. Martin Malia has called it the 'first – and only – case of all-European revolution'.[34]

What, meanwhile, of the country that in 1776 commenced our age of revolution? In 1848, the United States of America was the country where labour, in the form of slavery, was less free than anywhere in central and Western Europe. It was also more numerous than in the previous century, for the slave population had increased from 700,000 in 1790 to 3,200,000 in 1850. Yet even so in the United States, the franchise extended lower down the social scale than in most of Europe,[35] and the first stirrings of organised feminism had been made with the Seneca Falls Declaration of 1848. There was also slavery in Brazil while serfdom, which could sometimes come near to being the same thing, still existed in Russia.[36]

One view of the major political theory texts is that any difficulties of understanding can be resolved by simply reading them again and thinking more deeply. I have no objections to re-readings or to deeper thinking, but also believe that a text is illuminated by its context. All writers on politics, and even political theorists, however abstract their work may seem, are reacting, and so contributing, to the events of their times. One understands them better if one bears that in mind. For that reason, this chapter constitutes an attempt to overview the period with which this book is concerned. The following chapter moves to the period of our starting point in the late eighteenth century.

2
Modern Society and Modern Thought

Modernity

In his classic work on the outbreak of the French Revolution, the French aristocrat Alexis de Tocqueville wrote of 'the belief that what was wanted was to replace the complex of traditional customs governing the social order of the day by simple, elementary rules deriving from the exercise of reason and natural law.'[1] This transformation encapsulates much of the political aspect of modernisation. In medieval societies, the social order was taken as static and God-ordained. It could be presumed that the life of one's grandchildren would be much the same as that of one's grandparents. Hierarchies seemed immutable. Their gradations were steep and distinct. The aristocracy were unlikely to have considered their peasantry as belonging to the same people as themselves; in some instances, they did not even speak the same language. Jurisdiction was less standardised. Certain provinces, cities and religious authorities had their own particular rights and privileges. In time, these were mostly swept away by the rise of central state power.

The period with which we are concerned, then, witnessed a massive challenge to traditional attitudes and the hierarchies that benefited from them. A succinct expression of this can be found in the Preamble to the French Constitution of 1791:

Nobility no longer exists, nor peerage, nor hereditary distinction of orders, nor feudal regime, nor patrimonial courts, nor tithes, denominations or prerogatives deriving therefrom, nor any order of chivalry... Property in office, and its inheritance, no longer exist.[2]

Monarchy is merely the upper echelon of nobility, operating on the same principle of hereditary privilege. It too came under attack, dispensed with in America and France and, consequently, more insecure elsewhere. In 1791, Thomas Paine noted that 'If I ask a man in America, if he wants a King? he retorts, and asks me if I take him for an idiot?'[3] While monarchy and aristocracy were reduced, the people, however defined, were elevated. Subjects were reclassified as citizens and granted what were called the rights of man, since renamed as human rights, and now a significant principle in world politics.

Concurrent with decisive shifts in political power, fundamental socio-economic changes were also occurring. We have noted the rise of industrial society but must also mention the change from feudal to capitalist methods of production and management. Writing on France but perhaps with Britain also in mind, Edmund Burke famously declared that the 'age of chivalry is gone. That of sophisters, economists and calculators has succeeded, and the glory of Europe is extinguished for ever.'[4] His contemporary, the anarchist William Godwin, made a similar point, but less emotionally: 'I perceived that we were grown a commercial and arithmetical nation... Contractors, directors, and upstarts – men fattened on the vitals of their fellow citizens – have taken the place which was once filled by the Wentworths, the Seldens, and the Pyms.'[5] Wealth creation, once regarded as rather vulgar, came to provide an index of national status.

Modern society, then, may be described as capitalist, industrial and also significantly urban. The UK population in 1780 has been estimated at 12.98 million. It had almost doubled by 1831. The census of 1851 put the population at 27.39 million. Britain famously became the first country declared to be predominantly urban, although on what now seems the extremely low benchmark of 4000 people. Even so, 'No other country in the world approached such a condition until after 1900.'[6] Less well-known, but more indicative of the transformation involved, in 1851 England and Wales became the only European countries where 20 per cent of the population lived in cities of over

100,000 inhabitants. One year earlier Charles Kingsley allowed the eponymous Alton Locke to explain the advantages of this transformation:

> It is the cities, John, the cities, where the light dawns first – where man meets man, and spirit quickens spirit, and intercourse breeds knowledge, and knowledge sympathy, and sympathy enthusiasm, combination, power irresistible; while the agriculturalists remain ignorant, selfish, weak, because they are isolated from each other.[7]

Britain might have led the way in terms of population increase, but the same phenomenon was evident elsewhere. It has been estimated that between 1800 and 1850, the French population increased from 27.3 to 35.8 million and that of the Germanic states from 22 to 34 million.

Yet even before the urban mass came into existence, the modern individual was born. Tocqueville noted that the 'word "individualism"... was unknown to our ancestors, for the good reason that in their days every individual necessarily belonged to a group and no one could regard himself as an isolated unit.'[8] Modern society contains the individual who pursues his own economic advantage, self-interest and happiness, and who is questioning in relation to both political and ecclesiastic authorities. The masculine pronoun is appropriate in that female rights had scarcely been articulated let alone recognised. In terms of formal arrangements, the age of modern democracy had not yet dawned; it could, however, be clearly foreseen.

To summarise on our understanding of modernity, we can say that:

Modern society is capitalist, industrial and urban.

Modern politics is decreasingly aristocratic and moves towards becoming liberal democratic. Power shifts from hereditary monarchs to popularly elected parliaments. Written constitutions become normal for all new regimes.

The *modern state* is proportionally less military and more bureaucratic than its predecessor; more the welfare state than the warfare state.

Modern thought is relatively secular and rationalistic.

The Enlightenment

The rise of modern thought is inextricably linked to the eighteenth-century Enlightenment. Though sometimes traced back at least as far as the 1670s, it has been associated primarily with the famous French *Encyclopaedia*, edited by Denis Diderot and Jean D'Alembert in 17 volumes between 1751 and 1765. These volumes constituted not merely an enormous compendium of knowledge but, more significantly, they encouraged a rational and critical evaluation of all social mores and institutions. They were, consequently, viewed by their opponents as subversive of both states and churches. Other significant writers associated with the Enlightenment include Montesquieu, Holbach, Helvétius, Voltaire, Turgot and also Rousseau, who, confusingly, can also be linked with the counter-Enlightenment.

The immense influence of the *Encyclopaedia* is just one of the factors behind the traditional identification of the Enlightenment with France and the French *philosophes*. It was France where Voltaire and Rousseau, the most colourful and, from some points of view, notorious writers were given prestigious outlets in the salons of the aristocracy they were busy undermining. Voltaire, certainly, became a national, if not international celebrity to an extent highly unusual before our own time. With hindsight, their significance appears all the greater in that their writings were soon followed by the most dramatic revolution of modern times.

However, the too exclusive classification of the Enlightenment as French was not shared by the French writers themselves. In the mid-eighteenth century, both Montesquieu and Voltaire praised England as the land of liberty. Its foremost scientist, Isaac Newton, had in *Principia* (1687) revealed the laws of nature. Voltaire thought Newton a greater man than Caesar, Alexander, Tamburlaine or Cromwell and also that 'never, perhaps, has a wiser, more methodical mind, a more precise logician existed than Mr. Locke.'[9] John Locke had been an opponent of Stuart absolutism, and in *Two Treatises of Government* (1690), he had undermined the theory of the divine right of kings and replaced it with that of government deriving from a social contract formulated by those who would be bound by it. On some accounts, Newton and Locke are precursors or 'early Enlightenment'. In the late eighteenth century, Jeremy Bentham and Thomas Paine, both of whom were made honorary French citizens after the revolution, shared much of the Enlightenment mentality.

Scotland too played an important role; unsurprisingly, as it had long enjoyed a more inclusive educational system than England. Its foremost philosopher, David Hume, befriended Rousseau, before being denounced by him,[10] and in 1763 became secretary to the British Embassy in Paris and so, more fruitfully, made friends with Denis Diderot and Baron d'Holbach. We should also mention Adam Smith and Adam Ferguson, pioneering figures in the creation of both political economy and historical sociology. Adam Smith's *The Wealth of Nations* is probably the most famous and influential economics textbook ever written.

A recent tendency has been to stress the specific particularities of each nation's Enlightenment, but the movement was self-consciously international. Just as the aristocracies of the various countries identified more with each other than with their own lower orders and communicated with each other in French, so too did the philosophers. In Germany (which was then more a cultural than a political unit), the main figures were Christian Thomasius, Christian Wolff, Gotthold Lessing, Frederick the Great and, above all, Immanuel Kant. In Holland, the seventeenth-century philosopher Baruch Spinoza was massively important;[11] in Italy, Cesare Beccaria; in Russia, Catherine II. Perhaps, the most remarkable American figure was Benjamin Franklin – scientist, philosopher and statesman, and also a direct link between European and American developments. The American Declaration of Independence, its constitution and system of government and even the planned, geometrical layout of its capital city can all be regarded as enduring monuments to the Enlightenment mentality.

Recent scholarship has undermined long-standing categorisations about the Enlightenment, making it risky to say anything general at all. Such scholarship has suggested that we pluralise the term; enlightenments rather than enlightenment. Also, as already indicated, the chronology of the movement has been pushed backwards into the seventeenth century. Thus far we have named the dominant thinkers rather than their thoughts. One recommendation is to define 'enlightenment as an attitude of mind, rather than a coherent system of beliefs'.[12] There is certainly no catalogue of opinions to which all subscribed, but the following views and concerns have usually been associated with the movement.

The recommendation of 'Enlightenment' assumes that darkness had previously prevailed. From this perspective, inherited values no longer provided a repository of accumulated wisdom. They were seen more as superstitious encumbrances from which emancipation was needed. Authority, then, was no longer enough; tradition was no longer its own justification. In *Zadig*, Voltaire asked the inconvenient rhetorical question: 'Is there anything more respectable than an ancient abuse?'[13] Open debate and rational investigation were recommended to filter our intellectual inheritance and determine what still qualified as acceptable. The Enlightenment mentality here followed the lead of René Descartes (1591–1650) who, in his *Discourse on Method* (1637), formulated the following rigorous project:

> I could do no better than to undertake to rid myself, at least once in my life, of all the opinions I had hitherto accepted on faith, in order to replace them with better ones or to restore them to their former place, once I had brought them to the level of my reason.[14]

Another major figure of the early Enlightenment, Benedict de Spinoza, directed this approach explicitly to the sensitive issue of religion: 'I resolved in all seriousness to make a fresh examination of Scripture with a free and unprejudiced mind, and to assert nothing about it, and to accept nothing as its teaching, which I did not quite clearly derive from it.'[15] This approach was also adopted by Kant a century later:

> Our age is, in every sense of the word, the age of criticism, and everything must submit to it. Religion, on the strength of its sanctity, and law, on the strength of its majesty, try to withdraw themselves from it; but by doing so they arouse just suspicions, and cannot claim that sincere respect which reason pays to those only who have been able to stand its free and open examination.[16]

Three year later, Kant had moved from description to more explicit recommendation, declaring that for Enlightenment 'all that is needed is *freedom* ... freedom to make *public use* of one's reason in all matters',[17] a mentality that was clearly subversive of the established institutions of the old regimes.

There is a famous German folk-song, *Die Gedanken sind frei* (Thoughts are free), which dates back to the peasant wars of the sixteenth century. The song lauds the security of private thought, *innerlichkeit*, which is held to be immune from the control of state and social authorities. Kant referred to this mentality in acknowledging that 'We do admittedly say that, whereas a higher authority may deprive us of freedom of *speech* or of *writing*, it cannot deprive us of freedom of *thought*.' However, he explained that this was only a very limited victory, for freedom of thought cannot properly exist without the nourishment of actual expression.

> But how much and how accurately would we *think* if we did not think, so to speak, in community with others to whom we *communicate* our thoughts and who communicate their thoughts to us! We may therefore conclude that the same external constraint which deprives people of the freedom to *communicate* their thoughts in public also removes their freedom of *thought*, the one treasure which remains to us amidst all the burdens of civil life, and which alone offers us a means of overcoming all the evils of this condition.[18]

Thus rational enquiry, to be effective, needed an environment of tolerance and permission to develop one's ideas in whatever direction reason might lead. This is exactly what established states and religions had traditionally opposed. No wonder that both Voltaire and Diderot, like Locke before them, wrote treatises on tolerance. They were, to put it at its most self-interested, trying to secure their own working conditions. And with good reason. In 1717–18, Voltaire had been imprisoned in the Bastille for his satire against the Duc d'Orleans. Diderot's *Pensées Philosophiques* was burned by the Parliament of Paris in 1746, and three years later, he was imprisoned for his *Letters on the Blind*. The case for toleration seems not to have convinced the French authorities, for in 1757, the death penalty was ordered for writings critical of government and religion, although arrest was the more common penalty. Still, on 'the eve of the 1789 Revolution more than 160 censors were on Louis XVI's thought-police payroll'.[19]

On this issue Prussia, for a while, did better. In 1740, the year of his accession to the throne, Frederick II decided that 'All must be tolerated... here everyone must be allowed to choose his own road to salvation.'[20] At his invitation, Voltaire went to Berlin in 1750 and, until they fell out 3 years later, enjoyed a generous pension and lodging in one of the royal palaces.

The writer Horace Walpole, youngest son of Britain's first prime minister, reporting from France in 1765, had asked: 'Do you know who the philosophers are, or what the term means here? [It] means men, who avowing war against popery, aim, many of them, at a sub-version of all religion, and still many more, at the destruction of regal power.'[21] This certainly accords with a long dominant image of the Enlightenment, but one that now requires modification. Among those whom Walpole met was Baron D'Holbach, regarded as the first avowed atheist writer, whose *Système de la Nature* was published in 1771. D'Holbach, however, was on the extremes of theological criticism. Though atheism was much suspected, not all theological criticism was atheistic. Tzvetan Todorov has recently reminded us that the 'majority of Enlightenment thinkers identified not so much with atheism as with natural religion or deism.'[22] It was actually a ploy, honest or otherwise, to label as atheist those whose religious views differed from one's own. This was applied to non-Christians, like the Deist Thomas Paine, who held that God was discernible not in the books of men but in the products of nature.

Such beliefs clearly downgraded religious establishments. Much of the opposition was less to religion as a body of beliefs than to pow-erful church institutions. In France, the Roman Catholic Church functioned as an ideological support of the regime, an opponent of free discussion of religious issues and a major landowner. In his *Philosophical Dictionary*, Voltaire boldly declared that 'the true vam-pires are the churchmen, who eat at the expense of both kings and people.'[23] David Hume once described religion as 'a Source, which has, from uniform Prescription, acquird a Right to impose Non-sense on all Nations and all Ages...in all ages of the world, priests have been the enemy of liberty.'[24] The Roman Catholic Church hit back in a manner that proved Hume's point, for by the end of the century works by Locke, Voltaire, Diderot, Rousseau, Gibbon, Paine and Kant had all been banned by the Papal index. Roy Porter has summarised the situation as follows:

What angered the philosophes above all was that churches – opulent, and a drain on the economy – were still exercising mind-control and political power. The Catholic Church in particular continued to outlaw other faiths. It largely monopolized the education system... It censored books.... Only where the wings of churches had been clipped by the civil authorities, as notably in the Dutch Republic and England, was progress assured.[25]

Thus, this conflict was fought out more fiercely in Catholic France than elsewhere. Philosophical debate in both Prussia and Scotland in the 1780s and 1790s, for example, shows that there, at least, the dividing line was not between Enlighteners and the church, but ran *within* the *Protestant* church. The American colonies derived, of course, from people fleeing religious persecution, so unsurprisingly freedom of worship was given prominent legal expression. The 1786 Virginia Statute for Religious Freedom, written by Thomas Jefferson, demanded that 'our civil rights have no dependence on our religious opinions' and, in the same manner, the US Constitution, of 1 year later declared that 'no religious Test shall ever be required as a Qualification to any Office or public Trust under the United States.' In 1791, a Bill of Rights was added to the Constitution. Its first article was as follows: 'Congress shall make no law respecting an establishment of religion or prohibiting the free exercise thereof; or abridging the freedom of speech, or of the press; or the right of the people peaceably to assembly, and to petition the Government for a redress of grievances.'[26]

One concern of Enlightenment thinkers was to delve below the surface manifestations of human cultural forms and unearth human nature as such. This required undertakings both geographical and historical. Of the former, our thinkers took note of the findings of those who had travelled to distant continents and contacted 'natural man'. Rousseau drew on reports of the Caribs of Venezuela and the Oroonoko Indians; Voltaire had a Huron land in St. Malo bay and make a number of perceptive comments on the hypocrisies and inconsistencies of the French. David Hume, in contrast, looked to ancient history. There he found the nature of man to be no different from that of his own time.

Would you know the sentiments, inclinations, and course of life of the Greeks, the Romans? Study well the temper and actions of the French and English: You cannot be much mistaken in transferring to the former *most* of the observations you have made with regard to the latter. Mankind are so much the same, in all times and places, that history informs us of nothing new or strange in this particular. Its chief use is only to discover the constant and universal principles of human nature.[27]

This was just one view, though one shared by Helvétius and Kant. It was part of a wider endeavour to delineate the nature of mankind and, consequently, its prospects. The traditional belief in original sin had led to a restricted view of human potential. Enlightenment thinkers, in contrast, paid greater attention to Locke's famous formulation, according to which the mind was originally a blank slate, a *tabula rasa*. Its character was determined by the individual's particular experiences. This was something which could be controlled. The consequences of this were enormous. Humankind was now malleable, so, under the right controls, development could take place and, ultimately, the world could be modified. From these presuppositions stemmed the immense concern with education.

Kant had defined Enlightenment as 'man's emergence from his self-incurred immaturity'; its motto as 'Have courage to use your own understanding!'[28] The basic project, then, had education at its base. Mankind's subservience to obsolete forces was held to be mental in nature, or ideological, as we would now put it. Ignorance aligned with unthinking obedience to traditional authority, whereas to change consciousness was to change the world. Enlightenment thinkers saw themselves as in the vanguard of liberation. Education, said Helvétius, 'can do all';[29] it was the prerequisite for social progress. For François Quesnay 'When a nation is fully educated, tyranny is automatically ruled out.'[30] The Marquis de Condorcet put it more positively: 'Nature has indissolubly united the advancement of knowledge with the progress of liberty, virtue, and respect for the natural rights of man.'[31] Knowledge, then, was a revolutionary force; its own power was enough to create a more liberal society. Even Robespierre, not primarily associated with such views, once announced that the 'power of reason, and not the force of weapons, will propagate the principles of our glorious revolution ... All fictions disappear before truth, and all follies fall before reason.'[32] Schools were, of course, the institutions through which rationality was to be propagated but, in the eighteenth century, where they existed they were overwhelmingly under the control of the churches. So began the long battle for the secularisation of schooling, a struggle that in many countries continues to this day.

An educated society was an improved or more civilised one. This was a time when Europeans were discovering and colonising other parts of the globe. Travellers reported back on the strange, exotic and, in their view, primitive peoples they had encountered. Such peoples were unlike them in terms of opulence and mores, but they were of the same species. They were as we had once been, so in them we witnessed our own previous condition. Adam Ferguson explained that

> the inhabitants of Britain, at the time of the first Roman invasions, resembled, in many things, the present natives of North America: they were ignorant of agriculture; they painted their bodies; and used for cloathing [*sic*], the skins of beasts.[33]

The designation of such peoples as relatively backward led to the notion of there being a ladder of human development and even a rudimentary science of social change. This is where modern sociology and social science really began. This aspect does not apply to Voltaire or Diderot, let alone Rousseau, for whom decline was more evident. The key figure here is the under-acknowledged Anne-Robert-Jacques Turgot, for a few years a minister under Louis XIV, who in 1750 outlined the sequence of societal development as hunting, pastoral and agricultural societies leading progressively to the modern commercial age. This pattern, furthermore, had a logic; a kind of chemistry of development. 'All ages', said Turgot, 'are linked together by a chain of causes and effects which unite the present state of the world with everything that has preceded it.'[34] Turgot clearly pre-empted the similar categorisation in the Scottish Enlightenment and, furthermore, anticipated Auguste Comte, the acknowledged founder of sociology, in outlining the intellectual phases of human advancement as religious, philosophical and ultimately scientific.

A designation of past progress, however, provides no guarantee that it would continue into the future. For Hume and Vico, social change was cyclical, and for Rousseau, the 'body politic, as well as the human body, begins to die as soon as it is born, and carries in itself the causes of its destruction.'[35] Voltaire's eponymous Zadig 'pictured to himself men as they really are, insects devouring one another on a tiny fragment of mud'.[36] Turgot, again, was unusual in believing that mankind 'continues its onward march, albeit with tardy steps, towards an ever-nearing perfection'.[37] It was his biographer and disciple, the Marquis de Condorcet, who went one step further and delineated the next stage to which mankind was ineluctably ascending. It seemed to him, as to Joseph Priestley in England, that peace, harmony and social equality were all attainable social achievements.

In spite of their criticisms and expectations, we find Enlightenment thinkers having scant expectation of changes in the social structure: a significant downward diffusion of power was not expected. More general was the belief in reform through benevolent despots receiving rational advice from their intelligentsia. Democracy, then, was not explicitly rejected because the idea rarely made it onto the agenda. In Voltaire's view, 'truth is not for everyone: the mass of the human race is not worthy of it.'[38] He also has 'The Philosopher' arguing that the 'general population still remains in a state of deep ignorance to which the need to make a living condemns it...but the middle class is enlightened.'[39] In his classic work on the background to the French Revolution, Alexis de Tocqueville noted that the philosophers showed 'an uncommon want of faith in the wisdom of the masses. I could mention several who despised the public almost as heartily as they despised the Deity.'[40]

Voltaire also thought that the 'number of those who think is exceedingly small, and they are not interested in upsetting the world.'[41] In spite of this, the Enlightenment has often been blamed for the French Revolution, especially by those who were opposed to both. In fact, the idea of violent revolution hardly entered the heads of the major Enlightenment figures and would certainly not have been approved; violence, after all, represented the antithesis of rationality. The linkage with revolution has most often been made in respect of Jean-Jacques Rousseau, elevated by the Jacobins into an iconic figure. He, however, had little faith in revolution as the means to social progress:

> People once accustomed to masters are not in a condition to do without them. If they attempt to shake off the yoke they still more estrange themselves from freedom, as, by mistaking it for an unbridled licence to which it is diametrically opposed, they nearly always manage, by their revolutions, to hand themselves over to seducers, who only make their chains heavier than before.[42]

This view was echoed by his disciple, Kant: 'A revolution may well put an end to autocratic despotism and to rapacious or power-seeking oppression, but it will never produce a true reform in ways of thinking. Instead, new prejudices, like the ones they replaced, will serve as a leash to control the great unthinking mass.'[43] And yet we can't quite leave it at that; though not advocates of actual revolution, there can be little doubt that Enlightenment thinkers contributed to the process that de-legitimised the old regimes.

At this stage, it is worth reiterating the significance of the Enlightenment legacy for modern societies. Alfred Cobban once expressed it as follows:

> If we look for rational, physical causes of misfortunes instead of attributing them to witchcraft, if we accept the impersonal wage system in place of personal slavery, if we reject the torture of individuals as a means of eliciting the truth and use instead the impersonal rules of the law, if we do not regard personal salvations as so important that we are prepared to burn people in order to achieve it for them as well as for ourselves, if we do not believe that the stars are concerned with our individual fortunes, and so on, we are tacitly acknowledging the influence of the Enlightenment over our assumptions and actions; for the opposite was in each case the normal view before what has so often been condemned as the abstract thought of the Enlightenment extended the scientific, generalizing approach from physical nature to human actions.[44]

These points are particularly worth making now that a current fashion criticises the Enlightenment for racism, sexism and incipient totalitarianism. The approach of such critics is often based on a narrow and very selective reading of the main sources. It is also usually quite unhistorical in that it judges the movement by the values of two centuries later. What is thereby overlooked is how progressive the Enlightenment was in its own political and cultural context.

Revolution, Radicalism and Reaction in the Late Eighteenth Century

There are many ways in which the start of our period is resonant with tendencies that have become more pronounced ever

since. With the American revolution of 1776, we have the first colonial liberation movement. Having seen off their colonial power,
the 13 former British colonies then spent over a decade sorting
out their internal relationships. Wishing to avoid both the loss of
their separate powers and the re-establishment of monarchy, the
states, in 1787, agreed upon a constitution with a federal basis
and an elected President. It forms a major landmark in political
history, not only as an act of codification but because, probably
for the first time anywhere, it totally dispensed with hereditary
offices. John Adams, the second President of the United States,
envisaged what was then a most strange thing: a country of 'twenty
or thirty millions of freemen, without one noble or one king
among them'.[45] Part of the case of the North American colonists
against the British Crown had been that they were merely seeking the normal rights of Englishmen. In this sense they did not
see themselves as a different people from their distant rulers. However, their Constitution was a very un-English thing, in that their
former homeland had, and still has, a hereditary head of state,
hereditary and un-elected appointed members of the House of
Lords and an unwritten Constitution. The British Constitution is
as much a symbol of the past as the United States' one became
the symbol of the future. The Americans provided an example
that was followed both immediately and ever since. 'About fif-
teen new written constitutions were proclaimed in America, and
ten in Europe, in the quarter-century ending in 1801',[46] and
from then onwards any newly independent state or any state
changing the nature of its regime, marked that change with a
constitutional document outlining the powers and responsibilities
of the main state and parliamentary institutions. Britain is now
alone among the major western powers in not having such a
document.

In another part of the Americas, an equally momentous uprising took place, the 1791–2 slave revolt in Haiti against French rule.
This was true anti-imperialism, in the sense of rejecting rule from
a *different* people. The revolt, however, was not based on a different ideology, but marked the acceptance by the slaves of the French
revolutionary creed of the rights of man. This irony was obviously
inconvenient for what C.L.R. James called the 'maritime bourgeoisie ... [who] put the Rights of Man in their pockets whenever
the colonial question came up'.[47]

It was not, of course, only overseas that uprisings were occurring. The 1789 French Revolution was the most profound and resonant social upheaval that Europe had ever known. Its impact was all the greater for occurring in the country that pre-eminently represented aristocratic splendour. For the aristocracies and people of Europe, France was still seen in the image created earlier in the century by Louis XIV, 'the sun king', with his splendid palace at Versailles. France, then, set the tone for all of Europe in culture, fashion, philosophy, manners and food.

> The nobility of Europe talked French, wore French clothes, sat on French furniture, bought French pictures, collected French porcelain, read French books and pretended to believe in French philosophy. No one was educated until he had lived in Paris, visited Versailles, and listened to the gossip of the famous *salons*.[48]

As well as quality, France was also predominant in quantity. It was the most populated country in Europe, containing about 20 per cent of the continent's population, so any major changes in France were bound to have wider repercussions. As Burke was quick to notice, the new ruling ideology had application beyond France's borders.

In place of prescription and divine right, the National Assembly drew up its 'Declaration of the Rights of Man and of the Citizen'. Men, they announced, 'are born and remain free and equal in rights...These rights are liberty, property, security and resistance to oppression...The source of all sovereignty is essentially in the nation; no body, no individual can exercise authority that does not proceed from it in plain terms.' On the basis of popular sovereignty, aristocracy and monarchy were both undermined. From this emerged a nationalism that presented the people as, whatever their other differences, essentially united by their common rights. This nationalism seemed liberal in the sense that its ideological base was the rights of man. Consequently, other peoples had equal rights to similar arrangements. From this postulate derived the attempt to export the revolution across the continent. This involved some of the less endearing aspects of modernity; the military coup, as demonstrated by Napoleon Bonaparte in 1795, and, if not total war, then the whole life of a nation being geared to war to an unprecedented extent.

England, too, witnessed the emergence of radical lower class politics, though in far less dramatic form than in France. In January 1792, Thomas Hardy founded the London Corresponding Society, a centre of radical agitation in England. Members corresponded with the French and with its numerous affiliates at home. The society was composed of craftsmen and small tradesmen. One social historian has described it as the 'first political association of working-men to be formed in any country'.[49] Though its supporters defended the principles (not the practice) of the French Revolution, its aim was the right to vote. It was, thus, very English; a forerunner of both Chartism and the Labour Party. A clearer precursor of revolutionary socialism emerged in France with the 1796 conspiracy of Babeuf and the Equals for communal sharing and ownership of property. Here, we already have a criticism of the French Revolution from the left; one that declared class struggle the basis of social change and saw the French aristocracy as having been replaced by the rich.

The 1790s also produced the first feminist classic, Mary Wollstonecraft's *A Vindication of the Rights of Woman*. Her basic claim was that the rationality that men attribute to themselves could be equally attained by women were it not for 'a false system of education'.[50] In terms of potential, women and men were equal and should, therefore, be granted equal rights in society. In France, the Declaration of the Rights of Man prompted from Olympe de Gouges the lesser-known Declaration of the Rights of Woman (1791), but apart from abolishing male primogeniture, the French revolution did little for women. In France some privileged women had, for over five centuries, been allowed to vote at local and national levels. Women had participated in revolutionary clubs and societies and sat as spectators in the galleries of the National Assembly, but in the constitutions of 1791 and 1793, the political rights of women were explicitly denied. Then in 1804, the Code Napoleon categorised women as legal minors and forbade them the right to appear as civil witnesses. Wives were obliged to obey their husbands and so, among other limitations, could not own property without their husbands' consent.

In such a period of social transformation, it is unsurprising that several familiar concepts relating to social and economic affairs were first introduced into the language. Eric Hobsbawm once drew up a catalogue of the terms that 'were invented, or gained their modern meanings' between 1789 and 1848. These included: 'industry', 'industrialist', 'factory', 'middle class', 'working class', 'capitalism', 'socialism', 'aristocracy', 'railway', the political usage of 'liberal' and 'conservative', 'nationality', 'scientist', 'engineer', 'proletariat', 'utilitarian', 'statistics', 'sociology', 'ideology', 'strike' and 'pauperism'. As Hobsbawm notes, 'to imagine the modern world without these words ... is to measure the profundity' of the transformation that took place within these years.[51]

These are all the further varied signs of what we call modernity breaking through, creating the world with which we are familiar. However, one must not look at this question too one-sidedly. Many attitudes and practices were not that modern at all. Our period starts in 'a world in which "Americans" were native tribesmen, "citizens" were select and exclusively male, and "war" could imaginably pass for a good thing.'[52] The Enlightenment, furthermore, only made limited inroads into traditional attitudes among society at large. Thus in 1777, the Elector Maximilian of Bavaria followed his doctor's orders in swallowing a picture of the Virgin Mary as a supposed cure for smallpox. In 1780, a 'witch' was killed near Angers. Two years later 'a maid servant was executed as a witch in the Swiss canton of Glarus.'[53] In 1783, when a balloon landed just 12 miles from Paris, it was destroyed by a group of peasants who mistook it for the moon.[54]

Furthermore, the modern world includes more than the radicalism we have just outlined. It also comprises the reaction against it, for resistance occurred all along the line. The counter-Enlightenment rejected the notion that there was any one universal standard to which all societies should subscribe. Where the radicals were universalistic, the conservatives were particularistic: each society had its own laws, norms and values, which were a product of its own unique history and so appropriate to it. To a considerable extent, the French Revolution created modern conservatism, for it was through that fundamental challenge that the defenders of the old order were stimulated to present their world-view in relatively systematic form. Its foremost spokesman was Edmund Burke, whose *Reflections on the Revolution in France* will be considered in the next chapter.

Another aspect of counter-revolutionary ideology was the emergence of right-wing nationalism. The attempt to spread the revolution by armed force produced the obvious disability that the revolutionary doctrine was associated with alien rule. In Germany, in particular, this produced a nationalism that countered the inferiority of its troops with the claim to the superiority of its thoughts. Here the alleged purity of its language became the basis to a claim of having a special spiritual mission to fulfil.

Conservatism's prime task was to maintain the traditional social hierarchy, and so once workmen were beginning to organise it was but a short step to legal limitations. In this way, the French Revolution demonstrated the limits of its social radicalism. In 1791–2, the French passed the Le Chapelier laws which forbade trade unions, picketing, strikes and any form of collective bargaining aimed at the raising of wages.[55] Here, we have a rare instance of the British copying the French, for in 1799 and 1800 William Pitt's government also passed a law against combinations. Yet there were worse places to be a labourer than England or France. According to de Tocqueville, serfdom survived in Hohenzollern-Sigmaringen until 1833, in 'Saxony for Lusatia' until 1832 and in Mecklenburg until 1820.[56] In Russia, serfdom was not abolished until 1861; in the United States of America, slavery was not abolished until 1865, and then only after a bloody civil war. In Prussia, 'right up to 1918, the *Gesindeordnung* bound so-called farm servants to a regime which was very far from that of free labour.'[57] In Austria, the status of serf survived until 1919.

Political legitimacy claimed on the basis of the divine right of kings lasted well past our period and into the twentieth century in the Russian and Austro-Hungarian regimes that were overthrown during the First World War. Military defeat led to what is now called 'regime change' and so, in one way or another, produced adjustments to modernity. This same impetus was absent from the victorious countries. During the First World War, British officers still carried swords in combat. They no longer do, but Britain's system of monarchy can be regarded as a feudal remnant, for it is based on the pre-modern notion that positions are inherited firstly by the eldest son and otherwise by the eldest daughter. Similarly, the House of Lords has not quite thrown out all those who got there merely by being their fathers' eldest sons.

The unprecedented nature of the French Revolution was such that it made an immediate and dramatic impact on thinking people throughout Europe, and particularly so in those countries nearest to France. The fall of the Bastille was at first widely welcomed as a heroic manifestation of will in action, a long-awaited synthesis of theory and practice, as a breath of fresh air and an intoxicating springtime of mankind. The appropriate and most frequent metaphors recounted the removal of chains and shackles. To those of a different political persuasion events in France appeared to signal the outbreak of a dangerous disease in need of urgent elimination. On the English side of the Channel, the French Revolution provoked a political debate of a quality and intensity unequalled in our history.

To Wordsworth, in the first flush of excitement, the revolution held out the promise of a new and better age for mankind:

> Bliss was it in that dawn to be alive,
> But to be young was very Heaven! – Oh! times,
> In which the meagre, stale, forbidding ways
> Of custom, law, and statute, took at once
> The attraction of a country in romance!
> When reason seemed the most to assert her rights,
> When most intent on making of herself
> A prime enchantress – to assist the work,
> Which then was going forward in her name!
> Not favoured spots alone, but the whole earth,
> The beauty wore of promise – that which sets
> (As at some moments might not be unfelt
> Among the bowers of Paradise itself)
> The budding rose above the rose full blown.[58]

The preacher John Wesley saw events in France in a different light. To him, only the direct intervention of Satan could have produced such a cataclysm. Religious interpretations were commonplace and hardly surprising in reaction to events that seemed beyond the scale of human instigation. They could, however, be used in support of either side. Thus on the 4 November 1789, the Rev. Richard Price, a Welsh non-conformist minister, preached a sermon in London, (to which Burke responded), full of millenarian expectation, even invoking a comparison with the response of Simeon in Luke, ch. 2.

> What an eventful period is this! I am thankful that I have lived to it; I could almost say, Lord, now lettest thou thy servant depart in peace, for mine eyes have seen thy salvation. I have lived to see a diffusion of knowledge, which has undermined superstition

and error. – I have lived to see the rights of men better understood than ever; and nations panting for liberty which seem to
have lost the idea of it. – I have lived to see thirty millions of people, indignant and resolute, spurning at slavery, and demanding
liberty with an irresistible voice.[59]

Apart from the context of religion, there was also a marked attempt
by the British to judge the French Revolution in terms of their
own history. One of the central reference points was the comparison between France in 1789 and Britain in 1688. To Richard Price
the liberties currently being sought in France were similar to those
achieved by the English in 1688, when William and Mary had succeeded James II, Protestant succession had been assured, and the
rights of parliament against the monarch asserted. Thus, concluded
Price, admirers of the so-called Glorious Revolution of 1688 ought
to welcome the revolution in France. In taking this attitude, Price
was adopting the characteristic approach of British radicals, many
of whom had also shared his defence of the American colonies in
their resistance to King George III just 13 years earlier. Similarly, in
the United States, Thomas Jefferson viewed the French Revolution
as a French version of the American one.

The first chapter attempted an overview of the whole period
covered by this book. This chapter, in contrast, has outlined the
issues, assumptions and challenges with which our period begins.
We can, then, now move on to our array of major theorists whose
ideas set the debate on emerging and developing modern society.
We start with a thinker who argued for the wisdom and stability
of traditional arrangements, a reminder that there were those for
whom modernisation was more a dangerous threat than a positive
promise.

3

Edmund Burke

Life

Edmund Burke (1729–97) was born in Dublin, one of fourteen children, only three of whom survived infancy. He was educated at a Quaker boarding school at Ballitore in County Clare and then at Trinity College, Dublin. Like many young men of ability in Ireland and Scotland, he came to London to advance his career. His first intention was to study law but gradually he became more interested in literature, aesthetics and then politics, becoming the Member of Parliament for Wendover (1766–74), then Bristol (1774–80) and finally Malton (1780–94). He became Secretary to Lord Rockingham, who was twice Prime Minister (1765–6, 82) and was appointed Paymaster-General in 1782 and again the following year. For someone of his background, it was a remarkable achievement to rise so high in the British establishment. Burke was a commoner and an Irishman with Catholic connections on his mother's side, whereas the governing class was overwhelmingly aristocratic, English and Protestant.[1] Furthermore, Burke made only a limited effort to accommodate himself to those in power. One might say that he often denounced the political practice of his time for failing to live up to its declared norms. It is this that gives his apparent early radicalism the conservative base that only later become fully apparent. Nowhere is this more evident than in his bold attacks on the growing powers of the Crown. As a Whig, Burke was committed to the settlement of 1688, when James II fled the country to be replaced by William and Mary. This 'Glorious Revolution' had curbed monarchical power, established the rights of parliament and assured the Protestant succession. Nearly a century later, in

'Thoughts on the Cause of the Present Discontents' (1770), Burke claimed that once again the monarchy was subverting the British constitution by its excessive influence over Members of Parliament. Then in his 1780 'Speech on the Economical Reform', Burke criticised the expenses of the Royal household, arguing, with almost Benthamite zeal, that many offices were survivals from a history that time had rendered redundant.

Burke is best known for his massively influential *Reflections on the Revolution in France* (1790). At the age of 61, he suddenly became the foremost defender of the old order in its hour of greatest danger. That he could play this role was far from obvious from his earlier political campaigns, particularly his defence of the American colonists in the 1770s, so, more than most politicians, Burke had to face the charge of inconsistency.

Burke is also known for attempting to remedy the grievances of Irish Catholics and for the classic statement of the belief that a Member of Parliament cannot be mandated by his constituents but should vote according to what he thinks best for the country as a whole. He told his constituents: 'You choose a member indeed; but when you have chosen him, he is not a member of Bristol, but he is a member of *parliament*.'[2]

The American Colonies

In the 1770s, Burke was also on the anti-monarchical side in the dispute with the American colonies. He thus became identified with radicals like Thomas Paine who favoured American independence. This was misleading, for Burke supported the colonists not in what they were for but in what they were against – a government in London that looked more to force than to conciliation.

In common with the other British colonies, eighteenth-century America was held in the economic grip of the mercantilist system. This stipulated that colonies should only produce the goods needed by Britain, should export their goods to Britain, in British or colonial ships, and should accept only the manufactured goods that Britain produced. The object of this policy was to keep a complete monopoly of the trade of the colonies to the exclusion of outside powers. Such a system was, as intended, highly profitable for Britain, colonial customs revenue contributing a vital part to the Crown's income. At a certain stage, it also suited the American colonists. Its indefinite continuation, however, would have required a permanent restriction of North American economic expansion and broader development. Acts passed forbidding the colonial manufacture of woollens, in 1669, and of iron goods, in 1750, were almost doomed to failure, and were actually disregarded from the start. One-crop colonies suffered particularly from the curb on economic development. Thus Virginia had taken almost 50 years to recover from the effects of the 1668 fall in tobacco prices.

Now Edmund Burke, commonly regarded as a supporter of the American Revolution, actually accepted the basic assumptions of eighteenth-century mercantilist imperialism. He believed that the colonies should be governed according to the principles of 'equity' and 'lenity' but not that they could have full control of their own affairs. In 1769, he announced that the American colonies should continue to be governed according to 'that great object for which alone the colonies were founded, navigation and commerce'.[3]

However, as he was continually to emphasise, the American colonists were Englishmen, and so it was unbecoming for them to be kept in a condition of subjection, which was anyway unnecessary for apparently colonialism and freedom could be reconciled. As Burke told his Bristol constituents:

> I have held, and ever shall maintain to the best of my power, unimpaired and undiminished, the just, wise, and necessary constitutional superiority of Great Britain. This is necessary for America as well as for us... But, – I have ever had a clear opinion... that this superiority is consistent with all the liberties a sober and spirited America ought to desire. I never mean to put any colonist, or any human creature, in a situation not becoming a free-man. To reconcile British superiority with American liberty shall be my great object... I am far from thinking that both, even yet, may not be preserved.[4]

The freedom of the American colonists consisted, according to Burke, in being governed according to the old, acceptable, procedures. Britain had for years controlled American trade but had not imposed taxes on them. The attempt to do so through the Sugar Act of 1764 and the Stamp Act of 1765, repealed in 1766, was a blunder, not because it was inherently wrong, but because it was inexpedient.

The criterion of governmental action is not what is abstractly right but what is practicable. Out of the plausible policy alternatives, Burke favoured following the line of least resistance. 'People must be governed in a manner agreeable to their temper and disposition; and men of free character and spirit must be ruled with, at least, some condescension to this spirit and this character.'[5] The tax on tea in itself was relatively trivial, but Lord North's government insisted on its enforcement in order to maintain the principle of Britain's right to tax the colonies. This stance was one of the causes of the 1773 Boston 'tea party' and helped provoke the colonists' demand for independence.

Burke consistently opposed these measures and gave Lord North's government his usual advice that they should not rule according to abstract principles but rather according to prevailing conditions.

> Whoever goes about to reason on any part of the policy of this country with regard to America upon mere abstract principles of government, or even of those of our own ancient constitution, will often be misled ... All the reasonings about it that are likely to be at all solid, must be drawn from its actual circumstances.[6]

Burke's conscience on this matter was clear, for the Rockingham administration of 1765–6 had repealed the hated Stamp Act, but their position with regard to taxation of the colonies was rather ambiguous. Replying to the attacks of Grenville, Burke noted that before proposing the repeal of the Stamp Act, the Rockingham Whigs had asserted 'in the fullest and least equivocal terms the unlimited legislative right of this country over its colonies; and, having done this, to propose the repeal, on principles, not of constitutional right, but on those of expediency, of equity, and of lenity'.[7]

So according to Burke the Rockingham Whigs believed in the abstract, because not enforced or enforceable, 'unlimited legislative right of this country over its colonies'. This right is certainly of an unusual kind, for it is a claim only to be asserted in the virtual absence of opposition. Burke insisted on the right but then opposed attempts to enforce it. He believed that the manner of its enforcement was inexpedient, but one might ask what rights are for if not to be implemented. For Burke, however, there was no choice. 'No way is open, but...to comply with the American spirit as necessary; or, if you please, to submit to it as a necessary evil.'[8]

Burke's concern for the American cause stemmed partly from the fact that he regarded their claims on taxation and representation as being no different from those formerly claimed and attained in England. Already at the Albany Congress in 1754, Benjamin Franklin had stated that 'Compelling the colonies to pay money without their consent would be rather like raising money in an enemy's country than taxing Englishmen for their own public benefit.'[9] Ten years later James Otis, of the Massachusetts assembly, also attacked the British government for failing to abide by the principles of their constitution. He regarded the colony as being an integral part of the mother country. The colonists were therefore entitled to 'the natural, essential, inherent, and inseparable rights of our fellow subjects in Great Britain'.[10] On a similar basis, Burke spoke of the conflict as a civil war; a dispute where both sides belonged to the same people.

Burke was in fact rather proud that the colonists were acting on British principles. He was later to remind them that 'That very liberty, which you so justly prize above all things, originated here.'[11] He viewed them as attempting a defensive revolution, in support of the traditional procedure which George III and his ministers were trying to undermine. Writing of himself in the third person, Burke declared that 'he always firmly believed that they [the Americans] were always purely on the defensive in that rebellion. He considered the Americans as standing in that time, and in that controversy, in the same relation to England, as England did to James II, in 1688.'[12]

However, colonial adherence to the traditions of the British constitution was short-lived. Abstract principles began to seem more appealing. In 1774, James Wilson of Pennsylvania declared that 'All men are, by nature, equal and free: no one has a right to any authority over another without his consent: all lawful government is founded on the consent of those who are subject to it...the happiness of the society is the *first* law of every government.'[13] Similar sentiments were expressed in the more famous 1776 Declaration of Independence.

It is noteworthy that Burke, who so vehemently opposed the abstract principles of the French revolutionaries, had been less upset when equally abstract principles were proposed by the American colonists. The difference, no doubt, was that he saw the American

Revolution as more justifiable and so was less inclined to emphasise the intellectual discrepancies of its leaders. Burke sympathised with the revolutionary movement, but not always for the same reasons, nor in the same manner, as many of its other adherents. In fact, Burke did not so much support the revolution as agree with the colonists in their grievances against the British government. His sympathy with what the colonists were against – unwise policies – tended, for most people, to align him with what they stood for. This, however, was misleading. Burke regarded American independence as no more than the unfortunate consequence of a regrettable policy. He would have preferred the uprising to have been truly defensive; thus merely restoring the *status quo ante* of British colonial rule without imposing new taxation. 'We have wished to continue united with you, in order that a people of one origin and one character should be directed to the rational objects of government by joint councils, and protected in them by a common force.' He regarded the separation as 'a heavy calamity', the sole consolation being that 'we had much rather see you totally independent of this Crown and kingdom, than joined to it by so unnatural a conjunction as that of freedom with servitude.'[14]

After the loss of the American colonies, India was gradually to emerge as the colonial jewel in the British crown. Here also Burke, the advocate of benevolent, paternal imperialism, regarded the British rulers as failing to meet their obligations.

The East India Company

In the 1780s, Burke worked prodigiously, but unsuccessfully, to secure the impeachment of Warren Hastings, the Governor-General of Bengal. Hastings appeared to be at the apex of British exploitation, whereby Indian principalities were impoverished by officials whose wealth then corrupted the politics of their home country. Burke believed that the East India Company had ruined every prince and state that trusted it. He wrote more on India than on any other issue and his powerful indictment of British rule by the East India Company significantly prefigured some of the themes of *Reflections on the Revolution in France*. The British in India seemed scarcely less revolutionary than the Jacobins later in France in their disregard for long-established norms and practices. The East India

Company seemed to have provided India with 'an oppressive, irregular, capricious, unsteady, rapacious, and peculating despotism, with a direct disavowal of obedience to any authority at home'. Burke wanted 'power to be taken out of their hands'[15] and into those of parliament, which is what eventually happened as a consequence of the 1857 mutiny.

Just as Burke later feared that the Jacobin contagion would spread to England, he here warned that British misgovernment in India would rebound to produce corruption in the home government. He supposed that the sudden wealth attained by those despoiling India would infect British society when they returned home. As later in France, a too sudden elevation in wealth, power and status would produce a class of people badly under-prepared, and hence totally unsuitable, for the exalted positions which they had attained. This was exacerbated by the apparent youthfulness of those governing India. 'Schoolboys without tutors, minors without guardian, the world is let loose upon them, with all its temptations, and they are let loose upon the world with all the power that despotism involves.'[16] To accuse British imperialism as debilitated by juvenile inexperience neatly inverts the dominant mentality which justified imperial rule on the notion that the conquered countries were infantile in terms of social development. Burke, however, contrasted the youth of the British occupiers with the antiquity of the country they ruled. India was no immature society; it was, on the contrary, an ancient civilisation: 'This multitude of men does not consist of an abject and barbarous populace ... but a people for ages civilized and cultivated; cultivated by all the arts of polished life, whilst we were yet in the woods.'[17] These extracts on India formed part of speeches that were 'often met with derisive laughter',[18] but to a later age, they exalt rather than diminish Burke's reputation. Uday Singh Mehta has noted that 'None of the well-known liberals or socialists of the nineteenth century expresses anything like Burke's indignation and searching critique of the empire.'[19] To those cultural relativists who believed, then as now (for they are still with us), that practices abroad need not comply with our values at home, Burke replied:

> This geographical morality we do protest against ... the laws of morality are the same everywhere, and that there is no action which would pass for an act of extortion, of peculation, of bribery, and of oppression in England that is not an act of extortion, of

peculation, of bribery, and oppression in Europe, Asia, Africa, and all over the world.[20]

Burke, then, on the eve of his greatest crusade, appeared as a radical critic of both the British monarchy and the ruling class. When, however, they came under fundamental attack, he became their foremost defender.

The French Revolution

Eighteenth-century book titles were often significantly longer than we are now used to. The commonly abridged title of *Reflections on the Revolution in France* actually continues as follows – *and on the proceedings in certain societies in London relative to that event in a letter intended to have been sent to a gentleman in Paris.* The *Reflections*, then, apparently grew out of a reply to a young Parisian acquaintance, Charles-Jean-Francois Depont, who had sought Burke's comments and approval of affairs in France. As Burke warmed to his topic, the normal scale of a letter was rapidly transcended, though the outline of the original intention remained spasmodically apparent. The first part of the *Reflections*, in the Everyman edition, takes up 160 pages, with no chapter divisions or sub-headings. Burke then began the second part with the following justification: 'This letter is grown to a great length, though it is indeed short with regard to the infinite extent of the subject.'[21] He might, at this point, have conceded that he was no longer really writing a letter but, rather, a book, especially so as he had actually written a long letter of reply to Depont in October 1789.[22]

At one level, the duality of intention between a personal letter to a young Parisian and a book for a general British audience appears stylistically unsatisfactory. Burke conceded as much at the beginning of the book when, referring to himself in the third person, he acknowledged that a 'different plan, he is sensible, might be more favourable to a commodious division and distribution of his matter.'[23] Nevertheless, the 'different plan' was never produced, possibly because it suited Burke's purpose to let this ambiguity remain; for it enabled him, *vis-à-vis* a young Frenchman, to pose as an accredited interpreter of the British constitution, a stance that would have been very much harder for him, as an Irishman, to maintain in a purely British context. In this way, he was able to present his own chosen strand of the Whig heritage as representing the true meaning not only of that heritage but of the British constitution itself. In fact, the letter from Charles Depont merely provided the convenient context that encouraged Burke to elaborate concerns that were deeply troubling him in any case, for his interest in France was anything but academic.

Burke, clearly, had been in the thick of political life prior to 1789. His earlier campaigns no doubt steeled him for his greatest battle, for he became the spokesman of the European traditional order against the ideas of the Enlightenment and the French Revolution. Many who later turned against the revolution had at first welcomed it as a long-awaited synthesis of theory and practice and a liberating springtime of mankind. Burke, however, saw the revolution presciently, less as it then was and more as it was to become. His *Reflections on the Revolution in France* reads as if the great terror of 1793–4 had already occurred, though it still lay 3 years in the future.

Similarly, Burke was among those who were almost immediately aware of the extraordinary nature of the French Revolution. He knew from the start that it was an act of fundamental historical significance. 'It appears to me as if I were in a great crisis, not of the affairs of France alone, but of all Europe, perhaps of more than Europe. All circumstances taken together, the French Revolution is the most astonishing that has hitherto happened in the world.'[24] As the first major literary attack on the revolution, the book made an immediate impact and 'sold about 19,000 copies in the first year and probably 30,000 over the next five'.[25] These are quite extraordinary figures, both in view of the length and style of the work itself and of the relatively low population and literacy levels at the time. Burke unwittingly initiated the greatest political debate in British literary history. The responses from Tom Paine and Mary Wollstonecraft were just the most famous of the many publications answering Burke.[26] By 1791, the *Reflections* had been translated into French, German and Italian and was to have a significant influence on emerging European conservatism.

One of Burke's new admirers was King George III, who thereby, for the first time, brought Burke to a position of favour with the Court. George III regarded the *Reflections* as a book that 'Every gentleman should read.'[27] That the unfortunate king had lost his sanity the previous year, when he mistook an oak tree in Windsor Great

Park for his cousin Frederick the Great of Prussia, did nothing to lessen his influence on the Court in this respect. That the Establishment had been correct in identifying their foremost defender was clear to the radical lawyer Horne Tooke, associate of William Godwin and Tom Paine. He described the *Reflections* as 'the tears of the Priesthood for the loss of their pudding'.[28]

Winning the approval of the court meant losing that of the radicals. In the immediate aftermath of the revolution, the British political divide of 1789 was fairly similar to that of 1776; supporters of the American cause were expected to be sympathetic to the French experiment. Here, Burke seemed not to have maintained a consistent line. For him, the French Revolution did not herald a better age, a kingdom of heaven on earth or even a version of the British 1688 revolution. To the radicals, then, Burke seemed a deserter from their cause. Paine began his Preface to *The Rights of Man* (1791–2) with the grievance of abandonment: 'From the part Mr.Burke took in the American Revolution, it was natural that I should consider him a friend to mankind.' [29] So began a strand of radical thought, reaching from Paine through to Cobbett and Marx, that assumed Burke was a bought man who changed his opinions as he changed his paymaster.[30] What actually caused Burke to adopt an explicitly conservative position was that the social order of Europe seemed more fundamentally endangered than ever before.

One aspect of this related to France itself, the country where aristocracy seemed the most resplendent, where the 'sun king' Louis XIV had established the magnificent palace of Versailles. France at the time was the most populous country of Europe and already set the fashion in food, philosophy and much else. The attack on the French aristocracy raised the fear of similar attacks on other aristocracies.

The fury, then, with which Burke attacked the revolution stemmed largely from the supposition that the whole social order was being threatened. A key sentence to the understanding of Burke's whole outlook occurs early in the *Reflections* when he declares himself 'solicitous chiefly for the peace of my own country'.[31] This was endangered in three different ways:

Firstly, It had supporters on the English side of the Channel. The concern with this aspect is already evident in the second part of the book's full title – *Reflections on the Revolution in France* AND *on the proceedings in certain societies in London relative to that event*. Here, we have Burke's real prime motive for writing the book. In November, 1789 the Welsh non-conformist minister Richard Price had preached a sermon 'A Discourse Upon the Love of Our Country' to the Revolution Society, an organisation formed to celebrate the centenary of Britain's so-called Glorious Revolution of 1688. Price had argued that the French Revolution was an attempt to win the liberties that the British had gained a century earlier and so ought to be welcomed:

> I have lived to see a *diffusion* of knowledge, which has undermined superstition and error – I have lived to see *the rights of men* better understood than ever; and nations panting for liberty which seemed to have lost the idea of it – I have lived to see *thirty millions of people*, indignant and resolute, spurning at slavery, and demanding liberty with an irresistible voice.[32]

Burke read the sermon 2 months later and immediately began to outline the contrary view; that the French Revolution was the absolute antithesis of British political practice. The *Reflections*, then, is a book about both France and England, written for an English readership and warning them against those like the Rev. Richard Price, a minister who preached in support of French atheists. That Price's attitude was shared by many British radicals suggested to Burke that Britain also possessed the kind of politicised literati that had plotted the downfall of Old Regime France. He later warned that 'To us it is a Colossus which bestrides our channel. It has one foot on a foreign shore, the other upon the British soil.'[33]

Thus, *secondly*, the revolution was a particular danger to Britain because of its proximity: it was too close for comfort. This was not an outbreak far away by people of whom we knew little and felt slight connection. The revolution broke out among Britain's nearest neighbour, against whom, admittedly, they had recently been at war in both India and North America, but France was, nevertheless, at the forefront of the European and Christian civilisation that both countries shared.

Thirdly, Burke understood that what made the revolution attractive outside of its own country was a peculiarity of its doctrine. In their appeal to 'The Rights of Man', the revolutionaries proclaimed a universal ideology that transcended all particular and local attachments. National frontiers, religious allegiances and even class

interests all seemed threatened by the invisible contagion of revolutionary ideas, for 'Man' was everywhere. For Burke, these ideas
constituted 'an *armed doctrine*' that 'has by its essence, a faction of
opinion and of interest, and of enthusiasm, in every country'.[34] He
believed that the only hope was to destroy the revolution before it
destroyed Europe. Burke later attempted to organise anti-Jacobin
resistance, and was increasingly incensed by the failure of the British
government to take the defensive measures he thought necessary.

In the last years of his life, Burke became increasingly prone
to see 'the hand of God' behind the turbulence of revolutionary
France. As he despaired of the feeble attempts at counter-revolution,
he came to suspect that the whole cataclysm represented divine
punishment upon an erring humanity. In the *Reflections*, however,
the revolution was seen as having primarily intellectual and anti-
religious origins. Abstract ideas, stemming from the pens of Voltaire,
Diderot, Rousseau and D'Alembert, had, over a few decades, perverted the mind of France and sown a restless and threatening
discontent. These men had, ironically, been granted a prestigious
platform by the aristocracy they were so busy undermining. The first
and fatal false assumption of the salon literati was the illusion that
abstract reason in itself provided a sufficient basis for reorganising
the state. With quite sublime presumption, 'the aeronauts of France'
sought to transform their metaphysical dreams into a system of government, assuming as they went that reason began with themselves
and that all knowledge derived from the past was mere superstition.
As an explanation for the revolution, Burke fell back upon conspiracy theory. He saw respect for tradition pushed aside as the 'political
men of letters', of whom 'a spirit of cabal, intrigue, and proselytism,
pervaded all their thoughts, words and actions', carried out their
'plan for the destruction of the Christian religion'.[35]

In Burke's view, the evil intentions of anti-religious, plotting
factions, rather than genuine social grievances, gave rise to the revolution. The new morality of the Jacobins had replaced customs
hallowed by ancient usage. A new type of person had arisen, using
Rousseau as their 'standard figure of perfection', a man 'totally desti-
tute of taste in any sense of the word',[36] yet regarded as an adequate
guide for the reconstruction of the state. Practical knowledge was
discarded and replaced by 'a geometrical and arithmetical constitution'. Burke was aghast. 'They despise experience as the wisdom of
unlettered men.' The sheer conceit was more than he could take.

'I cannot conceive how any man can have brought himself to that pitch of presumption, to consider his country as nothing but *carte blanche*, upon which he may scribble whatever he pleases.' The new morality was that of the 'academies of the Palais Royal, and the Jacobins.'[37] It relied on that old enemy of Burke's, abstract principles. Customs hallowed by ancient usage had been replaced by the rights of man. All this in Burke's view was totally unnecessary. He declared himself reasonably acquainted with France immediately before the revolution. It was not perfect, for no human constructions ever were. Nevertheless, the country was in good commercial order. Nothing could be seen to justify the cataclysm that was soon to occur.

For Burke, it was sheer, unwarranted presumption to discard ancient wisdoms. The rules of acceptable social life had been forged by all our ancestors over many generations and had been slowly adapted to society's practical needs. Already years before the French Revolution, Burke's policy had been to 'put my foot in the tracks of our forefathers, where I can neither wander nor stumble.'[38]

Quite central to Burke's approach is the view that

We are afraid to put men to live and trade each on his own private stock of reason; because we suspect that the stock in each man is small, and that the individuals would do better to avail themselves of the general bank and capital of nations and of ages.[39]

So the individual is relatively foolish because, inevitably, less experienced than the species. For Burke society is the carrier of wisdom. Folk wisdom, derided by the literati, actually carries, transmits, modifies and transforms into knowledge the experience of many people over many generations. It is without parallel as a resource to draw on during the exigencies of life.

It looks as if, on this view, wisdom comes from not thinking. That would be a partial and limited summary of Burke's view. The wider context is that the thinking has already been done. It is not merely that 'we have made no discoveries,' but that 'we think that no discoveries are to be made, in morality; nor many in the great principles of government, nor in the ideas of liberty, which were understood long before we were born.'[40] Any individual thinking is, consequently, puny and unserviceable as against the aggregated wisdom of the community that has reached its conclusions after many ages and in adjustment to innumerable actual situations. Tradition, then, is preferable to innovation as it is more tried and tested and draws on infinitely more experience.

Yet, these guidelines were being torn asunder in the name of a spurious rationality. Burke's rejection of the Enlightenment is sometimes taken as an attack on rationality itself, yet from his perspective it was actually more rational to stick to tried and tested methods than for people to treat their country as empty terrain upon which they might construct whatever they fancied. Society, then, was there to be accepted and not to be treated as an object of experiment.

To Burke, the revolutionaries were like sailors who had thrown their compass overboard in mid-ocean. Their self-conceit allowed them to elevate their own particular ideas above the wisdoms embodied in their heritage. Burke, then, was a defender of traditional culture. It contained all the wisdom that a society needed for 'the great principles of government' and 'the ideas of liberty... were understood long before we were born.'[41] The implication of this is a much more modest style of politics than the revolutionaries were attempting. Each generation, then, had the predominant obligation to merely hold and transmit the heritage that it had acquired.

This, of course, assumed the fundamental importance of continuity. The revolutionaries believed that the old regime was based on oppression and superstition and so introducing the rights of man required a clean break. Burke declared himself acquainted with the faults of the previous French government but suggested that the country build upon its sound and established foundations rather than tear them down for replacement by a merely 'theoretic, experimental edifice'.

The core of Burke's case is that the revolutionaries were guided by theory rather than practice, by an 'armed doctrine'. Their maxim was 'liberty, equality and fraternity'. In respect of the former, Burke merely saw liberties being taken. Was he to congratulate an escaped convict on attaining his liberty? Charles Depont, in the letter to which we have referred, had asked Burke whether 'the French are worthy to be free.' In his reply, Burke had explained

what the freedom is that I love and that to which I think all men are entitled. It is not solitary, unconnected, individual, selfish Liberty. As if every Man was to regulate the whole of his Conduct by his own will. The Liberty I mean is *social* freedom. It is that state of things in which Liberty is secured by the equality of Restraint; a Constitution of things in which the liberty of no one Man, and no body of Men and no Number of men can find Means to trespass on the liberty of any Person or any description of Persons in the Society. This kind of liberty is indeed but another name for Justice, ascertained by wise Laws, and secured by well-constructed institutions.[42]

Meanwhile, of fraternity there was no sign; rather was there civil war, if not the Hobbesian war of all against all. No liberty; no fraternity. What about equality? This was a quite different matter. Of this, the revolutionaries were in serious and thorough pursuit. It is to this issue that significant parts of *Reflections* are devoted.

Though Burke did not separate them in this way, he provided two different arguments rejecting equality, each of which can stand or fall on its own. We shall turn first to the sociological answer before considering the theological one.

The sociological case against equality is based on the revolutionary transition necessary to achieve it. Burke was keenly aware that unprecedented social mobility was occurring in France, to 'the utter ruin of whole orders and classes of men'[43] and that, as a consequence, the traditional and hierarchical 'natural order of things'[44] was being perverted. To go against nature was to court disaster, as Burke immediately perceived when he considered the social and occupational background of the new National Assembly. 'From the moment I read the list, I saw distinctly, and very nearly as it happened, all that was to follow.' The new men seemed to be 'a handful of country clowns...mere country curates...men who had never seen the state so much as in a picture; men who knew nothing of the world beyond the bounds of an obscure village' and who represented no more than 'the fomentors and conductors of the petty war of village vexation'.[45] The old aristocratic class had been trained to rule; their very socialisation from their earliest years had supposedly accustomed them to the breadth of vision and the leadership that a great country requires. Burke thought that parochial mediocrity had taken over, for the new men apparently knew of little outside their own localities and so their rule was bound to be disastrous. Men of theory there certainly were, and in abundance, but none with any practical experience of affairs of state.[46]

The inevitable result of entrusting government to those with theory but without knowledge was that they would disregard the specific realities of each situation and solely try to apply their blueprints. In their approach, the situation counted for too little and their ideals for too much. In Burke's opinion, governments should act more in accord with circumstances and take greater account of the particular situation and dispositions of their own unique culture.

The importance of experience is thus a strong factor for leaving things as they are. Any change of ruling personnel could only elevate inexperience and so lead to deterioration. So Burke viewed with contempt the provincial attorneys and minor civic dignitaries whose grandiose plans were in inverse proportion to their ability to implement them. 'Who could flatter himself that these men, suddenly, and as it were, by enchantment, snatched from the humblest rank of subordination, would not be intoxicated with their unprepared greatness?'[47]

So, on this aspect of what is wrong with equality, Burke thought it ludicrous to discard ancient wisdoms. Experience was the truest guide, but the revolution had abandoned it. Burke was sure that the attempt at levelling would fail. It was against nature. Bringing down one class would merely lead to the rise of another, and he was not alone in predicting that when all authority is undermined then force would prevail, and soon the head of the army would become the ruler of the country, as the rise of Napoleon soon demonstrated.

It was Engels who later declared that in France the class struggle always appeared in the clearest outline. Certainly, and perhaps surprisingly, Burke's account of the French revolution has some similarities to the Marxist perspective, for out of the final destruction of feudalism Burke perceived the rise of financial interests. 'The age of chivalry is gone...and the glory of Europe is extinguished forever.' In its place had emerged 'sophisters, economists, and calculators'.[48] Clearly, a rudimentary notion of bourgeois or capitalist revolution is evident in Burke's understanding that out of the period of 'assassinations, massacre, and confiscation'[49] was emerging a new order with quite different priorities from those of its predecessor.

We now turn to the theological argument against equality. The view here is that there is a natural order of things, a hierarchy of nature of which human arrangements, and Burke specifically singles out the state, are a part. It is all God's creation. The levellers, therefore, are blasphemous. They are attempting to undo God's work. Burke, then, claimed to be defending Christian civilisation and so to have God on his side. In spite of pages devoted to the loss of church lands, Burke did not confine his argument to the local level of defending French Catholicism. This would not have been helpful in rallying the English against the revolution. Burke, then, glossed over the divide between Catholicism and Protestantism and presented the revolution as an attack on Christianity as such.

A social order which is divinely ordained is one in which people are obliged to accept their place. Consequently one's social position and political obligations are determined in advance by the structure and institutions of the society one grows up in. Burke assumed that God having 'disposed and marshalled us, by a divine tactic, not according to our will, but according to his, he has, in and by that disposition, virtually subjected us to act the part which belongs to the place assigned us'. Against this, neither metaphysical reasoning nor individual consent should be of any consequence. Running counter to the major political trends that were then emerging, Burke declared that 'Duties are not voluntary ... Men without their choice derive benefits from that association; without their choice they are subjected to duties in consequence of these benefits; and without their choice they enter into a virtual obligation as binding as any that is actual.'[50]

Burke's arch-enemy Rousseau put all the major problems of the state directly to each individual conscience. There are no representatives. All must apply their individual reason. Burke's view was directly contrary to this. For him, problems of allegiance and affiliation should not arise. Individuals find themselves in a particular social situation and are merely obliged passively to act out the social role they inherit. All this means that there is not too much to be done politically, certainly nowhere near as much as the revolutionaries had on their agenda. This is all in accord with the pre-modern disposition that politics is not about going anywhere or instigating anything but rather about keeping the ship of state afloat on an even keel.

This mentality is seen in Burke's idiosyncratic usage of the idea of contract. 'Society is indeed a contract',[51] he tells us. There was nothing surprising about this as term had a significant place in seventeenth- and eighteenth-century political thought. Social contract was said to be the basis from which society had emerged.

A pre-social condition had existed – a state of nature – from which, because of its inconveniences, people had come together to inaugurate an acceptable political order. The connotations of contract, then, were those of consent, choice and rationality. These ideas were part of the Whig ideology of the time. As a Whig, Burke held to their key concepts, but totally subverted their meaning. David Hume had undermined John Locke's belief in the actual historical occurrence of a social contract, but to Burke, this was beside the point. He believed authority accrued to institutions gradually over a long passage of time. It was prescription which, 'through long usage, mellows into legality governments that were violent in their commencement'.[52] In a way, wrong becomes right, but Burke's approach is more that origins, contractual or otherwise, don't matter. It is the long-term weathering of institutions that renders them optimal. The process of becoming is one in which institutions, values and patterns of behaviour gradually become appropriate and favourably serviceable to the people in question.

Furthermore, at the point of being made, a contract signifies free choice: that was the normal Whig sense. Burke, however, was fundamentally opposed to the radicals' view that forms of government were a matter of choice.[53] His contract, then, is one that *has been made*; one that holds you to its terms. Burke's contract, clearly, is the one that binds; it keeps everything in its place. It is, he says, between 'those who are living…those who are dead, and those who are to be born'.[54] It is a strange contract indeed, for as C.B. Macpherson once pointed out, it has three parties to it, two of whom are not alive![55] It is, then, not a contract that gives free choice but a contract as a tacit obligation to leave everything in its place; a very conservative contract indeed. So ends the theological case for inequality.

At this point, we should ask what can be said to those in the lower strata of an unequal society. Burke did not endear them to his cause when he called them a 'swinish multitude',[56] a phrase omitted from an abridged edition prepared for the lower orders.

Burke has an answer to our question:

Good order is the foundation of all good things…The body of the people must not find the principles of natural subordination by art rooted out of their minds. They must respect that property of which they cannot partake. They must labour to obtain what by labour can be obtained; and when they find, as they commonly do, the success disproportioned to the endeavour, they must be taught their consolation in the final proportions of eternal justice.[57]

This is a most revealing section. Burke here effectively concedes that the lower orders are normally exploited and that their hopes for justice must be postponed until the afterlife. This was not the only linkage Burke made between religion and the condition of the poor. He had earlier noted that monks 'are as usefully employed as if they worked from dawn to dark in the innumerable servile, degrading, unseemly, unmanly, and often most unwholesome and pestiferous occupations, to which by the social economy so many wretches are inevitably doomed'.[58] So, the many do appalling work to which they are 'inevitably doomed'. Clearly, the monks are doing significant ideological work in buttressing a social order that does little for the 'many wretches' on whose labour it is based. So, we see why atheism was such a threat; it weakened the ideological arm that supported an unequal society.

This all sounds like a very static notion of society. A charge sometimes levelled against Burke is that he so looked backward that he gave no chance for society to move forward. We must, then, ask whether he had a theory of social change.

Burke presumably knew that change occurred. The French Revolution, for example, was a change, but one for the worse. Was he so wedded to tradition that he opposed all change? It seems not. For him legitimate change is that which builds on a pre-existing tradition rather than discarding it and trying to start anew. Burke employed the metaphor of France as a castle in some disrepair but which still had the foundations from which a solid and reliable structure could be built. So when forced to clarify his views Burke could not condemn all change – or even, in certain circumstances, revolutionary change – for submission to the worst of tyrannies is obviously unacceptable. He had to admit that certain circumstances necessitate resistance: 'this, I think, may be safely affirmed, that a sore and pressing evil is to be removed.'[59] However, the removal operation should only commence when the possibility of replacing it with something better can be almost guaranteed.

The subversion of a government, to deserve any praise, must be considered but as a step preparatory to the formation of something better ... For instance, when we praise our Revolution of 1688, though the nation in that act was on the defensive, and was justified in incurring all the evils of a defensive war, we do not rest there. We always combine with the subversion of the old government, the happy settlement which followed. When we estimate that revolution we mean to comprehend in our calculation both the value of the thing parted with, and the value of the thing received in exchange.[60]

This was written in 1791. The French Revolution had not yet reached the worst of its excesses but had gone quite far enough for Burke. Revolutions tend to excess and so he warned: 'If ever we ought to be economists even to parsimony, it is in the voluntary production of evil. Every revolution contains in it something of evil.'[61] Thus Burke's theory of social change is that a society should build on what it has already established and grown accustomed to; and his 'ideal' tolerable revolution is one that is strictly necessary, defensive, as peaceful as possible, maintains the rule of law and has beneficial consequences.

In addition to 'liberty, equality and fraternity', the main declared principle of the revolutionaries was 'the rights of man'. This was not a new issue for Burke. He voiced his opposition to abstract speculation almost continuously throughout his writings. For example, in a 1774 speech on 'American Taxation' he declared: 'I am not here going into the distinctions of rights, nor attempting to mark their boundaries. I do not enter into these metaphysical distinctions; I hate the very sound of them.' Burke was keenly aware that ideas are intrinsically dangerous, for the mind can construct alternatives that are improvements on present conditions, and that this can have subversive consequences, for

if, intemperately, unwisely, fatally, you sophisticate and poison the very source of government, by urging subtle deductions ... from the unlimited and illimitable nature of supreme sovereignty, you will teach them by these means to call that sovereignty itself in question.[62]

As a conservative empiricist, Burke always declared for the concrete as against the metaphysical. For him, all questions of ethics were only meaningful when related to specific occasions. In response to the charge that he was against the rights of man, he replied that his allegiance had always been to *actual* rights rather than to merely abstract ones. An actual right is the claim of a power that is legally enforced by the state. It is a right which is specific and has long had official recognition. In this sense, Burke could present the British Declaration of the Bill of Rights of 1689 as a real right. In contrast, an abstract right is a claim that exists neither in law nor in the heritage of the country. It was the claim to abstract rights that was causing such havoc in France.

Abstract rights provide an insufficient basis for a stable political order as they have no grounding in the traditions of the people. A deep respect for tradition is the alternative and eminently preferable guide. As an example of this, Burke presents to the French people the respect for tradition embodied in the British Constitution. A constitution is now normally assumed to be a written document outlining the framework of the political structure. In Burke's time, the un-codified nature of the British Constitution was not abnormal; neither was his assumption that it provided a light by which its citizens were guided along safe and well-worn paths.

Time and again, Britain is held up as a model for the French. Change ought to occur gradually, peacefully, as in Britain, but Burke does not tell us much about British history. There is some discussion of the so-called Glorious Revolution of 1688. The reason such a vigorous opponent of violent change supported that event was because he saw the use of the term 'revolution' as being misleading – especially if it led to identification with current events in France. In 1688, according to Burke, the Whigs had actually acted in the spirit of the constitution. They had resisted an attempt by the king to subvert it. Thus their action 'was, in truth and substance and in a constitutional light, a revolution, not made, but prevented'.[63] Such was the only permissible type of revolution, a defensive one; a restoration rather than an inauguration. It consisted of no more that 'an irregular convulsive movement...necessary to throw off an irregular convulsive disease'.[64] In Burke's view that 'revolution' was not merely defensive but backward looking. 'The Revolution was made to preserve our *ancient* indisputable laws and liberties, and that *ancient* constitution of government, which is our only security for law and liberty.'[65] So, whereas the English Revolution had been strictly defensive, that in

France was entirely offensive, in both senses of the term. Where the English Revolution had been peaceful, that of France was violent.

For similar reasons, the American colonists of the 1770s were deserving of sympathy, for they were claiming for themselves nothing more than the continuation of their traditional rights. It seemed to Burke that, as in 1688, it was the king who was breaking with tradition. On 1688, we might add that the peaceful non-revolution was actually the culmination of a period of turmoil that began with the Civil War in the 1630s. Burke does not mention that the British had a civil war, let alone that they chopped the king's head off. Maybe in this way, the French were actually copying the British example!

In addition to the force of his political argument, a word should now be said on the power of Burke's rhetoric. Writing with the purpose of persuasion, of kindling in his readers passions approaching the intensity of his own, Burke composed passages of unforgettable splendour. Who, having once read them, could forget his recollection of Marie Antoinette besieged at Versailles: 'I thought ten thousand swords must have leaped from their scabbards to avenge even a look that threatened her with insult'; or his metaphor of the 'thousands of great cattle, reposed beneath the shadow of the British oak', as against the revolutionaries, those 'little, shrivelled, meagre, hopping, though loud and troublesome, insects of the hour'?[66] However, in later writings, frustration got the better of him, and Burke descended into grotesque bombast. In 1791, he described the Jacobins as 'Reptile Souls moving in the Dirt of the Obscure Vices in which they were generated... The stench of such an enormous Carcass as that of France is enough to poison all Europe.'[67]

Burke's Later Influence

It is hardly surprising that a writer as polemical as Burke should have received a mixed reception. To the lower orders, he became notorious for his denigration of them as a 'swinish multitude'.[68] To others, the *Reflections* seemed exaggerated and over-emotional. It immediately became the focus of debate but was certainly not accepted as an instant classic. However, as the

Napoleonic Wars continued Burke's reputation grew, for he had been the first to proclaim the cause of counter-revolution. He has been regarded as a significant influence on such conservative thinkers of the next generation as Wordsworth, Coleridge, Gentz, Müller, de Maistre and Bonald. Many Victorian liberals co-opted Burke to their cause, emphasising his suspicion of the Crown, his writings on the dispute with the American colonies, his unceasing preoccupation with the abuse of power and his defence of free market economics.[69] However, of all Burke's concerns, it was the French Revolution which sent the main shock waves into the nineteenth century, particularly as lesser versions were re-enacted in 1830, 1848 and 1871. Yet, it was during the Cold War period that Burke's reputation stood highest, his arguments against the French Revolution being seen as a model for the western case against communism. So Burke provided the basis of defence against all those who dreamt of overthrowing established systems and starting anew, or imagined that rationality alone provided sufficient criteria for political choice. Of such approaches, there were many, and so, for the conservative side, much use that could be made of Burke's counter-arguments.

So, it was that a man who initially appeared as the scourge of the Establishment became its foremost defender when it was under greatest attack. Burke's stand on the French Revolution is only one of the factors which have contributed to his historical significance. Of more durable effect is the supposition that in formulating a coherent response to contemporary events he also came to articulate the foremost account of conservative philosophy. In the words of a major spokesman of twentieth-century American conservatism, 'Burke's ideas...provided the defenses of conservatism on a great scale, that still stand and are not liable to fall in our time.'[70]

If Burke is really still of relevance, his outlook must be applicable beyond the particular circumstances of his time. For this to be so, his conservatism must be shown as more than the defence of the traditional European agrarian and aristocratic order. This has been argued by S.P. Huntington who points out that Burke impartially 'defended Whig institutions in England, democratic institutions in America, autocratic institutions in France and Hindu institutions in India'.[71] Burke, then, in each instance, defended what was traditional for that particular society. A procedure that had stood the test of time, that had developed gradually through a long historical process of small adjustments and changes, had, by virtue of that process, and whatever its precise content, become proper for the people and society in question. It is, then, this approach that has enabled Burke's writings to be used as a general conservative philosophy, even by those living in societies very different from anything he could personally have envisaged.

4
Thomas Paine

Life

Very few people ever have had as remarkable a public life as Thomas Paine. Having described our period as the age of revolution, we can designate Paine as the man of revolution – even more so than Marx – for he played an active part in both the great uprisings of the age. Paine's *Common Sense* (1776) did much to stimulate and solidify anti-British feeling in the American colonies. One historian has described it as 'the most effective tract of the American Revolution'.[1] Furthermore, Paine's participation in the actual fighting and his later election by Congress to Secretary of its Foreign Affairs Committee all served to give him a more comprehensive view than most of the problems of revolution and the inauguration of new political systems. Having returned to Europe in time for the French Revolution, Paine's *Rights of Man* (1791–2) was soon accepted as the foremost rebuttal of Burke's *Reflection on the Revolution in France*. This secured for Paine honorary French citizenship and, though he spoke very little French, he represented Calais in their National Convention. Here, he aligned himself with the Girondin faction and pleaded for the life of Louis XVI, arguing against the system of monarchy rather than the current incumbent. This relatively sophisticated point was lost on the Jacobins, who confined Paine in the Luxemburg Palace, which was then being used as a prison. Having been outlawed by the English for being too radical, he was imprisoned by Robespierre for being too conservative. Paine's life was saved by a lucky fluke and the end of the reign of terror. Later involvement with the French included being consulted by Napoleon (who can scarcely have needed help on this) on the art of invasion. This was just one of the ways in which Paine tried to foment revolution in Britain. To the charge of treason, and contrary to Burke's emphasis on local attachments, Paine wrote that 'my country is the world, and my religion is to do good.'[2]

Such activities and Paine's consequent fame all belong to the second half of his life and could hardly have been suspected from the insignificance of his youth. Paine was born in 1737 in Thetford, Norfolk, the son of a Quaker father and Anglican mother. He left school at 13 yet produced an impressive and highly influential body of writing.[3]

Paine found employment with the excise service in Grantham in 1764 only to be dismissed a year later. He was re-appointed in 1768 in Lewes, Sussex, where his house still stands. In 1772, he wrote an appeal to parliament on behalf of excise officers.[4] It was his first significant writing and may have contributed to his 1774 dismissal from the service. If so, this outcome of his state employment cannot have endeared him to the British state and his later writings might, in part, be seen as his revenge.

Anyway, 1774 was a particularly bleak year for Paine. Apart from dismissal from the excise service, his tobacco shop failed and his second marriage was dissolved: a triple disappointment. He was 37 in an age when life expectancy was considerably lower than today.[5] No one could have predicted the prominent future that lay ahead. In December, he reached North America, which was to be the making of him. He was soon into radical journalism, campaigning against slavery, privilege, monarchy and cruelty to animals. His writings on behalf of the American and French revolutions then followed.

At the age of 65, with his revolutionary adventures well behind him, Paine returned to the United States. He did not get the reception he deserved. His role in the independence movement now counted for less than his denigration of the late, great General Washington. His support of the French Revolution was now used to align him with Jacobinism, of which he'd actually been a victim. His dissection of Christianity in *The Age of Reason* led to him being denounced as an atheist, which he wasn't; and his heavy drinking had him derided as a drunkard, which he probably was. He died in obscurity, and only six mourners were at his funeral. However, he was not entirely forgotten by later generations, for during the

Second World War, American airmen donated a statue of Paine to his home town of Thetford.

The American Colonies

Paine's arrival in America in 1774 was not auspicious. He got ill on the sea crossing and had to be brought ashore on a stretcher. Once restored to health, he rented a room in central Philadelphia. Next door was a bookshop where Paine soon made friends with its owner, Robert Aitken. Aitken wanted to produce a journal called *The Pennsylvania Magazine* and offered Paine the post of executive editor. The repercussions of this were immense, for it marked the beginning of Paine's literary career. As the essays and reports in the magazine appeared anonymously, it is still not fully certain exactly which ones were written by Paine. What is certain is that he gained a valuable apprenticeship in political journalism. The issue of the day, of course, was the dispute with Britain and the dominant response was to work for conciliation. Paine, however, had a different view. For this, he required more than the length of a magazine article and so prepared a longer pamphlet.

Common Sense was published in Philadelphia in January 1776. The whole first edition, comprising 1000 copies, was sold within 2 weeks and 'perhaps half a million in the first year'.[6] As for its impact, *The American Annual Register* for 1796 contained the following account:

> When the first copies arrived in the American camp at Cambridge, they were perused with transport. An officer then in that army observed lately that a reinforcement of five thousand men would not have inspired the troops with equal confidence as this pamphlet did, in the justice of their cause and the probability of their ultimate success . . . Before the plain arguments of an obscure individual . . . the pensioned and titled advocates of royalty sunk into forgetfulness . . . The summons to liberty and to vengeance resounded from New Hampshire to Georgia. From the degraded appendage of a foreign monarchy, the thirteen United States rose to an independent existence. Thomas Paine was the Tyrtaeus of that revolution.[7]

Paine was suddenly famous on both sides of the Atlantic. This was the first time that most people in England had heard of him, so Burke was surely not alone in assuming that Paine was American.[8] This designation is one point of agreement between them both, for Paine soon identified with his fellow Americans, speaking of and for them in the first person plural.

Much attention has been given to contrasting Burke and Paine on the French Revolution; much less to their differences on the American Revolution. The common notion that they were on the same side on the American dispute must be modified by the basic differences of their approach: Burke's emphasis was on conciliation, Paine's on the irreconcilable differences between the two countries. The first few pages of *Common Sense* display a certain philosophical propensity on the common eighteenth-century theme of the origins of society and government. Paine's motives, however, were always more political than philosophical. Here, he suggested that society emerges from our virtues and government from our vices.

> Society is produced by our wants, and governments by our wickedness... Society in every state is a blessing, but government even in its best state is but a necessary evil... Government, like dress, is the badge of lost innocence; the palaces of kings are built on the ruins of the bowers of paradise.[9]

There is, perhaps, a slight anarchistic yearning in Paine's early writings but he did not, like Rousseau, trace the origin of government to a trick, nor, like Marx, to a defensive tactic by the rich. Rather, humankind was not good enough to remain in the state of nature. 'For were the impulses of conscience clear, uniform, and irresistibly obeyed, man would need no other lawgiver; but that not being the case, he finds it necessary to surrender up a part of his property to furnish means for the protection of the rest.'[10] The process of de-legitimising government had begun. It continued by rapid movement to the issue of monarchy. This he attempted both by biblical evidence and by enquiring into the origins of the British monarchy.

The crisis in the American colonies provided the first significant opportunity for the development of Paine's incessant anti-monarchical crusade. Most colonists blamed the British parliament rather than George III for the imposition of excessive taxation and controls of trade. Paine, however, was less concerned with the character of the man than with the origins and nature of the system. His condemnation commenced chronologically and in a surprising manner for an author who was later to become famous for denying the veracity of the Bible:

> In the early ages of the world, according to the scripture chronology, there were no kings...Government by kings was first introduced into the world by the Heathens, for whom the children of Israel copied the custom. It was the most prosperous invention the Devil ever set on foot, for the promotion of idolatry...for the will of the Almighty, as declared by Gideon and the prophet Samuel, expressly disapproves of government by kings.[11]

With reference to the British monarchy, Paine declared:

> In England a k[ing] hath little more to do than to make war and give away places; which in plain terms, is to impoverish the nation and set it together by the ears. A pretty business indeed for a man to be allowed eight hundred thousand sterling a year for, and worshipped into the bargain! Of more worth is one honest man to society and in the sight of God, than all the crowned ruffians that ever lived.[12]

This is followed by reference to 'the Royal [Brute] of Britain' and the conclusion that 'He, who hunts the woods for prey, the naked and untutored Indian, is less a Savage than the [King] of B[ritain].'[13]

Paine shared the radical individualism of a sub-culture strongly influenced by Puritanism and so joined the attacks against aristocratic luxury and wastefulness. The old regimes were condemned largely on account of the heavy taxes required for the court and the armed forces. The American War of Independence was seen as a resistance to British avarice and to the attempted imposition of English taxation levels, which in 1780 Paine presented as being 11 times heavier than those in the American colonies.[14]

Paine thought that even if conciliation brought peace, it would be in Britain's interest only. His call for American independence was the first plain avowal of such a policy. It came at just the moment when the course of events disposed people to accept it. For many, their approval was reluctant, as there was still immense respect for the laws and institutions of the ruling colonial power. The revolution, as has often been noted, was carried out by people with little revolutionary intent. Their distance from the mentality of the Jacobins was immense, as is made clear, for example, by the career and writings of John Adams, the second President of the United States.[15] As usual, then, Paine was on the radical wing of political debate, heartily welcoming the attempt to overthrow the domination of a system he despised. Independence was not to be viewed as an unfortunate necessity but as 'America's natural right and interest'. When the struggle was almost over Paine proclaimed the achievement the 'greatest and completest revolution the world ever knew, gloriously and happily accomplished'.[16]

In these writings on American independence, Paine hardly concerned himself with the rights and tactics of political disobedience, rather taking it for granted that colonialism and freedom were irreconcilably opposed. It was not until a few years later that he linked the appeal to force with the absence of representative institution.

> The despotic form of government knows no intermediate space between being slaves and being rebels ... the government which Britain attempted to erect over America could be no other than a despotism, because it left to the Americans no other modes of redress than those which are left to people under despotic governments, petition and resistance.[17]

Paine was not alone in regarding the American revolt as 'a new era for politics ... a new method of thinking hath arisen', for the myth of a new start, of removing the shackles of the past, was widespread. This 'new era' was not for America alone but also for the many other countries still ruled by monarchy, so, he declared, the 'cause of America is in a great measure the cause of all mankind.'[18]

Paine was not the first to argue for American independence, but he was probably the most significant. The North American colonies were soon overwhelmed with an almost millenarian faith in their own destiny and, once the struggle was over, Paine expressed his satisfaction:

> Never, I say, had a country so many openings to happiness as this. Her setting out into life, like the rising of a fair morning, was unclouded and promising. Her cause was good. Her

principles just and liberal. Her temper serene and firm. Her conduct regulated by the nicest steps, and every thing about her wore the mark of honor.[19]

But life is not that simple. Paine was soon involved in the murky business that politics so often is. Accusations of financial irregularities against Silas Deane led to Paine's forced resignation from the Committee of Foreign Affairs and attacks on him in the street. Perhaps, it is not surprising that so outspoken a figure should have generated opponents. This was becoming increasingly obvious and irksome. Paine had donated the proceeds of his writings to the American cause, but by the mid-1780s, he was short of both money and work. Neither the federal government nor the individual states compensated him to the extent he expected, so in 1787, he was glad to return to Europe, conveniently in time for the next great revolution of his life.

The French Revolution and the *Rights of Man*

Having played his part in North America, Paine felt distinct signs of change in the old world. Arriving in Paris in May 1787, he penned an essay to which events gave a prophetic ring: 'The people of France are beginning to think for themselves... It is a matter well known to every man who has lately been in France, that a very extraordinary change is working itself in the minds of the people of that nation.'[20] At this stage, Paine still felt sympathetic to the Bourbon regime. It had, after all, given support to the American cause. However, once the Bastille fell, Paine identified with the French revolutionary movement, though the Quaker in him set him apart from those who thrived on bloodshed and murder; and so from the Jacobins and the 'reign of terror', whose victim he so nearly became. Paine, then, was a revolutionary for whom a revolution did not have to be violent. He believed that where the strength of reason was sufficient to persuade, violence would become unnecessary. Paine's ideal was a 'passive, rational, and costless revolution' in which 'Reason, like time, will make its own way, and prejudice will fall in a combat with interest.'[21]

Paine's claimed right of revolution was always linked with the principle of government by consent. Whereas Locke, a century earlier, had envisaged resistance as justified only when the governmental 'trust' had been broken, for Paine the right to political self-determination was absolute. A 'Nation has at all times an inherent indefeasible right to abolish any form of government it finds inconvenient, and establish such as accords with its interest, disposition, and happiness.'[22]

Once he learned that Burke was writing against the revolution, Paine was determined to respond. Part One of the *Rights of Man* appeared in 1791. A thousand copies were sold in the first fortnight and 50,000 copies before the end of the year. Part Two was published in 1792, and by the end of the following year, 200,000 copies had been sold, making the book one of the publishing sensations of all time.[23]

This was a work for which its author was convicted of seditious libel and outlawed. He escaped prison thanks to a warning from the poet and artist William Blake which provided Paine with enough time to escape to France. This in itself indicates that Paine was no lackey of polite society presenting the literate public with the banal conventional wisdoms of his day. What nearly brought the full wrath of the law down on Paine's head was the fact that he had just delivered the whole British Establishment as outspoken, straightforward and censorious a broadside as they can ever have received. And this attack came at a moment when, whatever firmness may have been evident in their fabled stiff upper lips, the covered knees of the stiff upper classes were becoming distinctly wobbly. The collapse of the old regime in France, the humiliation of their aristocracy, the chaos and confiscation that had accompanied the arrival of the new ruling group had all served to encourage other kings to cling in fear and trepidation to their thrones, other nobles to their status and privileges, lest a similar fate befall them. A distinct chill shiver ran through the courts of Europe. The least spark of discontent was rigorously suppressed, lest it flare up into a conflagration beyond all possible control.

It was in such an atmosphere of wary tension that Paine decided to inform the British public that monarchy and aristocracy were expensive, illegitimate, belligerent and superstitious frauds, based on ignorance and opposed to all notions of reason; that realisation of the absurdity of such a pernicious system was merely the first step in replacing them with a qualitatively superior order – as had been done in France.

The monarchy and aristocracy were the possessors of power, so Paine turned his attention to systems of government. In his view, 'governments must have arisen either *out* of the people, or *over* the people.'[24] He regarded the latter form as being in the majority and classified the sources of government as either 'superstition', 'power' or 'the common interest of society and the common rights of man. The first was a government of priestcraft, the second of conquerors, and the third of reason.'[25] The latter form is one of social compact; the other two are not. Compact is 'the only principle on which they have a right to exist'.[26] Should there be any doubt about the nature of the compact, Paine makes it explicit that he is not referring to any agreement between the government and the people. This would be impossible because it is only as a result of the compact that government is formed. The act by which government is established is, as with Locke and Rousseau before him, one of 'trust'. The government is neither a superior body nor an equal partner with the people. It is deliberately put in an inferior position as a trustee, with duties rather than rights, obliged to serve rather than command. In his earlier writings, Paine had displayed anarchistic tendencies and clear traces of this are still evident in the *Rights of Man* where we are told that 'a great deal of what is called government is mere imposition. Government is no farther necessary than to supply the few cases to which society and civilization are not conveniently competent.'[27] However, following the American and French revolutions, Paine more generally came to see them as potentially doing some good. Nevertheless, governments always tend towards domination and so need to be kept firmly in their place.

The way to do this was to follow the Americans and have a written constitution. This contains the terms on which the people agree to structure their political system. It is the arrangement they make with each other; it also sets the limits within which government is contained. Without a constitution, a government has full legislative freedom, for good or ill, during its period of office. Where there is a constitution, this freedom is curtailed and the people maintain their basic rights. 'Government without a constitution, is power without a right.'[28]

The United States, of course, was in the vanguard. It was an exception to the normal rule. For Burke, actual origins were unimportant. For Paine, in contrast, they were crucial. They determined all that followed. A government based on false principles continues on false principles. Paine de-legitimised monarchy by asking how it originally emerged:

> It could have been no difficult thing in the early and solitary ages of the world, while the chief employment of men was that of attending flocks and herds, for a banditti of ruffians to over-run a country, and lay it under contributions. Their power being thus established, the chief of the band contrived to lose the name of Robber in that of Monarch; and hence the origin of Monarchy and Kings.[29]

Paine's prime example of badly constituted government was that of his own country of origin – England. He found English govern-ment deficient both in terms of historical origins and contemporary practice. The first step to rationality had never been taken. No con-stitution had been formulated. The resulting condition was that beneath the glittering but tinsel-thin façade of society there lay hid-den 'a mass of wretchedness that has scarcely any chance, than to expire in poverty or infamy.'[30]

Paine saw all these troubles as stemming from William the Con-queror, 'the son of a prostitute and the plunderer of the English Nation.'[31] The system's origins lay in conquest, and so throughout its subsequent history, servitude had frozen into the social structure. Paine believed that the descendants of the Norman conquerors still formed the ruling class in Britain. This is the theory of the 'Norman yoke', a notion that is still given expression as late as 1845 in Benjamin's Disraeli's *Sybil or the Two Nations*. For Paine, 'if the succes-sion runs in the line of conquest, the Nation runs in the line of being conquered, and it ought to rescue itself from that reproach.'[32] Paine, then, did not accept the Whig view that the 1688 revolution pro-vided a sufficient curb on arbitrary monarchical power. In spite of his avowed internationalism, he felt insulted that the British had sent for a foreigner to rule over them. That revolution still left Britain with monarchy and aristocracy, forms for which Paine felt nothing but contempt. Monarchy he saw as an empty form, based on igno-rance and force, inherently belligerent, necessarily conservative and often of foreign extraction. He believed that such a system impover-ished society, for it gathered around the throne a band of parasites living off public money. The only reason it survived was by giv-ing certain groups a vested interest in its continuance. It was 'the master-fraud, which shelters all others'; 'a thing kept up to amuse the ignorant and quiet them into taxes'.[33]

However, for Paine monarchy was a harmful and expensive luxury. Once dispensed with, its apparent necessity immediately disappears. 'If I ask a man in America, if he wants a King? he retorts, and asks me if I take him for an idiot?'[34] Similar criticisms apply to aristocracy. The practice of primogeniture, in dispossessing all younger sons, burdens the public with maintaining a group otherwise condemned to poverty. 'Aristocracy has never more than *one* child. The rest are begotten to be devoured.'[35] The French had shown that rigid class differentials were ludicrous and unnatural. 'The artificial NOBLE shrinks into a dwarf before the NOBLE of Nature.'[36] What divides a nation should be replaced by what unites it. The title of 'Man' was sufficient for this purpose. 'The French Constitution says, *There shall be no titles*; and, of consequence, all that class of equivocal generation, which in some countries is called "aristocracy" and in others "nobility", is done away, and the *peer* is exalted into MAN.'[37] As to the 'Nobility, or rather No-ability...the Nation disowned knowing anything of them but as citizens.'[38]

Such comments make Paine seem like an opponent of hierarchy. This, however, was not so. He was merely opposed to a hierarchy based on birth, which he wanted replaced by one founded on actual achievement. He was less in favour of an equal society than one that allowed equality of opportunity. Here, he adopted the French Revolutionary maxim of 'the career open to talent'.

Having informed us that most governments were wrongly constituted, Paine's examples of governments based on reason were the recently inaugurated ones of the United States and France. These were the two countries in which both monarchical and ecclesiastical power had been abolished and where political power derived from elections for freely chosen representatives. For much of the nineteenth century, the revolutions of these two countries were regarded as having instituted democracy and Paine, similarly, has been widely viewed as an advocate of democratic politics. This point needs some consideration, for Paine actually wrote very little on democracy. The *Rights of Man* contains just a few pages on the topic. As was then quite normal, he regarded democracy as an ancient form of government practiced for a time in Athens. Paine greatly approved of Athenian democracy – 'We see more to admire, and less to condemn, in that great, extraordinary people, than in any thing which history affords.' What he then referred to as democracy we now call 'direct democracy', a form suitable only for small societies where all citizens can assemble in one place. Once the population and area of the territory increased 'the simple democratical form became unwieldy and impracticable' and degenerated into monarchy. So, democracy for Paine was an ideal form of rule, but one confined to small societies at an early stage of their development: 'original simple democracy'[39] was how he sometimes referred to it. Athenian democracy, of course, had restrictions. Women, slaves and resident foreigners had no voting rights. So for Paine, unlike for us, democracy was a constitutional form which could have considerable restrictions.

Who, then, would have the right to vote in Paine's recommended system? In *Rights of Man*, Paine did mention that the French constitution imposed a tax qualification for voting and also suggested that in Britain the right of election should be 'as universal as taxation'.[40] He described the prevailing situation as one where taxation took a quarter of the income of 'a labouring man, with a wife and two or three children'. This surely implies that everyone is taxed, but the aforementioned labouring man does not realise this 'because it is disguised to him in the articles which he buys'.[41] Anyway, even if taxation were universal, it is noteworthy that the author of *Rights of Man* did *not* explicitly present the right to vote as a right of man. It is more evidently presented as a right of taxpayers. This, of course, was the significant linkage made in the American colonial claim of 'No taxation without representation'. In the *Rights of Man*, Paine was les radical about franchise rights than were the members of the London Corresponding Society, founded in 1792. They believed that 'every adult person, in possession of his reason, and not incapacitated by crimes, should have a vote for a Member of Parliament.'[42] It was not until 1795 that Paine explicitly rejected the prevalent notion that property should provide the basis of voting rights.[43]

Would women have the vote? They didn't in ancient Greece, nor in post-revolutionary France and the United States of America, yet obviously women, like men, paid tax on the goods they purchased, for Paine wrote that 'all the people of England pay taxes.'[44] So although Paine seems like one of us because he favoured representative government, we should not presume that this implied universal franchise, for after all Paine was capable of marvellously direct expression. If he had wanted women and the poor to have the vote, he was quite capable of saying so clearly, directly and unambiguously. It is significant that – at least in *Rights of Man* – he didn't.

One notable way in which Paine did foreshadow future developments was in his concern for welfare. The final chapters of *Rights of Man* contain financial tables outlining his plans for child allowances, subsidised schooling, birth, marriage and funeral grants, old age pensions and proposals for the 'Employment at all times for the casual poor in the cities of London and Westminster'.[45] Paine wanted no prohibition on the money accumulated through hard work but would limit the amount that could be inherited. This of course would, as probably intended, hit the aristocracy hardest. It is, then, no exaggeration to describe Paine as an under-acknowledged ideological precursor of the welfare state that came to his country a century and a half later.

Is this, then, the same Thomas Paine who favoured free trade and cheap government? Apparently so, for Paine believed that the overthrow of the aristocratic system would rid society of its particular costs. With the abolition of primogeniture, the aristocracy would have to pay for their own younger children rather than foisting them upon the public with 'useless posts, places, and offices'.[46] Furthermore, he believed that aristocracy meant war, while free commerce required peace. When the latter predominated, navies would become unnecessary and could be dismantled. Consequently, government would be no more expensive than before, for the money needed for welfare payments could 'be drawn from the excise collections, which are made eight times a year in every market town in England'.[47] In 'Agrarian Justice', written in the winter of 1795–6, Paine further developed his concern with social inequality. Here, he suggested paying everyone 15 pounds at the age of 21 and 10 pounds a year to all those aged 50 or over. These payments were to be financed by death duties and a 10 per cent tax on land. For Paine, the poor should not have to rely on charity and suffer the stigma with which it was associated. Welfare was a right, and the tax on land that funded it was the compensation that the landed owed to the propertyless, for land had originally been given by God to mankind in common. Its private appropriation had been necessary for agricultural productivity and development, but nevertheless those who lost out were entitled to recompense.

Though governments on the whole were bad, Paine had not given up hope. People, having previously created their state structure, were equally capable of altering it. Unlike Burke, Paine considered that each generation had the right of changing its whole form of government. The potential ability was there, lying dormant. Man's reason had only to be brought into operation for improved, legitimate government to follow in its wake.

There is a certain optimism inherent in acceptance of the possibility of social change – the bad does not have to be fatalistically accepted. Faults can be remedied, however bad, for basic human nature remains good. 'Man, were he not corrupted by governments, is naturally the friend of man' for 'human nature is not of itself vicious.'[48] That there is little evidence of this merely shows the extent to which people have been corrupted by governments. The disposition and capacity for rational government both prevail – all that is needed is rather more strength of will for the abstract vision to become a practical reality. Only then will the 'original inherent Rights of Man'[49] be introduced into society.

Paine did not hold his vision of the just future to be utopian for he had helped to inaugurate it – in North America. There the people had formed a constitution to control their government. From rational beginnings had stemmed rational conduct. The form of government decided on was republican, its interference in society was confined to those apparently few functions that could not otherwise be performed, 'order and harmony were preserved,'[50] and the economy prospered.

The significance of this change was seen as considerably greater than its local impact. It was the powder keg that would set Europe alight. French soldiers returning from the successful struggle in North America brought the good message of liberty back to their own country: 'A knowledge of the practice was then joined to the theory; and all that was wanting to give it real existence, was opportunity.'[51] It is characteristic of the thought of this period that Paine placed such stress on ideas as the major factor determining social change. Furthermore, these ideas were not exclusively external in origin. Within France itself, the major thinkers were preoccupied with some fundamental questions. Paine instanced Montesquieu, Voltaire, Rousseau, Abbé Raynal, Quesnay and Turgot as a revolutionary intelligentsia undermining the ideological foundations of the old regime.

With the examples before him, Paine was clearly aware of the possibility of radical social change. When he mentioned 'revolution', he wanted his readers to be quite clear to what scale of phenomenon he was referring. He was not concerned with those minimal changes which 'had nothing in them that interested the bulk of mankind' but with a complete 'renovation of the natural order of things'[52] Piecemeal tinkering would not get to the causes of the problem, for it was not the cogs of society that needed oiling, but the whole machinery which needed replacing. It was the system as a whole which was at fault.

In order that the tax burden might be reduced, that the dormant talents of the nation may be developed and that the new order in France might prosper in security, Paine saw it as necessary that the British should also assert their human rights by means of revolution. This, to Paine, did not necessarily imply violence. Where the strength of reason was sufficient to persuade, the force of violence becomes unnecessary. Whichever path the situation might dictate, Paine had no doubt that the destination would be reached. Reason would win through. Nothing could be the same again, for what is once known can never be lost. Society would be qualitatively and irreversibly improved for the age of revolution was at hand.

Just as the Bolsheviks, in the immediate aftermath of the 1917 revolution, expected similar outbreaks throughout the capitals of Europe, so Paine was convinced that regeneration would be so rapid that 'I do not believe that Monarchy and Aristocracy will continue seven years longer in any of the enlightened countries in Europe.'[53] 'The iron is becoming hot all over Europe. The insulted German and the enslaved Spaniard, the Russ and the Pole, are beginning to think.' It was even 'necessary to include England in the prospect of a general reformation'[54] for the French would take for Britain the role that the Americans had performed for them. All in all, Paine anticipated better times for the countries that concerned him. 'The present age will hereafter merit to be called the Age of Reason, and the present generation will appear to the future as the Adam of a new world.'[55]

Paine's declared purpose in *Rights of Man* was to reply to Burke's *Reflections*, so we should now ask how successfully he did so, focusing particularly on their differing views on the aristocracy, on human rights and on the condition of the poor.

To Burke, the advantage of aristocratic rule was that they were the class with political experience. This is the view that any task is better performed by those who have previously done it than by those who haven't. Paine's approach to the aristocracy was quite different. He investigated the norms by which they operated. One such rule was the hereditary principle by which leading positions were obtained by birth rather than talent. With characteristic clarity of mind, Paine reduced this idea to absurdity: 'The idea of hereditary legislators is as inconsistent as that of hereditary judges, or hereditary juries; and as absurd as an hereditary mathematician, or an hereditary wise man; and as ridiculous as an hereditary poet-laureate.'[56]

Paine's other main case against the aristocracy concerned primogeniture: inheritance by the eldest son. He declared that this system threw all the other children upon the community; they were 'begotten to be devoured'. The aristocracy, then, were fundamentally unjust in the way they treated their own class. Their 'ideas of *distributive justice* are corrupted at the very source.'[57] In how they treat their own, they demonstrated how fundamentally unqualified they were to be rulers of the nation as a whole. Finally on the aristocracy, we have already noted that their origins in conquest had long frozen society into a structure of conquest from which it should emancipate itself.

Paine's very title of *Rights of Man* indicated that this concept formed the core of his case. Burke had maintained that in 1688, the English had established 'for ever' the principle of hereditary monarchy. Paine took this to mean that the generation of 1688 enjoyed the right to determine their form of rule but that no later generations had a similar right, so that currently men had no rights.[58] Burke, then, seemed to be acknowledging the rights of the dead but denying those of the living. Paine, in contrast, accepted the right of the 1688 generation to establish their preferred form of rule, but then asserted that an equal right belonged to all subsequent generations. Furthermore, he thought it proper that these subsequent generations should fully use that right. Each generation necessarily had more knowledge than its predecessors and in this way government would be continually improved. We see on this issue the extent to which Paine's approach was geared to facilitating change and Burke's to resisting it. Precedent was Paine's deadly enemy: the legal barrier by which the mistakes of the past were repeated and in whose name all attempts at improvement were condemned. Where

Burke appealed to the authority of the 1688 settlement, Paine only regarded as legitimate the wishes of the current generation. 'Every age and generation must be as free to act for itself, *in all cases*, as the ages and generations which preceded it. The vanity and presumption of governing beyond the grave is the most ridiculous and insolent of tyrannies.'[59]

The differences between Burke and Paine on rights were geographical as well as historical. For Burke, rights were specific to the locations that had given them legal force. Thus, rights in one country could be quite different from those in another. For Paine, in contrast, rights were universal; there were no mere rights of Englishmen or Frenchmen, but rather the Rights of Man. Burke, as we have noticed, perceived the radical danger of universalist claims, an important difference that resonates through to the human rights debates of our own time. Another stark difference between Burke and Paine is in their attitude to the poor. Burke offered them the hope of justice in the next world; Paine wanted redistribution and welfare in this one.

Just as Burke's *Reflections* stimulated an immense response, so too did Paine's *Rights of Man*.[60] Of the 60 or so publications answering Paine, we shall attend solely to Burke's response. His opinion of Paine's writings was not favourable. Paine, he thought, was 'utterly incapable of comprehending his subject. He has not even a moderate portion of learning of any kind.' Any answer to his arguments should be made not by the 'speculatist' but by the 'magistrate'[61]

Burke and Paine had been personally acquainted. In a letter of August 1788, Burke wrote: 'I am going to dine with the D[uke] of Portland in company with the great American Paine.'[62] They made a tour of the northern iron foundries in 1788 and agreed to meet in 1790 but avoid the topic of France. There is a sense in which they both wrote extreme works and were ignorant of the full causes of the French Revolution. Here, their accounts had some similarity as for both the spread of ideas was fundamental, though, of course, they had contrary evaluations of the worth of those ideas. For Burke, the French Revolution signified the arrival of chaos, evil and disorder; for Paine, the millenarian arrival of a secular Jerusalem. Neither viewed the revolution as anything other than a simplistic and clearcut phenomenon – a force of unmitigated evil or of unstained virtue. Paine saw England and pre-revolutionary France as corrupt, expensive, aristocratic, tyrannical, belligerent and irrational. In contrast, the new regimes of America and France were essentially honest, cheap, free, representative, peaceful and rational. These distinctions were so clear to him that he too easily imagined they would be so to all. For this reason, Paine was able to suggest that the old regimes, once exposed, would no longer be tolerated, especially so as their first two successors had already appeared. Paine, in *Rights of Man* at least, was over-complimentary to America and France; their having disposed of monarchical power led him too easily to assume the absence of all other vices. Britain, by contrast, having a monarchy, was assumed to possess the full range of corruption in all aspects of its national life.

Paine's optimism was based on a number of assumptions which were common among contemporary radicals. *Firstly*, he assumed that prejudices were easy to remove. 'No man is prejudiced in favour of a thing knowing it to be wrong. He is attached to it on the belief of its being right, and when he sees it is not so, the prejudice will be gone.'[63] Clearly, here we find no awareness of the limited extent to which beliefs are dependent on rationality for their acceptance. *Secondly*, Paine assumed that the art of government would be simple and straightforward once the vested interests and intrigues of aristocratic rule were removed. In May 1804, in an 'Address to the People of England', who were presumed to be badly in need of this message, Paine described the experience of American settlers brought into their first contact with political activity. 'They soon found that government was not that complicated thing, enshrined in mystery, which church and state, to play into each other's hands, had represented...Common sense, common honesty, and civil manners, qualify a man for government.'[64]

This pleasing misconception popularised earlier by Rousseau and later by Lenin has been a recurrent myth among radicals; always exploded, forgotten or ignored when the actual burdens of government have to be borne. A similar recurrent myth was that of natural belligerency expressed in war and imperialism as belonging solely to the old regime. The arrival of liberalism was heralded with as many over-optimistic expectations as that of socialism. The benefit of hindsight makes Paine easy to criticise, so we must acknowledge that one could never apply to him the criticism he made of Edmund Burke, who, he said, 'pities the plumage, but forgets the dying bird.'[65]

Before leaving Paine and the two revolutions, we must note that his predominant optimism was not unalloyed. We have already noted his change of mood concerning the United States. In France also, he registered the turn that events were taking. In 1793, the desertion of General Dumouriez, the defeat of the expedition to Holland and the persecution of his Girondin friends, and then of himself, led him to modify his earlier hopes. In April 1793, he wrote to Jefferson that 'Had this revolution been conducted consistently with its principles, there was once a good prospect of extending liberty through the greatest part of Europe; but I now relinquish that hope.'[66] Paine also tended to blame the shortcomings of the revolutionaries on vestiges from the old regime or on continuing British intrigue. In *The Age of Reason*, he characterised 'the Terror', much of which he spent inside the Luxemburg prison, as a condition in which the 'intolerant spirit of church persecution had transferred itself into politics.'[67]

Paine never fully reconciled himself to Napoleon's regime, and in September 1802, he returned to the United States. To his surprise, republican government had not eradicated sectional intrigue, while his immediate arrest on a charge of indebtedness can have done little to improve his disposition towards his country of choice. He published seven 'Letters to the Citizens of the United States' in which it is clear that, in spite of all disappointments, the light of 1776 still shone clear enough to provide the necessary vision. Yet in these letters, Paine admits that Cromwell was a tyrant and that tyranny had emerged in republican France. In the *Rights of Man*, there is nothing on the English Civil War, Cromwell and the setting up of a Republic. This is a strange omission in that Paine recommended a republic but didn't consider what happened when his own country had one.

Both friends and foes regarded Paine's message as expressing both the discontents and aspirations of lower-class radicalism. In 1797, one observer noted that 'our peasantry now read the *Rights of Man* on mountains and moors, and by the wayside'[68] while, much later, E.P. Thompson described the book as 'a foundation text of the English working-class movement'.[69] The extraordinary extent of Paine's sales indicates the impact he made, highly regarded on one side but despised on the other. Paine was in fact one of the most vilified people in British history. In this, the government led the way. After the first part of *Rights of Man* was published, the government subsidised anti-Paine pamphlets and a hostile biography. In 1792, their proclamation against seditious writings was aimed primarily against Paine. E.P. Thompson noted that 'Agents were appointed in various districts to visit bookshops and prosecute any found selling *Rights of Man*.'[70] Among the prosecutions was that of the Leicester bookseller Richard Phillips, who in 1793 was imprisoned for 18 months while James Ridgway, a Piccadilly bookseller, received a 4-year sentence. Around the same time, Paine was given the Guy Fawkes treatment, burned in effigy in towns and villages throughout the country. Frank O'Gorman has counted 412 known burnings during the winter of 1792–3, but still thinks 'this figure...must be a considerable underestimate.'[71] One might, at this stage, have thought that Paine could not possibly cause more offence, but he did, and that by publishing on the touchy topic of religion.

The Age of Reason

Paine's book titles conveniently inform us of his key concepts. If 'rights' came first, then 'reason' was second. It was reason that would indicate the existence of our rights. This was a quality that Paine was sure he possessed. In the third paragraph of the very first number of *The Crisis*, he assured his readers: 'I have as little superstition in me as any man living.'[72] Reason demanded government according to the rights of man. Human capability was quite sufficient, but this potential was lying dormant, shrouded by a veil of prejudice. If reason were brought into operation, legitimate government would follow. Paine's opinions were symptomatic of the wave of optimism that accompanied the prevalent philosophical speculation: 'Reason is beginning to throw such strong daylight upon all political questions that we should boldly and magnanimously repulse every sort of fear lest man should sink back in the black night of ignorance.'[73] The reason to which Paine referred is not primarily connected with deeply thought out intellectual logic, nor with the empirical process by which opinions can be based on historical, archaeological, literary or legal evidence. Rather, he proposed the simple, straightforward common sense of an uncluttered, honest mind.

For Paine, the prevalent inherited irrationalities lay not only in the political and social structure of his time but also in the dominant religious institutions. Disentangling faith and reason is a contentious business. Locke thought religious beliefs could be a matter of reason. Burke would not have made such a calculated attempt, holding that fundamental religious values should not be laid open to speculation. Paine, in contrast, was contemptuous of almost all religious beliefs that imposed the least strain upon his credulity, though he held unquestioningly to a belief in God.

Paine's opposition to churches was based upon their demand for blind obedience, a process requiring the alienation of individual thought and conscience. In their place, he declared: 'My own mind is my own church.'[74] 'I have now gone through the Bible, as a man would go through a wood with an axe on his shoulder, and fell trees.'[75] Christian belief is declared 'little else than the idolatry of the ancient mythologists, accommodated to the purposes of power and revenue'.[76] The stories of Adam and Eve come in for easy ridicule, as does that of the virgin birth:

> Were any girl that is now with child to say, and even to swear it, that she was gotten with child by a ghost, and that an angel told her so, would she be believed? Certainly she would not. Why then are we to believe the same thing of another girl whom we never saw, told by nobody knows who, nor when, nor where?[77]

The miracles are totally discounted: 'The story of Jesus Christ appearing after he was dead is the story of an apparition, such as timid imaginations can always create in vision, and credulity believe.'[78] Paine's objection was not just to the Bible as fable, but as pernicious fable, relating 'obscene stories, the voluptuous debaucheries, the cruel and tortuous executions, the unrelenting vindictiveness...that has served to corrupt and brutalize mankind'.[79]

Having written the first part of *The Age of Reason* without a Bible, Paine obtained 'a Bible and Testament' before continuing his analysis and 'found them much worse books than I had conceived'.[80] What is significant is the manner in which Paine reiterated his belief in the anti-rationality of Christianity. This goes deeper than 'the Christian system of arithmetic, that three are one, and one is three'[81] for the very nature of the Church is assumed to have an inherent hostility to science:

> The age of ignorance commenced with the Christian system...
> The setters-up, therefore, and the advocates of the Christian system of faith, could not but foresee that the continually progressive

knowledge that man would gain, by the aid of science, of the power and wisdom of God, manifested in the structure of the universe, and in all the works of creation, would militate against, and call into question, the truth of their system of faith; and therefore it became necessary to their purpose to cut learning down to a size less dangerous to their project, and this they effected by restricting the idea of learning to the dead study of dead languages.[82]

Here, Paine clearly read back into early Christianity the theory of scientific progress held in his own century. The religion of the church, consequently, appeared as an opium of the masses, in which 'the people have been amused with ceremonial shows, processions, and bells.' These helped 'extract money even from the pockets of the poor, instead of contributing to their relief'. Paine's attitude on this question is clearly demonstrated by his belief that 'one good schoolmaster is of more use than a hundred priests.'[83]

Paine may have rejected miracles, but he did believe in God. His faith was simple, recalling Rousseau's Savoyard Vicar. Paine reduced religion to belief in God plus a rudimentary social ethic. 'I believe in one God, and no more; and I hope for happiness beyond this life. I believe in the equality of man; and I believe that religious duties consist in doing justice, loving mercy, and endeavouring to make our fellow-creatures happy.'[84] The theme of Paine's deism was that God could be found in the works of his creation; in nature rather than in the writings of men. 'The creation is the Bible of the deist. He there reads, in the hand-writing of the Creator himself, the certainty of his existence...and all other Bibles and Testaments are to him forgeries.'[85] Thus Paine gave theological significance to the study of natural science. Deism was presented not as a new religion but as the old truths with the redundancies and distortions removed. Paine, as we have seen, saw prime significance in origins, and so 'Adam, if ever there were such a man, was created a Deist.'[86]

Paine's form of deism was common enough in the eighteenth century. What was new was for such beliefs to be argued in a style that could gain a wide readership and thereby undermine the credentials of established churches. Little wonder that it was found convenient to denounce Paine as an atheist. In addition, of course, Paine's religious and political attitudes interlock. Where political order is seen as emanating from God's plan, there is no legitimate role for man to make or alter his situation. This was Burke's view. The maximum role for God implies a minimal role for humans. Paine's approach was directly antithetical to this for the deist position reduced the role of God in human affairs. Instead of the divine right of kings, it is human beings who are seen as the creators of their own society, endowed with rationality and capable of making political arrangements in accord with their own will. Furthermore, reducing the role of God undermines the position of the church. Church power was to be viewed with as much suspicion as the state power with which it was interlinked. For Paine, 'All national institutions of churches, whether Jewish, Christian, or Turkish, appear to me no other than human inventions, set up to terrify and enslave mankind, and monopolise power and profit.'[87] In place of the Bible and the church, Paine suggested that simple common sense could indicate the straightforward ethical system that all should follow.

So, Paine had once again offended dominant sensibilities. Bishop Beilby Porteous informed the London clergy that 'Publication of the most impious and indecent nature ... have even found their way into the very bowels of the earth, among the miners of Cornwall and the colliers of Newcastle, some of whom are said to have sold their bibles in order to purchase the *Age of Reason*.'[88] Also not for the first time, it was declared a criminal offence to publish one of Paine's writings. As late as 1823, the publisher Richard Carlile was in prison for re-issuing Paine's *Age of Reason*. He had been sentenced for 3 years, but as he was unable to pay the accompanying fine, he had to stay for 6 years.

Conclusion

With Burke and Paine, we have not just the great debate on the French Revolution but also clearly different attitudes to modernity as such. Where Burke, especially after the French Revolution, sounds the nervous cry of the old order, Paine clearly looks towards the modern world of liberal democracy. His writings, then, provide a significant contribution to liberal thought, particularly so as his emphasis on human rights clearly differentiates him from the dominant utilitarian strand of English liberalism, which is the subject of our next chapter. In Paine's writings, we find such components of modernity as the abolition of hereditary political power and the recommendation of representative government, human

rights, welfare, free trade, separation of church and state and freedom of religious opinions. One summary of Paine notes that he
'succeeded in creating an extraordinary amount of trouble in several countries'.[89] An alternative and fairer view is to say that Paine
was a great and pioneering advocate of freedom, national liberation, human rights, equality of opportunity and representative
government.

5

Jeremy Bentham

Life

Jeremy Bentham started his intellectual work at a young age, studying Latin when he was three. At Westminster School, he was known
as 'the philosopher', a sobriquet that the remainder of his life amply
merited. Already at the age of 11, he was writing letters in Greek and
Latin to his uncle. At 12, he was able to write in French. He entered
Oxford University at 12 and graduated when he was 15.

Bentham was the son and grandson of lawyers and was trained for
the legal profession, which he rejected. He was called to the bar in
1769 but never practiced. His father died in 1792, leaving him with
an income of nearly £600 a year, so satisfactory a sum at that time
that he did not need to earn a living. In others, this might have led to
a life of leisure; not so with Bentham, who remained throughout his
long life a prodigious worker for reform. He was one of a number of
foreign radicals made an honorary citizen of revolutionary France,
even though he was no advocate of violence and opposed the French
'Declaration of the Rights of Man and the Citizen'.

Bentham had a strong urge to codify laws. He not only volun-
teered to provide a complete penal law for Russia and for the United
States of America but also additionally made a 'Codification Pro-
posal ... to All Nations Professing Liberal Opinions'. His hubris is
evident in this self-description: 'the most ambitious of the ambitious. His empire – the empire he aspires to – extending to, and
comprehending, the whole human race, in all places – in all habit-
able places of the earth, at all future time.'[1] In 1814, he offered his
plan for codification to the Governor of Pennsylvania, telling him:
'Sir, it is to a feast that I am thus bidding you. Join hands with

me, you and I will govern the world.'[2] Similar vaunting ambition in pursuit of a good cause is evident in his 1789 'Plan for an Universal and Perpetual Peace'. In the preface to his first published book, he distinguished between the 'expositor', who outlines what the law is, and the 'Censor' who declares what it ought to be. Bentham's ambition was to fill the latter role, to rise from the particular to the universal. 'The *Expositor*, therefore, is always the citizen of this or that particular country: the *Censor* is, or ought to be the citizen of the world.'[3] Bentham was critical of religion and churches, referring to God as 'Jug', short for 'Juggernaut', or else as a 'superhuman inferential entity'.[4] Bentham wrote a vast amount, only a small proportion of which was published in his lifetime, and some of that was in the French abstracts, re-orderings and translations of his Genevan admirer Etienne Dumont. In a book published in 2008, Cyprian Blamires noted that as 'a global movement hugely influential in many countries of the world, Benthamism or Benthamite utilitarianism was established by Etienne Dumont in 1802' and that 'right down to today in several European languages Bentham can only be read through Dumont.'[5] Among the many famous people with whom Bentham associated, we can single out Peter Mark Roget (of the *Thesaurus*) as one of the few people ever who could match Bentham's urge for classification.[6]

Richard Layard mentions that Bentham was 'one of the first intellectuals to go jogging – or trotting as he called it – which he did until near his death'.[7] That must have seemed fairly eccentric at the time, though scarcely more so than also having a walking stick named 'Dapple' and a cat called 'the Reverend Dr John Langborn'. Bentham was nearer to the mainstream of our time than his in opposing cruelty to animals[8] and in accepting homosexuality as a victimless act. He made up new words: some, such as 'social science' and 'internationalism' have remained in use; others haven't. No one now refers to 'antejentacular circumgyration' for a walk before breakfast or 'anteprandial circumnavigation' for a walk round the garden after dinner, or 'cacotheism' for the belief in evil gods or 'holophthoria' for 'utter destruction', and his recommendation that the United Kingdom be renamed as 'Brithibernia' has not been followed.[9]

In accord with his will, Bentham is now in a glass box at University College, University of London, where he looks remarkably well for a man of his age. This is not so difficult as he has been given a wax head, the real one being kept in a fridge. Nearby, a pub has been named in his honour, the 'Jeremy Bentham'. It is, appropriately, dedicated to 'the greatest happiness of the greatest number'.

Early Writings

In a work of 1725, Frances Hutcheson wrote that 'that action is best, which procures the greatest happiness for the greatest number; and that, worst, which, in like manner, occasions misery'.[10] Here, we have the core of utilitarianism, traces of which can also be found in such other eighteenth-century writers as Lord Shaftesbury, David Hume, Claud Helvétius, Adam Smith, William Paley, Joseph Priestley and William Godwin. It was Jeremy Bentham, however, who attempted to construct a full utilitarian system and with whom the doctrine is most fully associated.

Many of Bentham's writings relate to the reform of the law and the pursuit of rational constitutionalism. This, he realised, was an immense task, for 'the English law is a great part of it of such a nature, as to be bad every where.'[11] 'Were there no architects who could distinguish a dwelling-house from a barn, or a side-wall from a ceiling, what would architects be? They would be what all legislators are at present.'[12] As a student at Oxford, Bentham had attended the lectures of Sir William Blackstone, the leading legal authority of the day. These were published as *Commentaries on the Laws of England* (1765–9). Bentham's *A Fragment on Government*, published anonymously in 1776, was a vehement attack on his former teacher for his 'antipathy to reformation'. Already on the second page of the Preface, Blackstone was denounced as 'a determined and persevering enemy' of all those trying to become 'better acquainted with the chief means of living happily in' their own country.[13] The modestly described *Fragment* was the first major work of English utilitarianism. In it, Bentham declared that every law and institution should be judged according to its utility and swept away if it failed the test. In his opinion, there was nothing to worry about in the free censure of institutions for 'a system that is never to be censured, will never be improved.'[14]

Bentham denounced obsolete and effete institutions. He derided the mysticism and corruption of the House of Lords as a sectional interest opposed to that of the whole society and believed that privilege was only justified if it made itself useful. He also criticised monarchy and religion, complaining that undue religious influence was exerted on children at school. Bentham opposed the Church of England because of its powerful social role and coupled his hatred of priests with that of lawyers, but saw both as only tools of the monarchy. These were all what he called 'sinister interests' which gave their selfish concerns priority over the greater good.

Bentham was more concerned with reform of the law and administration than of society as a whole. He complained that fees deprived 90 per cent of the population of any hope of justice. He wanted the judiciary reorganised so as to make it more intelligible to ordinary people. He also required the state to provide a system of public instruction, believing that ignorance was one of the major causes of crime.

Whereas Blackstone had defended precedent, Bentham was generally indifferent to history. He was unconcerned with how governments had originated; the important point was how well they operated. Consequently, obedience to government should not be based upon a supposed contract in the past, upon consent that *had* been granted, but solely upon current utility and self-interest. In a fundamental rejection of traditional modes of royal legitimacy, Bentham declared that subjects should obey kings only '*so long as the probable mischiefs of obedience are less than the probable mischiefs of resistance*'.[15] One might think it a prelude to anarchy were people individually to calculate whether their obedience were justified. Bentham, however, immediately turned away from the logical consequence of his own formulation, declaring that governmental authority was unbounded, 'unless where limited by express convention'.[16] Having already rejected social contract, it is hard to see how Bentham could then defend convention. Surely if utility overrides the one, should it also override the other? There were, then, many difficulties to be overcome, but at this early stage Bentham, in echo of Rousseau before him, and Paine just after, assumed that the art of government could be made simple and uncontentious: 'Men, let them but once clearly understand one another, will not be long ere they agree. It is the perplexity of ambiguous and sophistical discourse that, while it distracts and eludes the apprehension, stimulates and inflames the passions.'[17] Bentham was fortunate that no contemporary dissected his work as he had Blackstone's.

Bentham's next major writing was *An Introduction to the Principles of Morals and Legislation*, published in August 1789 although written 9 years earlier. It made no initial impact, with the only known review written some years later. In time, however, it gained acceptance as the basic statement of utilitarian philosophy. Its famous first sentence declares that 'Nature has placed mankind under the governance of two sovereign masters, *pain* and *pleasure*.'[18] We avoid the former and seek the latter. The pursuit of happiness is Bentham's first principle. Individuals decide for themselves exactly what brings them happiness or pleasure. As against the traditional view that it was man's lot to suffer, Bentham brought to the fore the idea of happiness as the aim of life. It was to be won by reason now and not merely, as with Burke, in the afterlife.

Bentham regarded himself as a scientist – the Newton of the moral world. For him, happiness was the gravity of moral philosophy. Here, we have an important step in the creation of the social sciences; the belief that society can be studied objectively. Bentham believed he was producing a science of morality. For this, the components of his science had to be measurable. He had a passion for quantification and produced a 'felicific calculus' for the measure of happiness, to which he gave seven dimensions: intensity, duration, certainty or uncertainty, nearness or remoteness, fecundity, purity and extent. Individuals should add up the expected pleasures on one side and expected pains on the other to ascertain whether any particular action would be beneficial.

In a strict sense, this would seem to be an unattainable objective, but the point for Bentham was that rational behaviour is calculated behaviour. He objected to impulsive or habitual behaviour, to all actions not subjected to the test of whether they would maximise happiness. Bentham did not really expect that people would continuously act in this calculated way, but thought that the arithmetical balance could 'always be kept in view'.[19] What was most important was that governments should apply the utilitarian arithmetic, for their decisions were the most consequential. Bentham saw government as a kind of 'super accountant'. It had the function of teaching people how to maximise happiness and should apply sanctions on actions judged not conducive to that end.

Bentham assumed that human nature was one and the same everywhere, with all individuals pursuing happiness and avoiding pain; in other words, utilitarianism was part of our nature.

This was presented as an ascertainable psychological fact about human nature. So, whatever people might think, whatever their self-consciousness, they actually were utilitarians. If that were so, what, then, was the point of propagating a creed encouraging people to do what they do anyway? After all, there's no need to tell people to eat, drink and breathe for the continuation of their lives, as they do that anyway. Bentham's response was that the utilitarian endeavour was one of what later became called consciousness raising. If people were made fully aware of their true motives, they would then be able to pursue them more effectively.

Seeing that both then and now there have been people uncon-vinced by this doctrine, what can Bentham say to them? It seems that he regarded them as reasoning falsely. To those who reject utilitarianism and declare duty as a basic motive, Bentham retorts that for such people it is duty that makes them happy, and so his theory is confirmed rather than refuted. He believed you could not consistently reject utilitarianism as it could only be opposed in utilitarian terms.

Bentham decided that opponents of his theory were of two types; *the first* were supporters of the principle of asceticism. This was a practice of certain individuals, though Bentham also mentioned 'the Spartan regimen . . . various monastic orders, and the societies of the Quakers, Dumplers, Moravians, and other religionists'. Such people 'have frequently gone so far as to make it a matter of merit and of duty to court pain', their motive being 'the fear of future punish-ment at the hands of a splenetic and revengeful Deity'.[20] Put this way, it would appear that these groups were primarily seeking to avoid pain in the future, a motive actually entirely consistent with utilitarianism. Perhaps, here Bentham unwittingly fortified his belief that utilitarianism could not be consistently opposed.

The *second* category of opponents were advocates of the princi-ple of sympathy and antipathy. These people punish as they hate. Their approach is based on mood rather than rationality; it is sub-jective rather than scientific and so, through its failure to engage in the required social mathematics, unlikely to achieve the greatest happiness of the greatest number.

One consequence of Bentham's legal training was his contin-ual concern with punishment. His brother Samuel, an employee of Prince Potemkin in Russia, invented what they called a panopticon. This was intended by the Bentham brothers as an

'Inspection-House', an architectural technique suitable for a wide variety of institutions. However, its fame, or notoriety, rests on its use as a model prison in which prisoners would be productive and could all be observed from a central point.[21] Bentham thought this would both solve a social problem and make a profit and so became its major advocate. He spent an immense amount of energy, time and money on this scheme, which was never fully put into operation in Britain in his lifetime. A panopticon was constructed in Russia in 1807, but it burnt down in 1818.

Largely through the influence of Michael Foucault, Bentham's panopticon is now widely seen as symbolic of the dark side of modernity; the desire to supervise and control.[22] This approach fortifies the link once made by Max Horkheimer and Theodor Adorno between Enlightenment and totalitarianism.[23] What is thereby overlooked, among other things, is the *relative* benevolence of Bentham's intentions. His purpose was to provide an alternative to the transportation of prisoners to Australia, where they often were compelled to remain even after their sentences had been completed. A cheaper form of imprisonment in the home country was not merely of benefit to the government and the taxpayers but even to the prisoners themselves.[24]

The American and French Revolutions

Two of Bentham's main works came out in the years of revolution 1776 and 1789. So, we can ask whether the great radical, who despised tradition for its irrationality, was delighted to find the world moving forward in so dramatic a form. 'Not quite' is the answer, for the Americans and French were basing their systems on the wrong principles, those of natural rights. Though an incisive critic of bad laws, Bentham was certainly not an opponent of law as such, for civilisation depended upon it. 'That inestimable good, the distinctive index of civilization, is entirely the work of law.' In an almost Hobbesian passage, he noted that 'Without law there is no security; and consequently, no abundance, and not even a certainly of subsistence; and the only equality which can exist in such a state of things is an equality of misery.'[25] This was anything but the greatest happiness of the greatest number. One of the many problems with natural rights was the unjustified claim that they were outside statute law, logically and/or historically prior to such law and even over-riding it. '*Rights*, properly so called, are the creatures of *law*, properly so called; real laws give birth to real rights. *Natural rights* are the creatures of natural law; they are a metaphor, which derives its origin from another metaphor.'[26] Bentham considered natural rights to be based upon implicit unstated assumptions that were devoid of the intellectual rationality that was basic to utilitarianism.

For this reason, Bentham was unsympathetic to the demands of the British American colonists, though he soon came to separate the worth of their cause from the metaphysical language in which it was argued. In 1780, he referred to the Americans as 'one of the most enlightened [nations], if not the most enlightened, at this day on the globe'; yet still, concerning declarations of rights he asked: 'Who can help lamenting, that so rational a cause should be rested, upon reasons, so much fitter to beget objections than to remove them?'[27] Bentham later became a great admirer of the United States; its peace, freedom and prosperity producing a high score on the felicific calculus. "Look to America" became a favourite slogan. Yet, his attitude to their Declaration of Independence remained consistently negative: a 'hodge-podge of confusion and absurdity, in which the thing to be proved is all along taken for granted'.[28] The United States, then, had done well in spite of a belief in natural rights. France was rather different; that country did badly precisely because of them.

On 11 July 1789, 3 days before the taking of the Bastille, Lafayette had submitted the first draft of the 'Declaration of the Rights of Man' to the French National Constituent Assembly. The Declaration was debated on 21 August and adopted 5 days later. From the safe side of the Channel, Bentham was prompt in telling the French that they were on the wrong track. This is from a letter to Jacques Pierre Brissot de Warville, written in mid-August, 1789:

> I am sorry you have undertaken to publish a Declaration of Rights. It is a metaphysical work – the *ne plus ultra* of metaphysics. It may have been a necessary evil – but it is nevertheless an evil. Political science is not far enough advanced for such a declaration.[29]

A society that had gone wrong clearly needed putting right just as one that has rejected its past needs to plan its future, and

Bentham was not someone to miss an opportunity. By April of 1790, he was writing to the President of the National Assembly with his 'Draught of a New Plan for the Organisation of the Judicial Establishment in France'. His recommendations were not heeded, but he had somehow won the approval of the new regime, for in October 1792, he was offered, and accepted, French citizenship. The offer would surely not have been made had the French government known that Bentham was housing refugees from their revolution in his Westminster home. The offer of citizenship was also made to, among others, Tom Paine, Joseph Priestley, William Wilberforce, James Madison, Alexander Hamilton and George Washington. Unsurprisingly, the award failed to align Bentham with the revolutionaries for in the following year he wrote: '*Apropos* of Jacobinism, I begin to fear with you it has taken too strong root in France to be exterminated. Could the extermination be effected, I should think no price we could pay for such a security too dear.'[30] Bentham drew a clear causal connection between the doctrine and violence, noting that 'when I hear of natural rights ... I always see in the background a cluster of daggers or of pikes introduced in the National Assembly with the applause of the President Condorcet for the avowed purpose of exterminating the King's friends.'[31]

In comparison with the turbulence in France, England suddenly seemed less appalling, and in the 1790s, Bentham relaxed his hostility to the British legal system, even voicing a rather Burkean reverence for a Constitution that had emerged slowly over time. *Anarchical Fallacies* was probably written in 1795, though not published until 1816. Its conclusion is not what would have been expected by those who granted Bentham French citizenship:

> On the subject of fundamental principles of government, we have seen what execrable trash the choicest talents of the French nation have produced ... – how much inferior has the maturest design that could be furnished by the united powers of the whole nation proved, in comparison of the wisdom and felicity of the chance-medley of the British Constitution.[32]

It was not until 1809 that Bentham's concern for parliamentary reform found fresh voice.

Representation and Colonialism

Like Robert Owen at about the same time, Bentham had originally hoped that the intrinsic rationality of his ideas would produce immediate support from the British parliament. Both men were to be disappointed. Having originally favoured enlightened despotism, Bentham came to realise that corrupt governments would not voluntarily reform themselves. He thus gave up hope of reform from above and, partially under the influence of James Mill, became more of a democrat. In Bentham's view, a government would only act in the interests of those who elected it, so the wider the electorate the wider the interests that government would pursue. In his *Resolutions on Parliamentary Reform* (1818), he advocated the secret ballot, annual parliaments and a universal male suffrage. At a time when some had multiple votes, through their business interests, Bentham called for an equal suffrage. At a time when constituency populations varied immensely, he called for them to be of fairly equal size. These recommendations approximate to the Chartist demands of 20 years later, and were, of course, very challenging suggestions in that period of heavy reaction in the year before the Peterloo massacre. These proposals were put before parliament by Bentham's collaborator Sir Francis Burdett and were defeated by 106 votes to none.

It might seem that at the age of 69, Bentham had reached his most radical position. He, however, thought he had been radical all along, for utilitarianism is clearly an egalitarian doctrine in that all individuals are the best and proper judges of their own happiness and one person's happiness counts as much as anyone else's. In Bentham's own much-quoted phrase: 'Pushpin is as good as poetry.'[33] In the late 1770s, Solicitor General Alexander Wedderburn said of utilitarianism: 'This principle is a dangerous one.' Bentham accepted the charge and launched a counter-attack: 'dangerous it unquestionably is, to every government which has for its *actual* end or object, the greatest happiness of a certain *one*.' He then turned to the wider legal profession:

Dangerous it therefore really was, to the interest – the sinister interest – of all those functionaries, himself included, whose interest it was, to maximize delay, vexation, and expense, in judicial and other modes of procedure, for the sake of the profit, extractable out of the expense. In a government which had for its end in view the greatest happiness of the greatest number, Alexander Wedderburn ... would not have been Attorney General with £15,000 a year, nor Chancellor with a peerage, with a veto upon all justice, with £25,000 a year, and with 500 sinecures at his disposal.[34]

So, how democratic was Bentham? He dealt with the issue of representation in his *The Theory of Legislation* of 1802. Abstract right, he suggested, led to the view that universal suffrage should be introduced. The principle of utility, however, led to a different approach. Here, we look to the consequences. On this basis, Bentham decided that the suffrage should only be awarded to those who had the confidence of the nation. This would exclude those deficient in political integrity and knowledge. Poverty was a disqualification as it deprived the poor of even elementary education. So there was no vote for those 'whom want exposes to the temptation of selling themselves; nor ... those who have no fixed abode; nor' criminals. As for women, 'We cannot presume a sufficient degree of knowledge in women, whom their domestic condition withdraws from the conduct of public affairs.'[35]

Two decades later, Bentham was well into the phase when he had despaired of benevolent despotism and realised that the people must be able to control their government; but clearly still not all the people. In his *Constitutional Code* of 1823, Bentham drew back from his radical proposals of 1818 as we see from his categorisation of those who could be 'deducted' from the body of legislators. The group of non-qualifiers was composed of:

1. Females.
2. Males, non-adult: that is to say, who have not attained the age of (21) years.
3. Non-readers: that is to say, those who have not, by reading, given proof of appropriate aptitude.
4. Passengers.[36]

These, presumably, are temporary residents without citizenship.

In the period of the Napoleonic Wars and for some years thereafter, British radicalism was under perennial suspicion of affinity with the French Revolution. Bentham, however, as we have seen, was no advocate of their rights of man; he had famously attacked natural rights as 'nonsense upon stilts'. This opposition to natural rights fortuitously became favourable to Bentham's acceptance in Britain, as for decades after 1789 utilitarianism provided an alternative doctrine of reform to the one taken to have caused such havoc in France.

Unsurprisingly, Bentham thought that British practices abroad were as much in need of reform as were institutions at home. In an essay published in 1782, he noted the common view that the 'passion of avarice has implanted among the inhabitants of English race in Bengal, two evil propensities; a propensity to practice extortion, to the prejudice of the subjected Asiatics; and a propensity to practice peculation, to the prejudice of the public revenue.' How, he then asked, must this have looked to the 'poor Hindus'? It must, he decided, have seemed like a 'deliberate plan for forcing' them 'without reserve, into the hands of the European professional blood-suckers, carrying on the traffic of injustice under the cloak of law'.[37]

Then in 1793, Bentham sent Talleyrand a pamphlet entitled 'Emancipate your Colonies.'[38] It was in some ways a rather strange piece. Bentham's advice to the French was argued on the basis of colonialism being in contradiction with their declared revolutionary principles. He did not mention that those principles, based on theories of abstract rights, were not actually ones he agreed with. In that sense, the pamphlet was rather opportunistic. He hoped that once the French had freed their colonies, the British would then follow their example. Bentham, says Elie Halévy, 'up to the end of his life stood as an adversary of the colonial system'.[39] Here, however, we must distinguish between two different kinds of colonial venture. What, on the whole, Bentham opposed was the imposition of European rule on non-European peoples. The British had exported to India the whole panoply of aristocratic privilege and corruption down to the fictions, delays and absurdities of their common-law courts. 'And who would think it? This mass of absurdity is the work of modern refinement, not of ancient barbarism.'[40]

The colonialism that Bentham came to approve was that of voluntary British settlement overseas as a means of dealing with what was then termed 'the surplus population'. Here a British overseas colony is ruling itself rather than imposing external rule on a foreign people. The difference between the two types is obviously obfuscated by them sharing a common term. In 1831, the last full year of his long life, Bentham was converted to Edward Wakefield's plans for systematic emigration and drew up a charter for a colony in south Australia. He gave it the splendidly utilitarian name of Felicitania. When 2 years later the South Australian Association was formed, its 42 members included a number of Bentham's followers, among them John Stuart Mill. The actual colony was founded in 1836 and so, according to Halévy, who obviously enjoyed the irony, 'it happened that the Benthamites were the founders of the English Australasian colonies.'[41]

Colonies of settlement, insofar as there are no indigenous people in the area, or – a dubious proposition – that such people are not affected, pose no great difficulties from a utilitarian perspective. Such colonies could be defended on the basis of the greatest happiness, both for those who remained in Britain and for those who formed the settlement. The situation of indigenous peoples who have foreign rule imposed on them was, of course, quite different.

But yet, in spite of the theory, 'Colonisation is a fact beyond which their logic capitulated... Bentham had always dreamed of making laws for India.'[42] Already in 1782, Bentham imagined replacing the narrow and archaic bounds of current colonial rule with governors able to ascertain the greatest happiness of the greatest number. Such legislators 'having freed themselves from the shackles of authority, have learnt to soar above the mists of prejudice, know as well how to make laws for one country as for another: all they need is to be possessed fully of the facts'.[43] Once James Mill was established in the East India Company, Bentham hoped that his own ideas might attain dominance. 'I shall be the dead legislative of British India' he decided. 'Twenty years after I am dead, I shall be a despot.'[44] For James Mill, too, in spite of his *History of British India*, the practice of imperialism posed problems for his philosophical system. Though the Indian people were regarded as backward and in need of development, it is hard to see how even Benthamite rulers could be trusted to serve a society that had not elected them.

Written Constitutions

India and Australia, large though they were, were far from the limits of Bentham's legislative ambitions. The United States, though now long independent of the British crown, had still not fully thrown off some residual inherited anachronisms. In October 1811, Bentham wrote to President James Madision offering:

> *a compleat body* of proposed law, in the form of Statute Law: say, in one word, a *Pannomion*, a body of Statute law, including a suc-cedaneum to that mass of foreign law, the yoke of which, in the *wordless*, as well as boundless, and shapeless shape of *common*, alias *unwritten* law, remains still about your necks.[45]

Surely, a country progressive enough to have a written constitution would be sympathetic to the idea of further codification! Alas, nearly 5 years elapsed before Madison replied. His letter was flattering and apologetic but failed to give Bentham the authorisation he required: 'a compliance with your proposals would not be within the scope of my proper functions.'[46]

At that point, a lesser man might have wilted; not so Bentham. He was undeterred and merely shifted tack, making his codification offer first to the separate American states and then directly to the people, but once again without a positive response. So much for the English-speaking world! It seemed more likely, however, that the idea of codification might be acceptable in some conti-nental European countries. His brother, the naval engineer Samuel Bentham, was working in Russia and Bentham hoped that through him an approach might be made to the Czar. By January 1814, he had completed a letter for Alexander I offering to draw up a Penal Code for Russia. This time he had to wait a mere 15 months for a reply, but the response, again, was disappointing. The Czar promised to direct his Commission for the Compilation of Laws 'to have recourse to you, and to address to you its questions'.[47] This was less than Bentham hoped. In his reply, he declared a willingness to tackle the more modest task of establishing Penal and Civil Codes for Poland.

Then in 1820, Bentham offered to draw up a code of laws for the new liberal government in Spain, and in the following year, a similar offer was made to the Portuguese. This latter sugges-tion was accepted and Bentham spent much of his last decade drafting a Constitutional Code for Portugal. Bentham's advice was also sought from various other countries, especially from South America where, following independence from Spain, new constitutions were being drafted in Argentina, Chile, Colombia, Guatemala and Mexico. 'With remarkable foresight he early realized the significance of the experimental republics of South America. Miranda,[48] Rivadavia,[49] Bolivar,[50] Santander,[51] José de Valle, and Andrade were all at one time or another his disciples.'[52] The controversy over Bentham was particularly acute in Colombia, where for some years, his writings were alternatively banned by the conservatives and recommended by the liberals. At the University of Rosario, Bogota, Colombia, the last nineteenth-century ban was not lifted until 2002.

What, then, of England? In June 1812, Bentham had a meeting with the Home Secretary, Viscount Sidmouth, concerning the panopticon but also offered to draw up a Penal Code for England. Nothing came of it. Finally, it's worth recalling the purpose behind Bentham's desire to replace traditional common law by codification. As he saw it, the common law based on precedent was obscure and convoluted. This served the lawyers' vested interests; it made them indispensable interpreters. Bentham, then, wanted codification not merely because he had a tidy mind, but as part of his campaign against the convenient obscurities that so suited the legal profession. Codification was intended as an act of liberation. It would make the law logical, coherent, visible, accessible and comprehensible to all.

Utilitarianism Debated

Utilitarian ideas have, for over two hundred years, provided a source of intellectual fascination, both for those who reject them and those who don't. Whereas in the nineteenth century, utilitarianism informed social and public policy, by the second half of the twentieth, its main use was as a bone on which philosophers could sharpen their intellectual teeth. We thus turn to some of the issues that have concerned them.

In a number of places, Bentham asserted that individuals are themselves the best judges of what tends to their own happiness. This issue is so crucial for our understanding of the doctrine that it is worth recording in his own words:

Now as there is no man who is so sure of being *inclined*, on all occasions, to promote your happiness as you yourself are, so neither is there any man who upon the whole can have had so good opportunity as you must have had of *knowing* what is most conducive to that purpose. For who should know as well as you do what it is that gives you pain or pleasure?[53]

Also: 'Every one makes himself the judge of his own utility; such is the fact, and such it ought to be; otherwise man would not be a rational agent.'[54]

In that case, we might ask why there should be law at all, for the main purpose of law is to stop people doing what they otherwise would. We should initially note that the establishment of government at all is problematic for, in one sense at least, the logic of utilitarianism points in an anarchistic direction.[55] So why does Bentham have governments imposing sanctions so as to alter the arithmetical scales? Punishment diminishes individual happiness. Indeed, if individuals are to be allowed to pursue their own happiness, surely it is wrong to threaten them with punishment at all? In that case, the state would lose its coercive function and collapse into anarchy. Bentham's answer is that people realise that although law may constrain them, they are, on balance, better off and happier with it than without it. 'The true political tie is the immense interest which men have in maintaining a government. Without a government there can be no security, no domestic enjoyments, no property, no industry.'[56]

However, if every person were a rational calculator, then incurring punishment by breaking the law would not happen, though law-breaking might occur among those who knew how to avoid being caught! Indeed, the very making of law, for the purpose of guidance towards the general happiness, assumes there are people who need such guidance. They perceive their own happiness but do not subordinate it to the general happiness. Bentham did mention that infancy and insanity were grounds for exclusion from political participation and in *The Principles of Morals and Legislation*, both asserted and then denied that women were incapable of making rational, utilitarian calculations. Women were granted greater 'sensibility' than men, but otherwise suffered from inherent disqualifications: 'in point of quantity and quality of knowledge, in point of strength of intellectual powers, and firmness of mind, she is commonly inferior.' Furthermore 'the female is rather more inclined than the male to superstition.' All of this is a great disadvantage in terms of the

prime tendency that utilitarianism requires, that of rational calculation. Bentham concluded that women's 'antipathetic, as well as
sympathetic biases, are apt to be less conformable to the principle
of utility than those of the male; owing chiefly to some deficiency in
point of knowledge, discernment, and comprehension.'[57]

Presumably, then, law has to exist not just for the sake of all but
particularly for those deemed incapable of both the right attitude
and of doing the utilitarian arithmetic. In a revealing section of *The
Theory of Legislation*, Bentham noted that not everyone could 'perceive this connection between the interests of others and his own'.
The requisite level of insight required 'an enlightened spirit and a
heart free from seductive passions. The greater part of men have
neither sufficient light, sufficient strength of mind, nor sufficient
moral sensibility to place their honesty above the aid of the laws.'
This was why government was required. 'The legislator must supply
the *feebleness of this natural interest* by adding to it an *artificial interest*, more steady and more easily perceived.'[58] And later: 'The more
ignorant a man is, the more he is inclined to separate his private
interest from the interest of his fellows. The more enlightened he is,
the more clearly will he perceive the connection between his private
interest and the interest of the whole.'[59] Only 'superior people'[60]
attained the outlook that Bentham required. For the remainder, law
must be used to elevate their senses.

So what is the government meant to do? According to some com-
mentators the task of the legislator is not, primarily and directly, to
make people happy, which they cannot do as they cannot know all
individual preferences, but to remove harm. It is assumed that while
people are greatly divided on what brings them pleasure, they are
far more united on what they regard as harm. Clearly, for example, physical injury is generally regarded as a harm (though this
does raise the problem of masochism). So legislators are expected to
fulfil the easier task of threatening pain as a deterrent. They, however, have to decide what actions should be punished. Therefore,
implicitly, they must have a notion of what actions are counter to the
greatest happiness, and so, by exclusion, what tends towards it.

There is a divergence which Bentham occasionally thought he
could harmonise:

(i) Individuals do and ought to pursue their own happiness.
(ii) Individuals ought to pursue the greatest happiness of the
greatest number.

In this formulation (i) has a descriptive element while (ii) is solely evaluative. In short, to what extent should individuals consider the pains and pleasures of others? Like Adam Smith, whose *The Wealth of Nations* was published in 1776, the same year as *A Fragment on Government*, Bentham sometimes assumed that the sum total of individuals pursuing their own separate interests would conveniently align with the aggregate general interest. 'Society is so constituted that, in labouring for our particular good, we labour also for the good of the whole.'[61] This is what Elie Halévy called 'the natural identity of interests'[62] as against the artificial harmony of interests, which we shall consider shortly. In the former, the 'good of the whole' seems to be an unintended consequence rather than an act of explicit altruism. Here, then, all individuals pursue their own happiness, and the greatest happiness of the greatest number is a fortuitous convenient result. General utility is achieved in the easiest possible way, without making any sacrifices for it and without even taking it into account. It can hardly be called a fully moral act when the beneficial consequences are unintended. Adam Smith was at least aware of the problem of explaining this happy alignment between selfishness and social welfare and produced the quasi-theological device of an invisible guiding hand that was conveniently available to harmonise the individual pursuit of self-interest with the collective interest of the society.[63]

For those who read Bentham as accepting a natural alignment of individual preference and optimal social outcome, a consequent difficulty arises. Punishment by the state occurs when society decides that certain actions have to be condemned, discouraged and punished. The belief that individuals are the best judges of their own actions, and that these aggregate out to the greatest happiness of the greatest number, gives a high credibility, if not sanctity, to individual actions. On this basis, there seems to be no justification for the state's coercive role. If the aggregate of individual preferences naturally and conveniently produced the greatest happiness of the greatest number, then the state's coercive apparatus would not be needed, though, of course, a state role in public and social administration could remain. This would not be full and pure anarchism (though it might unwittingly lead to it) but rather the 'administration of things', as recommended by Henri de Saint-Simon and Friedrich Engels. Personal preferences would align and individuals would not have to be curbed in their actions.

This conclusion is, however, incompatible with Bentham's unflagging advocacy of the panopticon. Prisons are only necessary when there are convicted criminals to be confined. For Bentham, human nature was everywhere and always the same. He had no utopian expectations on a par with those of his contemporaries Thomas Paine and Joseph Priestley. Criminals will always be among us, and so the panopticon will always be necessary. Presumably, those whose crimes are serious enough to necessitate confinement have not acted in a manner conducive to the greatest happiness of the greatest number, though we must assume, definitionally, that they have been pursuing their own individual happiness.

Therefore, the coercive functions of the state can only be justified if they are there to impose the greatest happiness *against* those individual preferences that would detract from it. This is not just an issue *vis-à-vis* the criminal classes. Bentham always assumed a government that needed to legislate in accord with the greatest happiness of the greatest number. The implication of this is that legislation is an imposition on society by those who are best able to recognise selfishness for what it is and rise above it. In 'Anarchical Fallacies', Bentham argued that the natural rights doctrine was one of a selfish individualism that ought to be transcended:

> The great enemies of public peace are the selfish and the dissocial passions – necessary as they are – the one to the very existence of each individual, the other to his security ... Society is held together only by the sacrifices that men can be induced to make of the gratifications they demand: to obtain these sacrifices is the great difficulty, the great task of government.[64]

We have drawn from *The Theory of Legislation* for Bentham's belief in the natural harmony of interests. It so happens, somewhat inconsistently, that in the same work Bentham used the term 'artificial interest'[65] by which the intellectual elite achieve the broader general utility through their heightened morality and awareness, which for the rest can only be attained through government legislation. This latter position assumes the probable incompatibility between the individual and the more general happiness: 'The assassin pursues his happiness, or what he esteems such, by committing an assassination. Has he a right to do so?'[66] Here, Bentham was demonstrating the subversive consequences of natural rights theory, but what is also plain is that individual preferences must give way when they clash with the general interest.

Bentham wanted to align human nature with the good society. This may seem a vain pursuit if you assume that nature impels us to self-interest, and ethics to the general interest. The theory of the natural harmony of interests assumes the alignment occurs because the former unconsciously produces the latter, whereas the theory of the artificial harmony of interests takes it as the task of government to facilitate such an alignment. Bentham seems to have forwarded both viewpoints, which seem mutually incompatible. They can, however, come near to alignment for Bentham explained that individuals can have a self-interested motive for 'consulting the happiness of others.' In addition to pure benevolence, there is 'private affection' regulating conduct with family and friends; most importantly, as affecting a still wider body of people, the 'desire of good repute, and the fear of blame'.[67] Social pressure, then, can induce selfish individuals to modify their preferences and take general utility into account.

Bentham had some difficulty with what lies between the individual and the society: the group interest, whether it be that of our occupation or class. This he sometimes denounced as a 'sinister interest' that ought to be expunged. He gave insufficient credence to the fact that the individual interest almost naturally produces a related group interest, for the group interest can be an aggregation of people with similar individual interests. This alignment is the basis of, for example, trade unionism. The individual's self-interest is served by any advantages accruing to the group to which he or she belongs. Indeed, the prime motive for joining such a group is to pursue one's own advantage by aggregating the strength of those who share similar concerns and values. If all individuals naturally pursue their own interest, and this produces groups of people defending their similar interests, then rulers are necessarily bound to form a partial interest against the majority. The pursuit of one's own interest, being part of human nature, necessarily becomes a characteristic of rulers as much as of ruled.

How, then, can rulers be made to act in the general interest? It was the attempt to answer this question that eventually pushed Bentham in a more democratic direction. Rulers wish to maintain their position, so to get them to act favourably to the greatest number they must be made answerable to them in frequent general elections. With the introduction of democracy, the government maintains its power only by pleasing the majority. Bentham assumed this would ensure the greatest happiness of the greatest number. However, in *On Liberty*, 1859, John Stuart Mill pointed out that whole ages can be just as wrong as single individuals. On this basis, we can ponder both whether individuals always correctly judge the means to their own happiness *and* whether governments, even democratic ones, can reliably ascertain the greatest happiness of the greatest number. In short, felicific calculus or not, there are no guarantees.

If the operation of the felicific calculus is as plausible as Bentham sometimes assumed, why then did he not provide, in his extensive writings, even one example of its application? The obvious answer is that not even Bentham was able to achieve the impossible. Jonathan Riley has referred to the 'complex utilitarian mechanics that no one can really carry out'.[68] Happiness simply cannot be measured in the precise mathematical sense that Bentham sometimes assumed. However, that's not quite the end of the matter, for surely we all implicitly do some superficial utilitarian calculation whenever we have a choice of actions. How, for example, do students choose between the alternatives of an evening in the cinema or in the library? Is not a choice made between immediate and delayed gratification: happiness now or happiness later in terms of improved exam results and career prospects? It is also not quite the end of the matter for another reason. What was impossible in Bentham's day may be more possible now. Science has moved on. Richard Layard has asserted the following:

> Until recently, if people said they were happy, sceptics would hold that this was just a subjective statement. There was no good way to show that it had any objective content at all. But now we know that what people say about how they feel corresponds closely to the actual levels of activity in different parts of the brain, *which can be measured in standard scientific ways.*[69]

This doesn't fully do what Bentham wanted for such measures of individual happiness don't in themselves provide a way of determining in advance the greatest happiness of the greatest number, which for him was the more important consideration.

Bentham looked at each act in terms of its consequences rather than its motives. On that basis, utilitarianism has been judged ethically impoverished and amoral in that it judges outcomes but ignores motives. In 1834, Professor Adam Sedgwick of Cambridge University (not to be confused with Henry Sidgwick, also of Cambridge University, a later utilitarian philosopher) decided that a Utilitarian 'will inevitably be carried down, by a degraded standard of action, to a sordid and grovelling life'.[70] He reaffirmed the old verities that religion and moral feeling should override calculation and self-interest.

A second difficulty with consequentialism is that it further reduces the already implausible scientific claims of utilitarianism. In the *Fragment on Government*, Bentham wrote that the 'footing on which this principle [utility] rests every dispute, is that of matter of fact; that is future fact – the probability of certain future contingencies.'[71] The obvious objection here is that presumed facts concerning the future cannot be amalgamated with mere probabilities. Facts about the future are probably few and would need to be more rigorously separated from suppositions, possibilities or probabilities. There are some certainties in life, but legislative endeavours would be immensely curtailed if they could only be applied where outcomes were certain.

Consequentialism, therefore, undermines the certainty that Bentham assumed in producing a supposedly scientific doctrine. The likelihood of unintended consequences of intended actions was better understood by the philosopher Henry Sidgwick, who in 1874 made the point that:

> The Utilitarian must represent as accurately as possible the total amount of pleasure and pain that *may be expected* [emphasis added] to result respectively from conformity or disobedience to any given rule, and adopt the alternative which seems to promise the greatest balance of pleasure over pain. That this method is liable to the most serious errors, and this comparison must generally be of the roughest and vaguest kind, we have already seen, and it is highly important to bear this in mind; but yet we seem unable to find any substitute for it.[72]

Critics have noted that some perverse decisions could derive from utilitarian logic. What if punishing an innocent man leads to general approval, but letting him free leads to major rioting, damage and violence? Then, the greater happiness might be achieved by punishing the innocent man. 'Thus, it is claimed, utilitarianism has the consequence that it can be morally correct to punish the innocent.'[73] Similarly, it is conceivable that slavery could be defended on utilitarian grounds, by arguing, for example, that the enslavement of 10 per cent of the population could be justified by the additional pleasures it brought to the remaining 'greatest number'.[74] Bentham did actually address this issue. He argued that

> if slavery were established in such a proportion that there was one slave for one master, possibly I might hesitate before pronouncing upon the balance between the advantage of the one and the disadvantage of the other. It might be possible, all things considered, that the sum of good in this arrangement would be almost equal to the sum of evil. But things cannot be so arranged. Where slavery is once established, it presently becomes the lot of the greater number.[75]

Note here that Bentham failed to find intrinsic utilitarian grounds for rejecting slavery. It is only the convenient, but unverified and unconvincing, assumption in the last sentence that allowed him to blatantly tip the scales of the felicific calculus against slavery. The intrinsic majoritarianism of the doctrine, then, provides no obvious defence for minorities or unconventional individuals. The alternative liberalism, based on the rights of man, clearly seems more satisfactory. Here, each individual is protected, whereas under utilitarianism, you are only safe when part of the majority. Under Rawls' famous 'veil of ignorance',[76] individuals unsure of their social location and standing would surely reject the Utilitarian Republic of Felicitania for the relative safety of a society committed to the Rights of Man. Near the end of his life, Bentham realised this and so felt uneasy about the principle of the greatest happiness of the greatest number. This is from 1829: 'Greatest happiness *of the greatest number*. Some years have now elapsed since, upon a closer scrutiny, reason, altogether incontestable, was found for discarding this appendage.'[77]

A further problem with utilitarianism is that it would, presumably, pardon the breaking of contracts at the point at which they reduce the happiness of a contracting partner or of the greatest number. Thus, in a society which explicitly recognised self-interest as a basic, over-riding principle, contracts and promises could be almost useless. This, as we have seen, was Bentham's case against the fiction of a social contract. It is here, however, that 'rule utilitarianism' comes in. This asserts that following general rules, rather than judging each case independently, would help attain the greatest happiness of the greatest number, for individuals need, and are happier with, the security of knowing that contracts have to be kept.

Legacy

In Britain, Bentham's greatest influence was on such politicians and reformers as Edwin Chadwick,[78] Francis Place (who led campaign against the Combination Laws and helped draft the 1838 People's Charter), Lord Brougham (who as Lord Chancellor, 1830–4, introduced reforms in the legal system and facilitated the passing of the 1832 Reform Bill through the House of Lords) and Sir Robert Peel (who as Prime Minister repealed the Corn Laws in 1846). Also, partially through his friend James Mill and John Stuart Mill, both of whom worked for the East India Company, Bentham came to have a considerable influence on British policy in India.[79] Nevertheless, Michael Oakeshott's point is apposite:

> It is all very well to see Bentham's influence everywhere in the legislation of the nineteenth century, but when we consider how extreme his views about English law actually were, what must be noticed is, not the number of his isolated suggestions which have been put into practice, but the total rejection which his fundamental principles have suffered.[80]

As a propagandist for his utilitarian doctrine, Bentham does not always seem to have been his own best friend for he only published a small proportion of what he wrote. He was, however, extraordinarily lucky in certain relevant respects. He inherited enough money to concentrate on his writing, he lived until the age of 84, and he gained a few devoted disciples who helped him spread the message. Bentham and Etienne Dumont were first in contact in 1788, with the consequences we have already noted. James Mill met Bentham in 1808 and soon became his friend, neighbour and major advocate of utilitarianism. Of particular note was the rigorous education James Mill imposed on his eldest son, John Stuart Mill, who was brought up to be the flag-bearer of utilitarianism for the next generation. In his influential essay on 'Utilitarianism' (1861), John Stuart attempted to meet the criticism that the doctrine was a hedonistic one worthy only of swine. For this purpose, he added a concern for the quality of happiness as an addition to Bentham's calculus based solely on quantity. This, of course, considerably complicated the utilitarian arithmetic and so, on some accounts, Mill's attempts to rescue utilitarianism from obvious objections merely landed it in still greater difficulties.

Later in the century, Henry Sidgwick suggested that utilitarians adopt a principle of justice in addition to the pursuit of pleasure. As with Mill's quality axis, this attempt to deal with standard criticisms only made the utilitarian arithmetic even more impossibly complex. In accord with the current 'New Liberalism', Sidgwick also suggested that, on utilitarian grounds, extended state activity was necessary to remedy the failures of the market.

In a celebrated account of nineteenth-century thought, A.V. Dicey, in 1905 described Benthamism as 'fundamentally a middle class creed', which had been at the height of its influence between 1825 and 1870 when the middle class was dominant in parliament. There were, said Dicey, unintended consequences of the greatest happiness principle. The greatest number in the society were the working class, so utilitarianism provided a justification for rule which favoured them rather than the middle class to which most Benthamites belonged. 'Benthamism', Dicey complained, 'had forged the arms most needed by socialists.'[81] It seems to have been the middle-class Fabian strand of British socialism which was most aware of this. According to one account, 'Fabianism was the new Benthamism, seeking the "greatest happiness of the greatest number," not by means of *laissez-faire*, but through the collective control of the economic forces of society, and regarding Socialism as simply the logical consummation of a progressive policy of social reform.'[82] Generally, however, the socialist tradition does not seem to have given utilitarianism any prominence. The doctrine has, however, been of significance in welfare economics and has found its most secure location in the university philosophy departments of English-speaking countries.

6

Georg Hegel

Life

Georg Hegel was born in Stuttgart in southern Germany in 1770. He was not only the son of a minor official in the government of Württemberg but also the descendant of a long line of bureaucrats and church officials. In that, he became a great advocate of rational administration, and so his political recommendations were in accord with the family heritage. Whether the same can be said for his religious views is much harder to determine. Hegel attended a secondary school from which more than half the pupils usually entered the church, and then the local university where higher education 'was virtually synonymous with theological training'.[1] Though an avowed defender of Lutheranism, the place he eventually gave to religion in his philosophical system was both more complex and idiosyncratic than his church was accustomed to. In that, religion was taken to express in mythical form the truths that are explicitly enunciated in philosophy; Hegel implicitly relegated religion to a lesser form of understanding. He believed that

> strictly speaking, philosophy's topic is God alone, or its aim is to know God. This topic it has in common with religion but with this difference, namely that religion treats the subject pictorially while philosophy thinks and comprehends it.... religion is that form of consciousness of truth which is available to all men.[2]

In addition to becoming a philosophy teacher, Hegel also found employment as a tutor in Berne and as an editor of a Bavarian pro-Napoleonic newspaper, *Die Bamberger Zeitung*. He also became the headmaster of a secondary school in Nuremberg. Hegel accepted an unsalaried teaching post at the University of Jena (1801–7) before being appointed to teach philosophy at the University of Heidelberg from 1816–18 and then at the University of Berlin from 1818 until his death in 1831. He was apparently not a popular lecturer. Anyone reading his works will understand why, for some key parts are incredibly hard to understand. There are stories, possibly apocryphal, of German philosophy students who have read him in English because they found it easier than the original German. John Stuart Mill, who was bright enough to have learnt Greek and Latin before his teenage years, 'found by actual experience of Hegel that conversancy with him tends to deprave one's intellect'.[3] During his first year at Heidelberg, Hegel wrote to his wife that for '*one* course I had only four listeners'. Popularity, of course, partially depended on what the course was about. He was more successful later at Berlin, where in 1829, 200 students came to hear his lecture 'On the Proofs of God's existence'.[4]

Hegel was 18 when the Bastille fell, so his adult life was dominated politically by the French Revolution, the Napoleonic Wars and the Napoleonic reorganisation of the many German principalities. He originally supported the French Revolution but like many others became disillusioned by the execution of the king in January 1793 and the Terror that began the same year. Nevertheless, on each anniversary of the taking of the Bastille, he drank a toast with his students commemorating the event. He became a great admirer of Napoleon, 'this world soul', whom he saw at Jena on the day it was occupied by French troops in 1806. Napoleon's place in Hegel's system was as a world historical individual, one of those few great men who embody the most progressive spirit of the age. This was a fine example of putting his philosophy before his personal circumstances, for one consequence of Prussia's defeat at Jena was that Hegel's 'own house was burned down by the French, the university was closed down and he was left without employment'.[5]

For our purposes, Hegel's most significant writings are his *Elements of the Philosophy of Right*, first published in Berlin in 1821 and *The Philosophy of History*, a series of lectures first delivered in 1822–3, but not published until 1837, 6 years after his death from cholera in 1831.

Germany

While the modern world in its various manifestations was being forged in America, France and Great Britain, the young Hegel became concerned with the anachronistic survival of Germany's many outmoded governments. He later described the United States as 'the land of the future, where in the ages that lie before us, the burden of the world's history shall reveal itself.'[6] The 13 former British colonies in North America had moved towards greater cohesion but, in contrast, the many German states had been content to slumber immobile within parochial particularisms that time had rendered ridiculous.

In the aftermath of Napoleon's conquests of Germanic territory on the left bank of the Rhine, Hegel commenced his investigation of *The German Constitution* (1799–1802) with the cryptic statement that 'Germany is a state no longer.'[7] France, England and Spain had succeeded in pacifying and uniting their territories under a central administration. In this development Germany, ever since the Thirty Years' War, had been left behind. Germany, without either a common military or financial system, remained hardly more than a cultural concept, suffering, like Italy, a fragmentation that left her open to foreign invasion and spoliation. This fragmentation, which cut one small principality off from another and made a common course of action well-nigh impossible, also generated an attitude that disengaged individuals from their own principality. Germany was modern solely in terms of its detrimental separation of the state from civil society. Hegel noted that 'the *bourgeois* sense, which cares only for an individual and not self-subsistent end and has no regard for the whole, began to become a power.'[8] Atomisation thus occurred both at the individual and the political levels as each individual gave priority to personal selfishness, while each state jealously guarded its autonomy. What was lost, and what had to be recovered, was a sense of the coherent whole.

Such was the lamentable German reality that generated in Hegel and his educated contemporaries a profound yearning for the supposed wholeness of life in ancient Greece. It seemed that the ancient *polis*, the Greek city-state, had a unity, form and coherence that modern society lacked. There, they believed, the soul of man had not been fragmented by the division of labour. At the political level, man and the citizen remained one, while between the individual and the state, there was perfect harmony. This no doubt idealised version of ancient Greece functioned as the yardstick by which contemporary Germany was found wanting. Modern fragmentation was seen as the culmination of a protracted decline originating in ancient Rome, then deepened by Christianity, the Reformation, the French Revolution and the increasing division of labour generated by modern capitalism. Ancient religion had been essentially civic and hence had helped to unify the polis, whereas Christianity, with its focus on the soul, concentrated the individual mind predominantly upon itself. Hegel's hope, then, was 'to combine the individual Greek's complete devotion to his city with the modern emphasis on the paramount importance of individual freedom'.[9]

A comparable attempt to look back to a period of community and wholeness can be seen in the medievalist tendencies of German romanticism. As with German Hellenism, apparently reactionary romanticism had a contemporary point. Frederic Beiser has reminded us that 'Ultimately, romantic medievalism was an expression of much deeper political ideals, ideals that are all too contemporary: the demand for community, the need for social belonging, the insufficiency of civil society and "market forces".'[10] In Great Britain, Romanticism is usually associated with Coleridge and Wordsworth and regarded mainly as a literary movement. In Germany, however, the main writers had a more explicitly social and philosophical tendency. Defining romanticism has been problematic for almost every writer who has tackled the subject. However, one can regard the following as among its significant characteristics:

a. Rejection of the Enlightenment and particularly its claims concerning the supremacy of reason. Politically the Romantics opposed the individualistic theories used to support the American and French revolutions. They rejected the notion that the social order could be constructed according to human desires.

b. The Romantics doubted the adequacy of science and brought back into social theory an appreciation of the irrational and emotional aspects of human behaviour. Sentimentality, intuition, faith and religion were all viewed positively.

c. A preference for the past, particularly the feudal past, which some saw as a golden age. They revered the monarchy and nobility as representing the best that remained of feudal society.

d. An organic concept of the state, with an emphasis on movement and historical growth rather than mechanical construction.
e. An appreciation of simple, 'unspoilt' rural folk and a love of nature.
f. A compulsive preoccupation with the hero and genius, the unique individual.

In Germany, Herder is regarded as a precursor of this movement, whose main figures were Friedrich Schlegel, his brother Wilhelm, Adam Müller, Friedrich Schleiermacher, Novalis and Friedrich Karl von Savigny. Their thought provided a significant part of the context of Hegel's intellectual development. He shared some of their concerns but developed his own unique position by working towards different conclusions.

For example, on the question of the codification of law, the Romantics thought that 'Customary law was of more importance than direct legislation'[11] and denied that the aspect of cultural legacy that law represented could be adequately abbreviated into a written constitution. Such an attempt smacked too much of the rationality blueprint of society proffered by the Jacobins. Hegel steered a middle way between these alternate views. For him, law could be codified but should only be given as much rational content as was consistent with the society's prevalent level of culture.

> For a constitution is not simply made: it is the work of centuries, the Idea and consciousness of the rational (in so far as that consciousness has developed in a nation). No constitution can therefore be created purely subjectively... What Napoleon gave to the Spanish was more rational than what they had before, and yet they rejected it as something alien, because they were not yet sufficiently cultivated... The constitution of a nation must embody the nation's feelings for its rights and [present] condition; otherwise it may have no meaning or value.[12]

Hegel also rejected the Romantic attempt to revive the German past.

> We must oppose this mood which always uselessly misses the past and yearns for it. That which is old is not to be deemed excellent just because it is old, and from the fact that it was useful and meaningful under different circumstances, it does not follow that

its preservation is commendable under changed conditions – quite the contrary... The world has given birth to a great epoch.[13]

On the possibilities of rational knowledge, the Romantics accepted the view 'that truth itself cannot be known but that truth consists in what wells up from each individual's heart, emotion, and enthusiasm in relation to ethical subjects, particularly in relation to the state, government, and constitution'.[14] Hegel rejected such ethical subjectivity because in allowing all actions, however absurd, to be defended according to the criteria of good intentions, law would be totally undermined.

Part of Hegel's critique of the Romantics stemmed from their desire to turn back to the political forms of medieval Europe. If that was impossible, how much less likely was it that the recreation of the even more distant condition of ancient Greece could be recovered. Raymond Plant has suggested that the 'whole of Hegel's philosophy may best be seen in terms of the pursuit of coherence.'[15] This the Greeks had attained on terms that were appropriate to their historical times and circumstances. Those times and circumstances, however, lay deep in the past. The medieval lay less deep and less far away, though equally irretrievable. There could, then, be no turning back. The contemporary challenge was to move towards coherence in a manner appropriate to the modern condition.

The French Revolution

For Germans of Hegel's generation, the most striking intrusion of the modern into their provincial repose was the French Revolution, in both its theory and its rather different practice. It embodied the sweeping away of medieval cobwebs and the introduction of the rights of man and the consequent tendencies towards democratisation. Pre-modern assumptions had regarded political rights as a privilege, and so properly confined to the deserving few. Now, though, rights were no longer to be unequally distributed on the basis of social position or exceptional desert, but were, in principle, granted to all alike in recognition of their common humanity. In place of the graded hierarchy of Estates, there came into prominence the egalitarian concept of 'Man'. Hegel noted that now

'*A human being counts as such because he is a human being*, not because he is a Jew, Catholic, Protestant, German, Italian, etc.'[16]

For the Germans, the French Revolution constituted what Burke described as 'an armed doctrine'. It imposed itself upon them not by its superior rationality but by the force of military conquest. What from one angle was a liberation from feudal obligation was, from another, the imposition of foreign rule and alien ideas. So whereas Paine was a prominent participant in the basic changes that France and America introduced, Hegel's situation placed him in the position of an observer of reforms imposed on his country from outside.

For many philosophers, widespread early enthusiasm for the French Revolution turned into its opposite with the onset of the Terror of 1793–4. Hegel was affected by both aspects of this process, but not to the extent of ever becoming the Revolution's opponent. At first, he had hoped for the 'recapture [of] something analogous to *polis* experience'[17] but, unsurprisingly, disappointment followed as an increasingly individualistic and atomised society destroyed all hopes of achieving genuine community. Yet even towards the end of his life, some four decades after the storming of the Bastille, Hegel, sometimes wrongly viewed as an ideologue of Restoration, could still justify the necessity for revolution and simultaneously evoke the exhilaration that accompanied its outbreak:

Before the French Revolution...the whole political system seemed one [great] injustice. The change was necessarily violent, because the transformation was not initiated by the government....the court, the clergy, the nobility, and even the parliaments were unwilling to give up their privileges either on grounds of necessity or for the sake of that right which has being in and for itself;...The thought and concept of right asserted its claims *all at once*, and the old framework of injustice could offer no resistance to it. A constitution was accordingly established on the basis of the idea [*Gedanke*] of right, and everything was supposed to be based on this foundation from now on. As long as the sun had stood in the firmament and the planets have revolved around it, it had never been observed that man stands on his head – i.e. [that his existence is based] on thought – and that he constructs actuality in accordance with it. Anaxagoras had been the first to say that the world is governed by *nous*; but only now did people come to recognise that thought ought to govern spiritual reality. This was accordingly a glorious dawn. All thinking beings shared in celebrating this epoch. A sublime emotion prevailed in those days; an enthusiasm of the spirit swept through the world as if the actual reconciliation of the divine with the world had only now been accomplished.[18]

To what extent, then, did Hegel share with the friends of the revolution the view that freedom was now at hand? Freedom, certainly, was a central concept of Hegel's philosophy. One aspect of it seems to consist of control over nature, and in this sense, freedom would be posited at the technological level. Technological mastery, however, does not of itself produce freedom; it is merely a pre-requisite. When controlling nature, freedom is possible, for a major obstacle to it has been overcome. In terms of individual choices, Hegel saw Luther and the Protestant Reformation as having achieved a great advance. The medieval notion of unthinking obedience to intermediaries between God and laymen was rejected. Freedom of thought now came into operation. There were two levels to this. What for Hegel was the lesser, and unsatisfactory, aspect he termed 'subjective freedom'. This was the ordinary view that freedom consists of an individual's subjective choice. The higher aspect was 'objective freedom', which consists of the self-determination of one's actions in conformity with reason. This is clearly a rather different (and more problematic) notion from the ordinary liberal view. It is also at variance with the views of the radical individualists of the era who regarded freedom as a trans-historical and natural right. For Hegel, as against Rousseau among others, man is not born free. As later with John Stuart Mill, so with Hegel, it was assumed that not all are fit for freedom. Rather than being an imperfectly recognised and wrongly withheld universally applicable human right, freedom, though the inherent destiny of man, is a hard-won and only gradually attained human achievement. Thus, for Hegel, the French revolutionary breakthrough consisted only of the *consciousness* of freedom, not the practice of it.

A characteristic of both proponents and opponents of the French Revolution was the view that it signified, for better or worse, a major breach, a wrenching free, from all previous history. We have seen that Burke regretted the rejection of accumulated wisdom and experience, while Paine rejoiced in the removal of ancient superstitions and privileges. Hegel, in contrast to both, saw the events in France, however momentous, as still part of the *continuity* of world history. In this dawning of a new age, 'the Germans went no further than theoretical abstraction', whilse the more audacious French immediately 'proceed[ed] from the theoretical to the *practical*'.[19] Thus, for Hegel, the French Revolution signified the rise to a position of pre-eminence of *the idea* that all are free. Whatever particular disfigurements occurred, world history had moved irreversibly forward under the sway of this new principle. This Hegel never sought to deny, and so he opposed the nationalist and anti-French countermovements which emerged in Germany between the defeat at Jena in 1806 and the victory at Waterloo 9 years later. There could be no turning back. The new principles were the basis from which all politics should henceforth proceed. The practice of The Terror had disfigured and dishonoured ideas of freedom that nevertheless remained valid. What Hegel wished to attain, then, was the rational implementation of ideas that the French had introduced, not for themselves alone, but for all mankind.

Greek culture, it seems, was to be praised rather than copied; for its exemplary achievements were appropriate only for their own far-distant age. The French revolutionaries had misguidedly adopted a practice corresponding to that of ancient Greece during its democratic moments. Modern France and the city-states of ancient Greece, however, differed not only in size but also in mentality. Democratic constitutions akin to those of ancient Greece 'are only possible in small states'. There continual personal contact and proximity to each other as well as to the political stage 'render a common culture and a *living* democratic polity possible'[20] in ways that cannot be reproduced in larger states.

In the simple springtime of mankind, direct individual participation was possible and acceptable because 'the citizens are still unconscious of particular interests, and therefore of a corrupting element: the Objective Will is in their case not disintegrated.' Such a condition did not last. The rise of subjectivity 'plunged the Greek world into ruin, for the polity which that world embodied was not calculated for this side of humanity'. Furthermore, Greek democracy was fundamentally dependent upon the small scale of the city state. In democracy, the citizen must be present at the debate, 'must mingle in the heat of action' and must be won over, if at all, by 'oratorical suasion'.[21] The written word does not produce the same effect, and the larger scale of the modern state diminishes the significance of the individual voter. The French revolutionaries, then, failed because they adopted an inappropriate model. Consequently, their 'republican constitution never actually became a democracy' as Hegel understood the term. 'Tyranny, Despotism, raised its voice under the mask of Freedom and Equality.'[22] Democracy in its pure form was thus seen as appropriate to a particular historical era long since departed.

> The idea... that all individuals ought to participate in deliberations and decisions on the universal concerns of the state – on the grounds that they are all members of the state and that the concerns of the state are the concerns of everyone, so that everyone has a *right* to hare in them with his own knowledge and volition – seeks to implant in the organism of the state a *democratic* element devoid of rational form, although it is only by virtue of the its rational form that the state is an organism.[23]

Hegel's basic complaint against the French revolutionaries was that they had destroyed without creating. They undid the old structures of society without putting any rational form in their place. Society had been left disaggregated and atomised. Individuals were disconnected from each other. The whole had no unity. 'The bad', he noted, 'is that whose content is entirely particular and distinctive, whereas the rational is that which is universal.'[24]

The French Revolution provided Hegel's modern warning example of a state organising its parliament in opposition to the idea of corporate mediation. In consequence, power was acquired by 'fanatical priests [and] riotous, revelling despots and their minions, who seek to indemnify themselves for their own degradation by degrading and oppressing in their turn – a distinction practiced to the nameless misery of deluded mankind'.[25] Such atomisation Hegel regarded as quite contrary to a rational, organic order. A political system based on the isolated individual and seen as a counter to the power of privilege fails to provide both a proper correspondence with the individual's real existence in a particular social context and the necessity for social unity. Hegel thought that 'electoral assemblies as unordered inorganic aggregates' have 'more in common with the democratic, even anarchical, principle of separatism than with that of an organic order'.[26]

At this stage, we must note that Hegel was quite wrong in assuming that the French had copied the practice of Greek democracy. Rather than direct democracy, they introduced what came to be called representative democracy, two forms that are immensely dissimilar. So, contrary to what Hegel indicated, there actually was a principle of organisation for elections to the French National Assembly. It was that of geographical constituencies, a form that was far from inappropriate given that allegiances were then much more regional than national. The view that the democratic element was void of 'rational form' is stated without an explanation as to why geographical constituencies don't qualify as rational, although such an explanation is not hard to surmise. A geographical constituency is 'merely assembled for a moment to perform a single temporary act and [has] no further cohesion'. In contrast, what Hegel wanted was political expression through 'associations, communities, and corporations which, although they are already in being, acquire in this way a political connotation'.[27] Hegel also seems not always to have distinguished clearly between the electorate and their representatives. Though all can 'share in deliberating' only the representatives actually legislate. However, whatever Hegel's errors concerning the revolution, and the errors of the revolutionaries themselves, in terms of his system the French Revolution signified a great step forward. It was part of the onward movement of world history.

World History

Hegel's own thought verifies his dictum that philosophy is its own time apprehended in thought. One aspect of contemporary philosophy was that it sought to package history into ascertainable stages. In the late eighteenth century, Turgot, Herder, Condorcet, Adam Smith and Ferguson were notable among those who sought to understand the processes of historical change. Perhaps none was so great a systematiser as Hegel himself. For Hegel, 'the history of the world is none other than the progress of the consciousness of freedom,' and each stage of consciousness developed its appropriate political form. 'The history of the world travels from east to west, for Europe is absolutely the end of history, Asia the beginning.' The Oriental knew that 'One is free' and thus produced political despotism.[28] 'Thus fear and despotism are the dominants in the

East. Either a man stands in fear, is afraid, or he rules by fear, and so is either servant or master...religion necessarily has the same character. Its chief feature is fear of the Lord.'[29] Religious consciousness seems to be basic to historical development. The Africans, in Hegel's generalisation, do not have this sense that there is something higher than man. Sorcery and magic dominate, but these are the powers of some people over others. The same is true of the worship of the dead, although that does at least point beyond this life. In Africa, the spirit was not developed, so Hegel declared the continent excluded from the world's history. The torch of history passed them by. It moved from the Orientals to the Greeks. The latter knew that 'some are free' and established democracy (as they chose to understand it). Philosophy and the world of freedom began in Greece but were restricted by the existence of slavery. European Christendom represents a further advance and knows 'that man as man, is free' and so established monarchy.[30]

The providentially ordained course of world history was one in which the state attains ever-closer proximity to its concept. In each stage, one national culture had the task of forwarding this development, which had followed the path of the sun in moving from east to west. During this journey, the foremost world-historical realms had been, successively, Oriental, Greek, Roman and then 'Germanic'. The last, in spite of its misleading designation, included European Christendom as a whole.[31] That Hegel saw an underlying mutuality among Europeans is evident from his belief that the 'European peoples form a family in accordance with the universal principle underlying their legal codes, their customs, and their civilization.'[32]

For Hegel, world history constituted the process of reason working itself out into actuality. Thought came first. It was the basis of historical change. To Friedrich Niethammer, a friend from his student days, Hegel wrote that 'Daily do I get more and more convinced that theoretical work achieves more in the world than practical. Once the realm of ideas is revolutionized, actuality does not hold out.'[33] This notion of historical change is only one part, and the simpler one, of Hegel's theory of history, for ideas work but in a mysterious way. Individuals and their beliefs are instruments of destiny whether they know it or not and in ways that they may not intend. The 'cunning of reason' operates in ways that are not always consciously understood, for the historical process does not depend on people's consciousness. A people's national aims may work towards ends of which they are unaware, so that what appears as accidental or fortuitous in history – such as war – may from the viewpoint of philosophy be seen as a necessity. Hegel's historical sense is fundamental to his whole philosophy. Shlomo Avineri has described Hegel as the 'first major political philosopher of modern society' in that he 'introduced the dimension of change and historicity which has since become central to modern political thought'.[34] We have seen that the French Revolution embodied a positive development in theory rather than in their practice. What changes in politics, then, did Hegel think appropriate to the new situation?

Political Recommendations

Hegel's theory of the state is central to his whole political philosophy and, hence, to the ideological disputes concerning his political affiliation. For a long time, Hegel was regarded not just as the ideological defender of the Prussian state[35] but, consequently, a progenitor of German nationalism and even nazism. Such an analysis failed to grasp that Hegel was writing of the idea of the state rather than the actuality; an idea or essence that may be implicit in any particular state but is not completely achieved. 'In considering the Idea of the state, we must not have any particular states or particular institutions in mind; instead we should consider the Idea, this actual God, in its own right.'[36] It is of the idea of the state that Hegel is reported to have said: 'The state in and by itself is the ethical whole, the actualisation of freedom ... The state consists in the march of God in the world, and its basis is the power of reason actualising itself as will.'[37] In consequence, men should 'venerate the state as an earthly divinity'.[38] The significance of the state is that it represents the highest point of reconciliation between the individual and society; the parts with the whole. In Hegel's view, men should identify with the universal, should be citizens rather than mere private individuals. 'It is necessary to provide ethical man with a universal activity in addition to his private end.'[39] In this respect, even war has a valuable social function.

Over the whole range of Hegel's writings, we find different designations of the state. His narrowest definition was that of a community organised for its self-defence; in short, a people who have an army. A second concept of the state was the sense that is now most familiar, that of the core political institutions of a society; what he called 'the *political* state proper'.[40] Thirdly, however, Hegel's fullest definition encompassed the people, the institutions and the ethics of solidarity [*Sittlichkeit*] that unite them. This broader understanding clearly indicates Hegel's prime concern with the integration of the people and their institutions. He was, however, aware of the modern condition in which integration was undermined by the rise of private interests. Between the state and the family had emerged what he called civil society. Its main feature was the economic life of the community in which particular needs, competition and divisiveness prevailed. The economy functioned largely according to a logic of its own which was at variance both with the ethical demands of law and with the love that prevailed in the family. Hegel had studied Scottish political economy, and had learnt from Adam Smith, Sir John Steuart and Adam Ferguson of the role of the market in modern societies. He believed, nevertheless, that it required close regulation. This was the job of what is usually translated into English as 'police', but, given the breadth of its functions, might be better understood as 'public authority'. Its tasks might include fixing prices of basic necessities, guarding the public against fraud, providing hospitals, supervising education and relieving poverty.

Competitiveness between individuals, then, could be modified and controlled. Nothing similar could be operated between states. Hegel rejected the recent notions of perpetual peace popularised by Rousseau and Kant and accepted that a state of nature would always exist between different countries. Treaties between states were agreements rather than contracts in that they could not be enforced and so war could not be superseded.

The main source for Hegel's views on monarchy is *The Philosophy of Right*, which originated in lectures he gave at the University of Berlin from 1818. The book, Hegel's last, was first published in 1821. It is issued with 'Additions' about a third as long as the main text, 73 pages in one English translation. These derive from lecture notes taken by Hegel's students. The status of these notes becomes a problem when, on certain points, there is a difference of emphasis from the main text. From the 'Additions', we learn that the institution of monarchy and its associated functions are more important than the particular incumbent. Hegel here denied that 'the monarch's *particular* character is of vital importance. In a

fully organised state...all that is required in a monarch is someone to say "yes" and to dot the "i".[41] The monarch's significance
is his ability to attain universality through his own person because
he is secure in his position which is raised above all classes and
groups. The advantage of hereditary monarchy is that it takes the
succession issue off the political agenda and thereby removes the
chance that cliques and factions will disturb the unity of the state
at its most precarious moment. Thus far, we appear to have something akin to a figurehead monarchy, but should note that the main
text of *Philosophy of Right* presents a considerably more powerful
monarch whose character is presumably much more significant, for
he may both appoint and dismiss members of the supreme council
or cabinet.

Hegel regarded monarchy as the essential characteristic of the
modern state, yet it is hard to resolve the uncertainties in his presentation of it, for the larger the monarch's role, the greater the
significance of his character and ability. Hegel wished to avoid the
element of chance that would result from elective (as had existed in
both the Holy Roman Empire and Poland) or contractual kingship,
but seems not to have recognised the extent to which hereditary succession leaves monarchy the victim of genetic chance. For most of his
lifetime, the English throne was occupied by King George III, (also
Elector and then King of Hanover) who, among other such indi-
cations of insanity, once emerged from his coach in Windsor Great
Park and addressed an oak tree as his cousin Frederick the Great of
Prussia.

Claims to objectivity and elevation above the strife of civil society
were also made on behalf of the civil service. Hegel described it as
a universal class in that it was placed above particular interests. Its
significance was such that it needed the best talents the society could
provide. Birth, wealth and other background factors were to be of
no consequence in recruitment. As against the still widespread pre-
modern practice of inheriting or buying positions, Hegel wanted
civil service posts determined by actual competence as demonstrated
in competitive exams. Here, he was in accord with the local situation,
for competitive entry into the Civil Service was introduced in Prussia
in 1807, though not in Great Britain until 1870.

That the task of administration requires certain qualifications is
now axiomatic. Hegel, however, also applied this concern to the legislature. It too had its own technical task; that of contributing to the

law-making process, which should only be entrusted to those capable
of dealing with its complexities. But, there is also a representative
function. This second task Hegel subordinated to the first. Representation, then, could only be granted to the extent compatible
with efficient, knowledgeable and rational fulfilment of law-making.
Entry into the administrative and legislative structures of the state
is now by quite different means. We might understand the inter-
connections between these areas but, as professions, treat them as
requiring different qualifications. The concern that Members of Parliament or Congress possess sufficient education and ability for their
task is never expressed in more than vague terms and without any
formal certificate of qualification.

Hegel reserved the upper house of parliament for the agricultural estate, which would include both peasant farmers and the
landed aristocracy. The advantage of the latter was that primogeniture placed them above the vagaries of fortune and so provided a
guarantee of political stability. Their particular qualities derive from
a guaranteed social position beyond all temptations of corruption
and ambitious self-advancement. Their lands could not be sold, nor,
because of primogeniture, could they exhibit any preference in the
distribution of their property at death. Thus, they were locked into
their social position. In the important matter of wealth distribution,
they were without free will and so beyond the temptations of modern life, 'equally independent of the resources of the state and of
the uncertainty of trade, the quest for profit, and all variations in
property'.[42]

The lower house represented the business class, the deputies
of whom were to be selected by the various corporations. These
are occupational groupings that could include both employers and
employees. Through earning their living in a similar way, they are
assumed to have common interests and outlooks. Through them
Hegel hoped to integrate society into the state, for he channelled
representation through social groupings that had already formed
naturally. So, for Hegel, the relevant unit was the social function
rather than the geographical area we have in today's constituencies.
The relationship between the state and the people should only be
mediated through an occupational interest group. These provide a
source of co-operation and experience in public affairs which lifts its
members above the level of personal selfishness and enables them to
cultivate a broader outlook.

An oddity of this system is that it structures society in terms of its separate social components and yet is still intended to overcome particularity. Hoping to overcome individual selfishness, Hegel provided instead a structure that looks bound to replace it with sectional rather than general interests. Particularity has not been overcome but merely elevated. This has the advantage of providing the individual with a mechanism of integration, but what one is integrated into is primarily one's occupational grouping and only secondarily, if at all, the state itself. To an extent, Hegel wanted rational, modern constitutionalism combined with a more traditional representation based on the Estates. This is a strange amalgam. Hegel wanted constitutions that overcame the imprint of a bygone age and were in accord with their times. This notion of appropriateness, which is so central to his social and political analysis, raises the problem of deciding how accord or coherence are to be determined and arbitrated. Hegel wanted monarchy and Estates representation in a modern state. In this respect, his own ideas of what politically accords with, or is appropriate for, a modern state are highly idiosyncratic.

The task of Hegel's lower house is merely deliberative; its role appears to be little more than advisory. It is subservient to the rational bureaucracy that was regarded as the prime characteristic of the modern state. Furthermore, the Crown provides the effective centre through which this influence operates, and thus the representative assemblies do not facilitate a pre-eminently parliamentary system.

Whereas entry to the upper house was hereditary, Hegel's recommended manner of entry to the lower house was by election, although the question of proper qualifications was equally important. 'People's representatives must not be picked at random, but rather one should choose the wisest from among the people, since not everyone knows, as it is his duty to know, what one's true and real will is, i.e. what is good for one.'[43] The approach here derives from Rousseau's notion of the 'general will' and is similar to Marx's view that the proletariat had a 'real will' which might well be different from their subjective preference. Hegel's deputies are charged less with representing the people's wishes than with doing what is right. Hence, their relation to their electors 'is not that of commissioners or mandated agents'.[44] Rationality and experience count above the representative function. Just as rationality was explicitly declared to have a particular social location, so we may suspect a corresponding limitation in terms of the importance

Hegel attached to governmental and administrative experience. 'The essential thing is to place *suffrage* in the hands of a corps of enlightened and honest men, independent of the court.' The required consciousness of the general and a fitting opposition to the particular are acquired by 'habitual preoccupation with public affairs'.[45]

In his *Proceedings of the Estates Assembly in the Kingdom of Württemberg* (1817), Hegel expressed distaste for the idea of salaried deputies. Without pay, one avoided the suspicion that office was sought for pecuniary reward. The consequence was to give 'preponderance in elections to property'.[46] Thus far entry to public office, whether to the bureaucracy or to the lower house, has exhibited a dual character. The concern with proper qualifications broadens opportunity beyond what can be attained by inheritance, nepotism or purchase, but simultaneously acknowledges the restricted social locations of those with the requisite rationality and experience. On Hegel's criteria the class basis of power might well remain unaltered from before, although the allocation of posts within that class would be far more discriminating.

In the *Proceedings*, Hegel also made some interesting and unusual comments on voting rights. In 1815, the monarch of the recently enlarged kingdom of Württemberg had summoned the Estates and presented them with a Constitutional Charter, the content of which gave rise to considerable conflict. The franchise, entirely normal for its time, was granted only to men over the age of 25 with an income of 200 guilders from real estate. These qualifications Hegel declared irrelevant to a properly ordered state. 'Age and property are qualities affecting only the individual himself, not characteristics constituting his worth in the civil order.'[47] Property as a commodity pre-eminently ties its owner to his selfish, individual interests, to the detriment of universal concerns. Inherited property in entailed landed estates apparently does not fall under this disqualification, for it is a source of stability and thus the appropriate qualification for aristocratic composition of the upper house. In contrast, the *fluctuating* fortunes of marketable property provide no guarantee of their owners' political reliability. Worth to the community, which is the qualification that really matters, derives from the nature of a man's office, social position, skill and ability. Age and wealth may be included as qualifications, but they should not be the only ones and certainly should not be dominant. In any case, Hegel noted that in more extended electorates, the citizen soon becomes relatively indifferent to his political rights, for as the number of voters increases so the real value of each particular vote is proportionately reduced. Thus in the end, one could expect popular suffrage merely to increase political apathy and so leave power in the hands of a narrow caucus, exactly the opposite of what its proponents intended. Hegel anyway regarded voting as a poor system of appointment. Its dependence upon 'an accidental attitude and a momentary preference'[48] seemed so much less satisfactory than elevation on the basis of objective qualifications. This disadvantage, however, is unlikely to be too detrimental as the assembly's task is little more than deliberative and advisory.

Below Representation

Hegel explicitly accepted conventional classifications which designated Greek democracy as a political form compatible with slavery. It was the form in which only 'some are free', and slavery in fact was its necessary basis. That the citizens could be released for democratic participation presupposed a lower order occupied with necessary labour. A corresponding situation still prevailed. Greek democracy was as outmoded and irretrievable as Greek slavery, but Hegel still recognised the inevitability of society containing an underclass precluded from political activity, although how community could be achieved across such a divide is far from clear.

Modern society seemed propelled towards inequalities that subjected the lower orders to poverty and ignorance. Their poverty leaves them 'more or less deprived of all the advantages of society, such as the ability to acquire skills and education in general, as well as of the administration of justice, health care, and often even of the consolation of religion'.[49] The 'rabble' were obviously precluded from any hope of qualifying for the bureaucracy or of gaining representation through the corporations. Hegel quoted the Italian poet Ludovico Ariosto: 'That the ignorant mass finds fault with everyone and talks most of what it understands least.'[50] Clearly, the lower orders were not seen as even having the right to form a corporation and so gain representation in the lower house. Not being possessed of rationality, they were destined to be mere objects of administration, however benevolent, rather than full participants in the public

life of their own community. Basic to Hegel's approach was his classification of the people as 'that category of citizens *who do not know their
own will*. To know what one wills, and even more, to know what the
will which has being in and for itself – i.e. reason – wills, is the fruit of
profound cognition and insight, and this is the very thing... which
the people lack.'[51]

According to one account, Hegel 'never entertains the idea
that... domestic servants, industrial proletariat, tenants-at-will, agricultural labourers, and so on, have any claims to be represented
separately'.[52] They were ruled out of contention just as obviously as
women and children. One critic has referred to Hegel's 'odd rejection of universal and equal suffrage'.[53] While the manner of rejection
may conceivably have been odd, the rejection itself was entirely normal at the time Hegel was writing. In the section of *Philosophy of
Right* on the state, Hegel mentioned the function of the Estates in
stimulating a consciousness of public affairs. His explanatory notes
take it as obvious that the political public normally excludes at least
children and women. Clarification of Hegel's ideas on the sexual
division of labour is provided in the section on the family. Here, we
learn that man's nature is fitting for the political sphere and woman's
is not. 'Man therefore has his actual substantial life in the state, in
learning... etc., and otherwise in work and struggle with the external world... Woman, however, has her substantial vocation... in the
family, and her ethical disposition consists in this [family] piety.'
Differences of nature produce different mental capacities.

> Women may well be educated, but they are not made for the
> higher sciences, for philosophy and certain artistic productions
> which require a universal element... When women are in charge
> of government, the state is in danger, for their actions are based
> not on the demands of universality but on contingent inclination
> and opinion.[54]

More extended justification for the political exclusion of women and
lower-class men was, at that time, not required. Ruling assumptions
concerning political access had not yet reached that crucial meridian
which changed the magnetic pull from one pole to the other; when
the onus of explanation rested on those who wished to restrict the
franchise rather than on those who hoped to extend it. Hegel obviously preferred the period when the desires of the masses had less

force and when the threat from the uneducated and unorganised was less apparent. Sound judgement was endangered by the falsity of public opinion. 'Whole peoples may often be a prey to excitement or be carried away by passion to a greater extent than their leaders.'[55]

Rational Bureaucracy

The intellectual background of both Hegel's thought and of the French Revolution was that of the Enlightenment. This tendency had both rationalistic and, to a much lesser extent, egalitarian elements. The effect of the former was to elevate intellect and education as the basis for political decision taking. The general effect of the latter, as primarily embodied in the notion of equal human rights, was to stimulate the movement towards wider parliamentary representation. A basic dilemma, then, was of how rationality and representation could be amalgamated. These are the questions we must consider in terms of Hegel's political recommendations. What level of priority was rationality to be granted? How was representation to be related to it? Was it rational to represent all? How was representation to be organised, and how could an objective will be elevated above the various particularities and gradations into which a modern society was divided?

In his Introduction to *The Philosophy of History*, Hegel noted that 'In a Constitution the main feature of interest is the self-development of the *rational*, that is, the *political* condition of people; the setting free of the successive elements of the Idea.'[56] Here, we have encapsulated the basis of his whole approach to politics. For Hegel, the central problem of human society was to facilitate the gradual realisation of rationality and, thereby, freedom. The political was both an agent of this process and a symptom of the extent to which the wider social and cultural milieu had developed its full potential. This prior teleological concern conditions the secondary question of the relationship of the populace to the state structure, for this is determined by the state's purpose. By declaring this to be the pursuit of impartial rationality, Hegel thereby opened up the question of how the society/state relationship should best be ordered, and what category of person could be granted political influence. He thought that access to formal politics should only be available to those capable of furthering its revealed purpose. Rationality, then, could only be advanced by those possessed of it. To those acquainted with the common identification of Hegel with conservative reaction, this might appear as the prelude to a rationale for keeping the rabble beyond the political horizon. It may function this way, but there is much else besides, for Hegel's thought does not facilitate simple one-sided categorisation. In his own distinct way, Hegel was clearly within the Enlightenment tradition and, in a manner reminiscent of Bentham, the call for rationality is simultaneously a criticism of outmoded institutions that have lost all purpose except the narrow defence of sectional privilege and all laws that are mere historical lumber and quite devoid of overall coherence.

Yet for a professed exponent of systematic rationality, Hegel's constitutional preferences seem beset with contradictions. Monarchy is attained by birth, but one joins the bureaucracy on merit. Only the corporations embody a representative aspect. Representation, then, has its place, but is merely one element of the system. And even within the representative sector, other qualities also have to exist. The popular will has to be countered and filtered. This concern for the politics of balance underlies Hegel's refusal to take a simple choice between monarchy, aristocracy and democracy. In spite of the primacy of monarchy, all three elements have their part to play. Hegel saw constitutional monarchy as the rational unity of the three forms. Democracy had its restricted sphere, but monarchy itself was also not without limitation, for legislative power was shared with the representative bodies. 'Without such a representative body, freedom is no longer thinkable.'[57] In accord with contemporary radical proposals, the French Revolution had produced a unicameral assembly. Hegel opposed this development. In his system, the Estates were divided into two assemblies in order to overcome the accidental character of 'the mood of the moment'[58] although given their powerlessness this precaution seems less than necessary.

If Hegel's system seems a strange amalgam of ancient and modern, hereditary and representative, this in no way detracts from its plausibility, for similar criticisms can still be made of the British parliamentary system with its elected lower house, its nominated and still partially inherited membership of the so-called upper house, and its hereditary monarchy. The influence of British practice on Hegel has often been noted. A major point of difference might be that Hegel regarded his system as an emanation of rationality, yet the British system has also been granted a comparable aura of excellence – that History as well as God or Providence have contributed to the emergence of a political pattern that rational constitutionalism alone would have been unable to match. Hegel's view was that political developments have their proper rhythm in which harmony is maintained with the prevailing cultural and historical context. A strong notion of ripeness is evident here. Retarded development is criticised on the same methodological grounds as attempted leaps into the future. Hegel thought it ludicrous to attempt any return to the constitutions of antiquity, so he also decried the utopian notion that the 'form of a constitution were a matter of free choice, determined by nothing but reflecting.'[59] This mentality, characteristic of emergent liberal thought, assumes that the individual could be a bearer of rights even before the creation of society and the state. For Hegel, on the other hand, it was only the existence of the state that made actual rights possible. Legitimacy for Hegel was not based on the modern notion of popular consent nor the ancient ones of prescription or divine right. He belonged to that strand of the Enlightenment tradition associated with reformist, bureaucratic autocracy. Improvement was possible only within the constraints imposed by existing conditions and the guidance of those with real understanding. Thus Hegel's basic attitude to both the individual and the state serves to differentiate him sharply from liberal individualism. It seemed to Hegel that liberalism, though it performed the necessary task of destroying outmoded institutions, was inadequate in replacing them with an atomised society possessed of a too-weak sense of community. For Hegel, the universal is represented by the state, and here too, the gulf between him and classical liberalism is wide. For the latter, the state was an object of suspicion, certainly necessary, for liberals are not anarchists, but equally certainly in need of curbs and limitations. It was from the state that the danger to freedom was thought to emanate. For Hegel, in stark contrast, the state was the source of rights and freedom. Whereas liberals wanted to limit the state's economic role, Hegel thought that it had a responsibility to regulate commercial relationships for the benefit of all.

Hegel's concern for representation was motivated by a strong desire to integrate all sections of society into a coherent whole. However, representation should be to a largely advisory chamber, and thus integration was intended to produce affirmation rather than general legislative powers. Political decisions should remain the preserve of the specially qualified. Clearly, Hegel belongs to a line of thought that stretches from eighteenth-century enlightened despotism through Saint-Simon and Auguste Comte to the English Fabians and even the Russian communists. This political tradition believes that bureaucratic power is not merely efficient but, even more controversially, simultaneously able to perceive and implement a general interest. The basic problem here, then, is the notion of bureaucratic objectivity. Hegel was aware of the danger of the civil service using its power in its own narrow interest and suggested controls by the monarch from above and the corporations from below. We see here how wide of the mark are any suggestions that Hegel's ideas can be linked with tyranny or even totalitarianism. His constitutional proposals, on the contrary, show a concern to maintain a balance of power through the acceptance of intermediate institutions.

Legacy

The placing of Hegel politically is no easy task. As Friedrich Engels was later to remark:

> Hegel's doctrine, taken as a whole, left plenty of room to accommodate the most diverse practical party views. And in the theoretical Germany of that time, two things were practical above all: religion and politics. Whoever placed the emphasis on the Hegelian *system* could be fairly conservative in both spheres; whoever regarded the dialectical *method* as the main thing could belong to the most extreme opposition, both in religion and politics. Hegel himself, despite the fairly frequent outbursts of revolutionary wrath in his works, seemed on the whole to be more inclined to the conservative side.[60]

On the conservative side, Hegel appeared to justify any *status quo* as necessary and hence rational in its historical context. That it failed to accord with the principle of rightness merely indicated the stage of development that the world spirit had reached. Thus at certain times 'the wrong is valid, so that the position it occupies is a necessary one.'[61] Patience rather than protest is sometimes presented as the appropriate response. 'As for the slowness of the world-spirit, we must reflect that it did not have to hurry; it had time enough – "a thousand years in thy sight are as one day" [Psalm 90:4]... in world history, advances are slow. Insight into the necessity for this long time is a remedy for our own impatience.'[62]

For a few years after his death in 1831, Hegel's influence was very strong in all German universities. Some followers regarded his work as the last word in philosophy. Soon, however, the Hegelians split into left, centre and right wings, divided at first on the question of whether traditional Christian beliefs were compatible with the Hegelian system and then on whether contemporary Prussia embodied Hegel's ideas. Yet not much later, in 1852, according to Karl Löwith, 'Hegel was as good as forgotten in Germany.'[63] From then onwards, Hegel's ideas have been co-opted for ideological purposes across the political spectrum. In respect of Germany, Hegel has been linked, quite misleadingly, first with Prussianism, then with German nationalism and later, by both advocates and opponents, with nazism. In England, in the late nineteenth century, T.H. Green, Bernard Bosanquet and F.H. Bradley adopted Hegel to bring to liberalism a stronger sense of community.

In 1837, an 18-year-old Rhinelander, Karl Marx, a recent arrival at the University of Berlin, had joined a Hegelian debating club. Out of this Young Hegelian debate on the place of religion in Hegel's system, the ideas that make up Marxism were soon to develop. Over a century later, in the radical 1960s and 1970s, interest in Marxism stimulated enquiry into its Hegelian roots. The influence of Hegel is, of course, part of his importance, yet it is also necessary to resist those who construct the Hegel that suits their ideological purposes. It is gratifying that a literature now exists which sees Hegel as interesting in his own right.

With Hegel, we come to thinkers for whom, in various guises, some transcendental or supra-human agency takes a hand and has mankind under its control. With Hegel it is the world-spirit, and, as we shall see, with Tocqueville it is providence, and with Marx and Engels it is the logic of history that moves society onward.

7

Alexis de Tocqueville

Life

Alexis de Tocqueville, politician, historian and sociologist, could trace his ancestors back to the time of William the Conqueror. His ancestral home was Tocqueville in Normandy though he was born in 1805 in Paris, the centre of the revolution that had broken out 16 years earlier. Though very much an aristocrat, Tocqueville was fated to live in the country where aristocracy had suffered its most spectacular defeat. Here, then, in the contrast between aristocracy and democracy, we find the polarity that informs all his major writings. The French Revolution of 1789 had culminated in the great Terror of 1793–4 when, among many others, half a dozen of Tocqueville's immediate relatives had been guillotined. His mother had watched her parents and grandfather being led to their deaths. Both Tocqueville's parents had been imprisoned but were saved by the fall of Robespierre in July 1794.

As a boy, Tocqueville was tutored at home by a priest, Abbé Lesueur, before going to a *lycée* in Metz. He then studied law in Paris from 1823–6 before serving as a judge in the Courts at Versailles.

The next French Revolution, that of July 1830, replaced the restoration monarchy of Charles X with the constitutional one of Louis-Philippe. It was less significant and violent than its predecessor yet still met with Tocqueville's disapproval. He reluctantly swore allegiance to the new regime but took the opportunity to leave France for the United States of America. His nominal purpose was to inspect American penal institutions and, with his friend Gustave de Beaumont, a report was produced in 1833. His real concern, however, was to investigate democracy in its most advanced form and thereby understand a trend already influential in Europe. Tocqueville was in the United States for less than a year, from May 1831 to February 1832. It was a short visit but one put to distinctly good effect. His report, *Democracy in America*, appeared in two volumes in 1835 and 1840. It won him instant celebrity and remains his most influential work.

Tocqueville married an Englishwoman, Mary Mottley, in 1836, to the disapproval of his family, perhaps more for her social class than her nationality. To some guests who spoke negatively of those who married below their own class, Tocqueville responded: 'I too married beneath me; and by God! it was worth it.'[1] He visited England in 1833, 1835 and 1857 and penned some acute observations about both England and Ireland. In Manchester, the first city of the Industrial Revolution, Tocqueville found confirmation of his ambivalent view of modernity:

> From this foul drain the greatest stream of human industry flows out to fertilise the whole world. From this filthy sewer pure gold flows. Here humanity attains its most complete development and its most brutish; here civilization works its miracles, and civilized man is turned back almost into a savage.[2]

Yet he was an admirer of British politics, praising the country's liberty and ability to reform in a gradualist manner. Though an opponent of slavery, Tocqueville was prepared to support French and other European imperialisms. France had conquered Algeria in 1830. Tocqueville visited there in 1841 and defended the situation on the basis of French national glory.

France was now experiencing revolution almost in each generation and, more explicitly than anyone else, Tocqueville foresaw the 1848 uprising. By then, he had been closely involved in political affairs, having been a member of the Chamber of Deputies since 1839. The February 1848 revolution rid France of monarchy for the last time. In May of that year, Tocqueville was elected to the new legislative assembly, and in June, he became Minister of Foreign Affairs. Tocqueville's elevation, however, was followed by rapid and self-induced decline. He resigned from ministerial office after just 5 months. Three years later, he opposed Louis Napoleon's coup of December 1851, was arrested and held for 1 day and then left public life for the tranquility of his study. This was of great benefit for the world of scholarship as Tocqueville commenced work on his planned history of the 1789 French Revolution. He was working on the second volume when he died of tuberculosis in 1859.

Democracy in America

Tocqueville's basic intention in visiting the United States was to view the democracy which had been established there, for it seemed also 'to be rapidly rising into power in Europe'.[3] He went, then, to see what the future of his own country might look like. His two volumes on *Democracy in America* were published in 1835 and 1840. As a result, Tocqueville became a celebrity and ever since, the book has been taken as the classic work on the United States by a foreigner.

Tocqueville confessed that 'in America I saw more than America,' for 'it appears to me beyond a doubt that, sooner or later, we shall arrive, like the Americans, at an almost complete equality of condition.'[4] Since 'no great democratic republic has hitherto existed in the world...The United States affords the first example of the kind.'[5] For this reason, its condition was of concern 'not only to the United States, but to the whole world; it concerns not a nation only, but all mankind.'[6] From this perspective, Tocqueville's interest was not only in America as America but in America as an example of the genus 'democracy'.

The peculiarity of the United States was the purity and extent to which it had developed the modern form of democratic society. 'The emigrants who colonized the shores of America in the beginning of the seventeenth century somehow separated the democratic principle from all the principles that it had to contend with in the old communities of Europe, and transplanted it alone to the New World.' There it developed with such particular rapidity that it 'seems to have nearly reached its natural limit'.[7]

The United States represented the most advanced stage of democratic development because it had been born free, without an indigenous aristocracy to overthrow. Circumstances had rendered it democratic from the start. Its general equality of conditions, egalitarian spirit and politically engaged citizenry signified, for Tocqueville, the essence of democratic life. He noted that public officials in the United States were all paid, and thus such posts were open to all members of the society. 'They have neither palaces nor guards nor ceremonial costumes' and so are 'not separate from the mass of the citizens'.[8] In the egalitarian townships of New England, Tocqueville found lively and effective local government operating in conditions of peace and tranquillity.

Tocqueville used 'democracy' to refer to the basic egalitarian tendency in society. It therefore encompassed far more than the formal political structure, for it also included the social, ideological and legal changes that were undermining the time-honoured formation of graded ranks and hereditary advantages enjoyed by his forbears. Democracy, accordingly, denoted not so much a precise constitutional arrangement as the general movement attacking the traditional system of inherited privileges. It can be best understood in terms of its antithesis for its primary definition derives from what it is not. Democracy had removed the fixed barriers to social mobility imposed by aristocratic societies. It is not that all immediately become equal but, rather, that all have a better chance to alter their social condition. From Tocqueville's perspective, democratic society seemed virtually classless for, in comparison with the Estates of medieval times, the social groupings of modern society were 'composed of such mobile elements that the body can never exercise any real control over its members'.[9]

Aristocracy and democracy are what Robert Nisbet refers to as Tocqueville's 'two great ideal-types' held 'in a kind of dynamic tension, a dialectical opposition'.[10] Democracy, defined as the anti-aristocratic movement, was certainly Tocqueville's basic understanding of the term. However, we must concede that his usage was not always consistent. Within Tocqueville's writings, democracy was sometimes specified as a social *condition*, sometimes as a social *tendency* and sometimes as a type of *government*. The latter usage might appear to be the same as that usually applied today, but that would be misleading. Even where Tocqueville referred to a democratic state or government, we are still not justified in regarding the nature of government as the only criterion. Democracy in government would be one part of democracy in society. This aspect is apparent in the following passage as also is Tocqueville's characteristic binding of origins and destinations:

Gradually the distinctions of rank are done away; the barriers that once severed mankind are falling; property is divided, power is shared by many, the light of intelligence spreads, and the capacities of all classes tend towards equality. Society becomes democratic, and the empire of democracy is slowly and peaceably introduced into institutions and customs.[11]

Tocqueville presented democracy less as a precise or attained condition than as a process. It signified the constant direction of social change. In the United States, individuals felt themselves to be as good as anyone else. In such a situation, traditional social deference could not long survive, so servants saw their position as merely temporary and hoped eventually to be masters themselves. In contrast to the norms of aristocratic societies, they did not submerge their individuality into that of the families they served. Similarly, farmers no longer deferred to their landowners nor workmen to their masters. The notion of equal human rights was slowly undermining the mind-set associated with differential and immutable birth rights. Society was correspondingly fluid for the social ladder could, in principle, be climbed by all. In the family, too, the modern mentality wrought its egalitarian consequences. Paternal authority was in decline for the distance between father and son was being steadily reduced. To Tocqueville's relief the division of labour between the sexes seemed unimpaired. While rising to the moral and intellectual level of men, American women still 'attach a sort of pride to the voluntary surrender of their own will and make it their boast to bend themselves to the yoke, not to shake it off'.[12]

By virtue of its origins, the United States of America was able to furnish the most advanced example of equality. Without an indigenous and entrenched aristocracy, it had not produced the same powerful and hostile counter-movements as in Europe. However its egalitarian process, though confirming the universal trend, was, necessarily, slight. A young and egalitarian nation had too short a history to furnish conclusive evidence of a long-term historical trend. For this reason, Tocqueville had to burst the bounds indicated by his book's title. America was broad enough to encompass sufficient material on the democratic *condition* but provided insufficient historical evidence of the democratic *process*. For this, he had to turn back to France.

As an aristocrat with a family line that could be traced to the court of William the Conqueror, Tocqueville brought to his investigations a profound sense of history. This perspective gave him many of his most valuable insights, provided a basic part of his comparative method and enabled him to construct a history of the *longue durée*. France lay next behind the United States in terms of democratic advance. In no other 'country in Europe has the great social revolution ... made such rapid progress'.[13] France's origins were utterly unlike those of the United States, yet 700 years of French history confirmed that similar processes were at work on both sides of the Atlantic. With its longer recorded history, France was better able to provide evidence of the durability of the democratic process. Tocqueville observed how gradually 'the value attached to high birth declined.'[14] At one time, French nobility could be inherited; by the thirteenth century, it could be purchased or conferred. In the conflicts of attrition between the crown and the nobility, either side might grant the common people influence in order to tip the scales in their desired direction. As a result, 'In France the kings have always been the most active and the most constant of levelers.'[15] In time, the invention of printing and the spread of learning 'opened the same resources to the minds of all classes'. From the Crusades through to the introduction of municipal corporations, fire-arms, Protestantism, commerce, manufacture and the discovery of America, the social consequences of this egalitarian trend appeared to have been consistent in their direction. Summing up the cumulative changes in France since the eleventh century, Tocqueville concluded that the 'noble has gone down the social ladder, and the commoner has gone up; the one descends as the other rises. Every half-century brings them nearer to each other, and they will soon meet.'[16]

Perhaps the most striking feature of Tocqueville's presentation of this process is his insistence upon its utterly inexorable character. To the reactionaries of his time, he framed rhetorical questions in a form which renders possible only negative answers.

> Would it, then, be wise to imagine that a social movement the causes of which lie so far back can be checked by the efforts of one generation? Can it be believed that the democracy which has overthrown the feudal system and vanquished kings will retreat before tradesmen and capitalists? Will it stop now that it has grown so strong and its adversaries so weak?[17]

The movement towards democracy was not, in essence, subject to the political will of statesmen. It was too deeply rooted for anything to be able to displace it. There is possibly an element of attempted self-persuasion as Tocqueville seeks to inform his fellow aristocrats, nostalgic for more congenial times, that any challenge is in vain. Basic acceptance is the only rational response. The democratic movement was long-term, all-powerful and inevitable. So much was clear from the evidence of French history. Yet from where or what did this powerful dynamic derive?

In his introduction to *Democracy in America*, Tocqueville emphasised that the whole book had

> been written under the influence of a kind of religious awe produced in the author's mind by the view of that irresistible revolution which has advanced for centuries in spite of every obstacle and which is still advancing in the midst of the ruins it has caused. It is not necessary that God himself should speak in order that we may discern the unquestionable signs of his will.... The gradual development of the principle of equality is, therefore, a Providential fact... Wherever we look, we perceive the same revolution going on throughout the Christian world.[18]

Here, it becomes apparent that Tocqueville, the cultivated aristocrat, held assumptions common among the upper classes of his time, that the world was divided into civilised and barbarian, or Christian and pagan. Whichever conceptual scheme had predominance was of little consequence for the one merged into the other. The favoured portion of the globe was progressive and predestined to dominate the stationary and backward regions. But what factors placed some countries on one side of this great divide and the rest on the other side? What moved some societies forward and what held others back? Nineteenth-century social science emerged, in large part, as an attempt to answer this important question. For Marx, social change derived from contradictions in the mode of production; for Mill, from the free development of ideas; and for Durkheim, from an increasing division of labour. For Tocqueville, the guiding hand of God lay behind the visible social processes. Christian equality was for him the basis of the democratic levelling process that he observed. In Tocqueville's scheme, God's providential plan is to history what continental drift is to geography; it is the basic law of movement to which all other changes are subordinate.

The God who set this process in motion, who watches over and guides it, is the God of Christianity. God had chosen to advance only the Christian nations. They were favoured with social progress denied to followers of other religions. This process within Christendom is one that simultaneously advances the democratising countries and increasingly differentiates them from the rest of the world. As Christendom becomes more alike, its distinctiveness as compared with the rest of the world is accentuated. An obvious disadvantage with providence as cause is that, like all theological explanations, it is not open to empirical verification. We may, however, surmise that this disadvantage was more than offset by the hope that the doctrine of providence could help reconcile members of Tocqueville's own class to the modern social order. The Roman Catholic Church had been the largest landowner of the old regime, and the monarchy had claimed to rule by divine right. In respect of both its property and its ideology, the Catholic Church in France was identified with the old order. Jacobinism, the agent of the new order, was seen as derivative from the impiety and heresy of Voltaire and Rousseau. The Enlightenment had upranked reason and downgraded faith. The revolution confiscated church lands, discarded the Christian calendar, closed the churches and substituted the cult of the Supreme Being for the worship of Jesus Christ.

All along the line, a simple equation seemed to hold good. On the one side, the old regime, monarchy, aristocracy and the Catholic Church; on the other, the *philosophes*, the Terror, democracy and secularism. Tocqueville's achievement was to break through these standard distinctions and to assert that God had not abandoned mankind; that all the attributes and changes of modern society were still part of His grand design. The consequence was inescapable. Christians should not oppose but rather should accept and come to terms with the modern world.

In like vein, we should understand Tocqueville's constant reiteration of democracy as not just providential but also inexorable. In the Preface to volume two, he declared himself 'firmly convinced that the democratic revolution which we are now beholding is an irresistible fact against which it would be neither desirable nor prudent to contend'.[19] Combining the inevitability thesis with the providential one implies that 'to attempt to check democracy would be in that case to resist the will of God.' This enabled Tocqueville to move towards his desired conclusion that 'the nations would then be constrained to make the best of the social lot awarded to them by Providence.'[20] We arrive, in consequence, at a theologically strengthened view that democracy is inevitable, the attempt to combat it both futile and heretical, and that the question of its acceptance should be taken off the political agenda.

Tocqueville's first impressions of American democracy had been favourable. In the townships of New England, he found a commendable level of participation, local government, civility, political morality and freedom. This implied a possibility of politics understood as more than just administration; it also involved discussion, argument, compromise, adjustment and exchange. It had to be extensive; not just a debate within the circle of the executive few, but the practice of involved citizenship by the whole community.

An advantage for the United States was that the townships existed before the states and the states before the federation. A strong tradition of municipal government had been established and a constitution created in which federalism and the separation of powers might combine to thwart all dangers of excessive centralisation. Provincial liberty appeared perfectly established and, in a country bursting with political debate, it had no opponents anywhere. Although the inherent general nature of democracy was to produce centralisation, in the American case, the opposite seemed to be occurring, for Tocqueville believed that the federal government was gradually losing strength. At the time of his visit, the United States had only 24 states. It was, one might say, less than half the country it is today, but still its relatively vast territory, its geography, combined with its history and its ideology to make it 'pre-eminently the country of state and municipal government'.[21]

The United States also had particular advantages that derived from its Puritan origins. In America, the spirit of liberty had always been combined with the spirit of religion. 'It must never be forgotten that religion gave birth to Anglo-American society. In the United States, religion is therefore mingled with all the habits of the nation and all the feelings of patriotism, whence it derives a peculiar force.'[22] Yet, though fundamentally religious, American society had established a formal separation of state and church. This was to the advantage of the church which was thereby freed from the uncertain fate of mortal institutions and united solely and unequivocally with permanent human needs.

Problems of Democracy

It was clear to Tocqueville that providence favoured democracy, yet it seemed to be working in a mysterious way for the society it advanced was beset with problems. The pre-modern order was held together by bonds of class that were legitimated by traditional usage. People knew where they stood, what they could do, how they should behave and on whom they could rely. Society appeared as an organic, cohesive totality in which certainty provided security and everyone knew their place.

The condition of democracy was very different. Tradition counted for little. Class ties had loosened if not disappeared. For Tocqueville, this development had its costs. In medieval society, individuals were bound up with, and into, their particular Estates. This gave them a sense of belonging that modern society could not equal. 'In periods of aristocracy every man is always bound so closely to many of his fellow citizens that he cannot be assailed without their coming to his assistance.' In modern society, each individual stood alone, cut off from wider supports and devoted increasingly to personal selfishness and material well-being. Such a person 'has no hereditary friends whose co-operation he may demand, no class upon whose sympathy he may rely; he is easily got rid of, and he is trampled on with impunity'.[23] Such people knew not with whom they could identify. Their society seemed atomised, fragmented, divided and unstable. The spread of opportunity was the greatest benefit but the cost, its inevitable consequence, was that of heightened insecurity. The chance to rise was matched by the risk of fall. This condition imposed a mental burden on those subject to it, and Tocqueville outlined a social psychology of democracy that was by no means favourable. He was constantly struck by the extent to which democratic societies appeared 'agitated by an ill-defined excitement and a kind of feverish impatience'.[24] All seemed 'bustle and activity'; 'everything is in motion around you.'[25] He decided that 'Agitation and mutability are inherent in the nature of democratic republics, just as stagnation and sleepiness are the law of absolute monarchies.'[26] The power and energy of democracy lay behind the wonders it achieved. 'Unquiet passions'[27] and restless ambition produced the progress attainable even by those of humble origins. Wealth they might secure, but not happiness, for 'in democratic times what is most unstable, in the midst of the instability of everything, is the heart of man.'[28] A vital question for democratic societies, then, was how they might combine equality with stable social cohesion.

Even a society that holds together is still not immune from the immense problems democracy carries in its wake. If society is united and similar but weak, it runs the risk of a despotic state rising unchallenged above it. If, on the other hand, it is united and strong, it produces and enforces a conformity that undermines the liberty democracy once sought to establish. Liberty, then, finds no security in the democratic condition. It is under permanent threat, for its structure is devoid of the safeguards which earlier societies had enjoyed. New dangers may come from above or below; either from the state or from the mass. It is to Tocqueville's suspicion of the possibly fundamental incompatibility of freedom and democracy that we must now turn.

In earlier times, the power of the state was relatively weak and its operations far from uniform. Governmental power was exercised predominantly at the local level and with very little standardisation. Some functions were left in the hands of the local aristocracy, and so 'the supreme power was always divided, it never weighed with its whole weight and in the same manner on each individual.'[29] In general, the aristocrats had enough wealth and influence to provide for themselves. This gave them a particular strength which they could put to good effect. 'Such persons restrain a government within general habits of moderation and reserve.'[30] The aristocracy thus came between the state and the individual, thereby rendering governmental power less immediate and oppressive. Furthermore, certain cities, corporations, families and people were granted special powers concerning the administration of justice, the imposition of taxes and the raising of troops. Charitable establishments were run either by the guilds or by private individuals. These all form part of what Tocqueville referred to as 'secondary powers' or 'intermediate institutions'. Though not established with any such intention, they came to function as preservers of liberty and guarantors of diversity. Their own powers curtailed, filtered and distanced those of the state. In providing countervailing institutions of power, wealth, influence, privilege, expertise and control, they furnished the space within which a modest but vital amount of liberty had been attained.

Democracy, by definition, has destroyed or nullified the powers of aristocracy. It introduces general human rights and destroys particular special liberties. Its tendency, then, is to reduce intermediate powers and leave the central government as the major, if not only, source of assistance. Tocqueville followed a long tradition in regarding republican institutions as most secure in small states. From this perspective, the geography of the United States threatened to undermine the success of its democratic experiments. In volume one, American democracy appears happily, and fortuitously, decentralised while democracy in the abstract was said to have the opposite tendency. In volume two, published 5 years later, Tocqueville was less optimistic and also less focused on the United States. His subject increasingly became that of democracy in general, and the basic tendency towards centralisation, if not despotism, was one from which the United States no longer seemed immune.

In volume one, Tocqueville wrote of the United States that 'In no country in the world do the citizens make such exertions for the common weal.'[31] In volume two, presumably based upon the same evidence but upon 5 years further thought, a different emphasis prevails. The active, public citizens have now found other pursuits. Their labours are increasingly directed towards material gain and their affections focused upon their families. Without class allegiance or corporate identification, the public man sinks within the narrow confines of private life. Democracy makes everyone alike, but the consequent individualism leads people

> to sacrifice their rights to their tranquility ... Each of them; living apart, is a stranger to the fate of all the rest; his children and his private friends constitute to him the whole of mankind. As for the rest of his fellow citizens, he is close to them, but does not see them; he touches them, but he does not feel them; he exists only in himself and for himself alone.[32]

This preoccupation with private concerns undermines the participatory virtues Tocqueville so admired. Now the scrutiny of public officials, the watchful suspicion and vigilance which was so central to the preservation of liberty, is sacrificed. Public needs are no longer met by the public themselves but by a growing band of officials upon whose shoulders tasks are willingly transferred and gratefully accepted. The power of the state is thus augmented by the complicity of both sides – an apathetic public who are happy to spare themselves the trouble of thinking and a government intoxicated with the delights of unlimited control.

In this situation, political democracy survives, but elections become a facade, a Potemkin village which barely conceals the civic devastation around it. Red-blooded citizenship has turned pale. Intermittent elections, once a mere part of wider citizenship, now become its whole. They salve the conscience of shallow democrats, for their intimation of participation makes it easier to evade the reality of the all-pervading passivity. Yet where humanity has so degenerated, and freedom has been so generally surrendered, its remaining occasional exercise merely confirms the incapacity of the people to make a proper choice. Tocqueville's final chapters seem to leave America behind as he rises to a more general level. We find a concern for 'the European nations of our time' or for 'democratic nations' in general. Tocqueville envisages a supreme power which

> covers the surface of society with a network of small, complicated rules, minute and uniform, through which the most original minds and the most energetic characters cannot penetrate, to rise above the crowd. The will of man is not shattered, but softened, bent, and guided; men are seldom forced by it to act, but they are constantly restrained from acting. Such a power does not destroy, but it prevents existence; it does not tyrannize, but it compresses, enervates, extinguishes, and stupefies a people, till each nation is reduced to nothing better than a flock of timid and industrious animals, of which the government is the shepherd.[33]

The danger from the state was only one half of the peril that democracy faced. It was, possibly, the less dangerous half, for its threat came from a familiar direction. Had not two centuries of emergent liberal thought warned of the hazards of unlimited state power? In democratic times, individuals are confronted by a new threat; one against which, in consequence, they were unlikely to be prepared. This was the omnipotence of society itself, now so flattened and featureless that any individuality stood out and found no secure refuge.

If the state and society were counterpoised, each might check the excesses of the other. There might then ensue a compromise

from which scope for some diversity might be found. This possibility, unfortunately, did not lie within the logic of the democratic
situation. We have noted that the people passively surrender their
liberties. They do so because, in democratic times, they see state
power not as an alien force but rather as an institutionalised expression of their own desires. Social pressures to conformity push in the
same direction and so reinforce the tendency of the laws. Against
this power, there is no defence, for the decline of intermediate institutions leaves only puny individuals. In this situation, only collective
strength could defend diversity.

Tocqueville's second volume begins with 21 chapters under the
general heading of 'Influence of Democracy on the Action of Intellect in the United States'. His findings form a catalogue of failures.
In the very first sentence, we read 'that in no country in the civilized
world is less attention paid to philosophy than in the United States'.
Later, we learn that the 'inhabitants of the United States have, then,
at present, properly speaking, no literature' and also 'no poets'. Also:
'in few of the civilized nations of our time have the higher sciences
made less progress than in the United States.'[34]

When Tocqueville turned from the cultural consequences of
America's situation in particular to that of the social structure
of democracy in general, his analysis became even more pessimistic. Now, it appeared that the democratic condition itself was
unfavourable to mental cultivation.

In aristocratic ages, the people had been accustomed to look up to
others. Just as there were certain bodies accorded political and social
authority, so also were there groups whose opinions or doctrines
were granted respect. Under democracy, in contrast, no particular
person, class or association is venerated. At first, the democratisation of values leads individuals to place intellectual authority in
themselves, but in time, they come to feel too isolated, weak and
insecure against the mass, and so their own self-esteem and self-
reliance are gradually replaced by an 'almost unbounded confidence
in the judgment of the public'. The tendency is one in which particular authorities come to be replaced by the unlimited authority of
the generality. No laws are needed to produce this effect, for public disapproval is enough. Against it, there is no alternative and no
appeal. So arises 'a new physiognomy of servitude' in which public
opinion becomes 'a species of religion, and the majority its min-
istering prophet'.[35] 'Variety', thought Tocqueville, 'is disappearing

from the human race; the same ways of acting, thinking, and feeling are to be met with all over the world.'[36] In Europe, as in the United States, secondary powers were losing their efficacy. The privileges of the old nobility and the powers of individual cities and other provincial authorities were all gradually being undermined. An omnipotent sameness was replacing them. This was not unprecedented. Tocqueville noted that in China, imitation had replaced innovation and consequently all progress had ceased. China was not a barbarian country; it had a developed civilisation, and so its fate provided an ominous warning. If diversity ceased to prevail it was evident that even a developed society could come to a standstill.

Tocqueville was not merely caught between aristocracy and democracy; he was, in his attitude towards democracy itself, caught between his hopes and his fears. Was it possible that democratic societies would play politics with such consummate skill that the advantages would be maximised and the disadvantages reduced? The interplay of democracy and liberty was one of Tocqueville's main concerns. The providential dynamic of democracy involved a broad determinism at the level of the general historical process. Its victory was assured. No such guarantee could be given to liberty. 'There is nothing,' thought Tocqueville, 'more arduous than the apprenticeship of liberty.'[37] Under modern democracy, it was particularly endangered. Survival would be possible only as a result of concerted and determined exertions. Equality was the most powerful demand. In a sense, this exertion was redundant for its victory was already providentially secured. Liberty was granted no divine advantage and so required the full strength of public support. Tocqueville saw little sign that this would be forthcoming. He warned that people who failed to attain democratic freedom would relapse into democratic despotism.

It is unclear to what extent Tocqueville was actually a friend of democracy. Other contemporary philosophers of history often conflated a prediction with an ethic and were prone to present as inevitable what for them was simultaneously desirable. This was not so with Tocqueville. Though inevitable, democracy carried intrinsic dangers. The examples of ancient times showed that democracy produced government in the interests of the majority, that is, the poor, who then abused their power by enlarging state expenditure to serve their own needs. Here, we reach the nub of Tocqueville's ambivalent attitude to democracy. Political life is a primary good.

He advocates politics as an activity of the people but is not sure if they can be trusted. Their self-interest and lack of wisdom might endanger both state and society. Consequently, the shoals through which the democratic current must pass require of it the most careful navigation. Democracy could be passive or active. Tyranny might be imposed on the passive many by the powerful few or by an active majority crushing all who think differently.

The danger of an unchecked majority was that it provided no guarantee for the liberty of the minority. This was the in-built limitation of democratic government. 'No obstacles exist which can impede, or even retard its progress, so as to make it heed the complaints of those whom it crushes upon its path. This state of things is harmful in itself and dangerous for the future.'[38] The constitutional means of alleviating this danger was by creating the greatest distance between the people and the executive consistent with the appearance of popular power. Consequently, Tocqueville favoured indirect and infrequent elections and the establishment of a bi-cameral legislature. He disliked the use of the referendum as this gave too direct an influence to the people. The requirement the times 'imposed upon those who direct our affairs is to educate democracy, to reawaken, if possible, its religious beliefs; to purify its morals; to mold its actions; to substitute a knowledge of statecraft for its inexperience, and an awareness of its true interest for its blind instincts'.[39] Otherwise democracy, which at best produces the finest examples of participatory citizenship, would, at worst, produce the opposite, a passive mass where diversity of opinion had become as flattened out of existence as diversity of rank.

We have indicated that the modern usage of the term 'democracy' involves a narrower conception than that adopted by Tocqueville. The term is now usually taken to describe not a type of society but a particular form of government. More specifically, western convention equates democracy with government freely chosen by the whole adult population. From such a perspective, Tocqueville's concept of democratic liberty is virtually a tautology. Conversely, democratic tyranny would appear a contradiction to those for whom the two terms are mutually exclusive. As Tocqueville saw it, democracy had two faces. One could be seen in the active yet peaceful citizenship of the New England townships; the other in the mass frenzy of the French Revolutionary Terror. It would, consequently, be illusory to allow the determinism of providence to lull citizens into a passive state of assurance concerning the future, for democracy alone was inadequate. Only when it was combined with liberty could democracy produce a situation adequate for mankind's dignity and continued development.

How, then, was liberty to be sustained in the age of the masses? Tocqueville's answers were both modern and ancient. The modern side was that he valued the practice of citizenship. This, however, could only have its proper effect if it found an efficacious context. Here, he drew on his analysis of medieval society and looked for actual or functional equivalents of the intermediate associations that had provided an assurance of liberty in earlier times. In this respect, he was pleased to find the Americans exhibiting a strong tendency towards association. 'They have not only commercial and manu-facturing companies, in which all take part, but associations of a thousand other kinds, religious, moral, serious, futile, general or restricted, enormous or diminutive.'[40]

The legal profession was not a particular friend of democracy, but in democratic times, it balanced the democratic element and so worked towards a plurality of influential opinion within society. The same was true of the freedom of the press. Newspapers were the necessary mouthpieces of the great national associations that a free society requires. By joining an association, individuals rise above the level of petty and selfish concerns; in pursuing communal goals, they learn the art of association and develop skills that fit them for higher levels of political activity. Associations, then, have paradoxical consequences for the state. On the one hand, they provide points of possible resistance to state power; on the other, they develop a pool of skilled personnel fit for absorption into direct governmental activ-ity. Either way, they represent the best chance of maintaining liberty in democratic times. Tocqueville's last chapters seem to be ones of increasing despondency, but he was unable to end on a defeatist note and so the final few pages of *Democracy in America* redress the balance. Freedom is hard-won and precarious, but its problems are not insurmountable. It is up to the individual nations themselves whether they will attain freedom, knowledge and prosperity rather than servitude, barbarism and wretchedness.

Tocqueville's priority was to secure liberty within democratic soci-eties. In this endeavour, religion had a vital role to play. It alone could impose limits on the passion for gratification that demo-cratic society legitimated. It alone raised people's minds above their own selfish concerns and imposed on them some obligations towards others. Though Tocqueville had doubts about the truth of Christianity, he was convinced of its social utility. In a democratic society, it became even more necessary than before, for as the external constraints of hierarchy became less severe, the internal imperatives of conscience needed to be more effective. Religion alone could provide a sense of boundaries and rules within which people might confine themselves and without which civilisation was unthinkable. In the United States, religion became 'the first of their political institutions; for if it does not impart a taste for freedom, it facilitates their use of it'.[41] In a manner slightly reminiscent of Rousseau, Tocqueville desired a civic religion which would bind people together to an extent which the laws alone could not guarantee.

The French Revolution of 1789

'The lot of the Americans is singular,'[42] wrote Tocqueville towards the end of his second volume. The more this is so the greater the implausibility of the broad theoretical structure he had created. The purpose of his in-depth investigation into American life had been to discover the reality which France and the rest of Christendom were destined to achieve. Tocqueville's comparative approach required him to ascertain which features of US society were general to the whole democratic process and which were particular to itself.

We should then, at this stage, ponder the question of whether the American experience could be amalgamated to the extent that Tocqueville originally assumed, for, even in his own account, beneath the general aspect of the broad democratic tendency, each country threatens to re-emerge with its own distinctive characteristics. *First*, the Americans began with very decentralised powers. At the time of their revolution, local autonomy was deeply entrenched. For the French, in contrast, decentralisation had already been undermined by the old regime. *Second*, in terms of the place of religion in society the United States had again done better. Religious ethics provided the ground upon which their social fabric rested. In France, in contrast, the triumph of unbelief among the upper classes and the intellectuals still endangered the moral basis of the civic order.

Tocqueville termed the people he studied in America as 'Anglo-Americans'. He gave due prominence to their Christianity but failed to give proper significance to their Protestantism. The Christian designation allowed him to align France with the Anglo-Saxon nations. Roman Catholic and Protestant categories would, of course, have set them apart. Tocqueville's work, with its strong emphasis on the social functions of religion, cries out for a fuller sociology of religion. Tocqueville might, for example, have turned his powers of analysis to the question of whether Catholicism and Protestantism had different propensities to produce a culture of citizenship and freedom. His few comments on this question seem to have been written for home consumption.

Third, Tocqueville did not view the 1776 American Revolution as comparable with that of France in 1789. In his opinion, America had achieved democracy peacefully, whereas France had moved towards it by way of revolution. Part of Tocqueville's task in studying America comparatively was to distinguish what was democratic from what was revolutionary.

These disparities between American and French democracy, then, lay behind Tocqueville's fear that the two countries were inclined to different types of democracy; that, by virtue of their respective traditions and values, the United States might have a better chance than France of keeping liberty intact even in a modern society. Tocqueville's retreat from the political scene in 1851 provided the opportunity to investigate these issues in the most dramatic event in French history.

Tocqueville's last major publication, *The Old Regime and the French Revolution*, was intended as the first volume of a fuller study of the 1789 revolution. It was not history in the conventional sense, as he himself realised. He saw himself outlining 'not so much the events themselves...as the spirit of these events...Until now its more visible history has been shown; I have turned it around to show what was beneath it.'[43] If the title had not already been taken, Tocqueville could quite accurately have called his book *Reflections on the Revolution in France*.

In *The Old Regime*, there is less emphasis on the theory of general historical development that had informed Tocqueville's writings on America and only one mention of divine providence. Nevertheless, Tocqueville was concerned to show how a trend common to all Christian countries had in France produced a revolution of unparalleled rapidity and violence. He noted how, over the previous three centuries, the French kings had detached the nobility from the people by drawing them into the court at Versailles. Gradually, the local functions of the nobility ceased while their privileges continued, a disparity which created particularly strong resentment. Tocqueville highlighted the regressive taxation system which exempted the nobility, precisely the social class most able to pay. He also noted that many members of the middle class and even lower middle class enjoyed certain tax exemptions if they occupied official positions. Meanwhile, the peasantry were being released from serfdom and many other antiquated restrictions, but still the burden of taxation 'fell most heavily' on them, 'the humblest members of the community'.[44] Tocqueville was certain that the peasantry had legitimate social grievances. Once the nobility had deserted the countryside, which they found 'profoundly boring', the peasantry were left 'more isolated from the rest of the community than the peasant of any other place or period'.[45] Additionally, the 'economic and social progress which was enriching other classes drove the peasants to despair; they were the downtrodden in the march of civilization.'[46] Tocqueville might regret the extent to which they became revolutionary, but he understood the cause, conceding that the 'common people (especially in rural districts) were seldom in a position to resist oppression otherwise than by a recourse to violence.'[47]

Revolution from those who do worst in any social system can be easily understood. What was more puzzling is the extent to which the old regime was undermined by those who most benefited from it. When elections to the Estates-General took place in March and April 1789, the practice of its distant predecessors was followed, allowing the people to list their grievances. Tocqueville carefully examined these *cahiers* and found that even the aristocracy shared the spirit of the times and so, fatally for them, 'touched off revolution'.[48] Furthermore, the fashionable aristocratic salons provided a platform for the radical writers who gradually became the leaders of opinion in the country.

This was probably as much contact with the middle class as the aristocracy desired, for, in Tocqueville's view, they feared being merged into them. However, the aristocracy was in decline and the middle class on the ascendant. The latter 'grew steadily richer and more enlightened' without aristocratic aid but 'at their expense'.

From the aristocratic standpoint, the middle class appeared first 'as their rivals, before long as their enemies, and finally as their masters'.[49] As to the occupational basis of this rising class, Tocqueville noted that '*rentiers*, merchants, manufacturers, businessmen, and financiers ... now proved to be the most strenuous and determined advocates of reform.'[50] This was in spite of the fact that the 'educated and wealthy classes, the *bourgeoisie* included, were far from being oppressed or enslaved under the old régime. On the contrary, they had generally too much freedom.'[51] From what, then, did their revolutionary dynamic derive? Here, Tocqueville made one of his most striking and innovatory contributions to sociological theory. Contrary to the view famously propounded by Thomas Carlyle in the 1830s,[52] the revolution occurred not because of how bad things were, but because of how much better they were becoming. What the revolution destroyed were merely the remnants of feudalism. Serfdom in Germany had survived much longer than in France, yet the revolution occurred not where oppression was greatest but, rather, where conditions were rapidly improving. This situation produced a powerful mood of expectation. As the regime got less repressive, hopes were correspondingly raised, and it was these which the state and government could not keep in check. So, Tocqueville concluded, 'the most perilous moment for a bad government is one when it seeks to mend its ways.' On this logic, we can understand the rather counter-intuitive point that at 'the height of its power feudalism did not inspire so much hatred as it did on the eve of its eclipse.'[53]

Tocqueville was also innovatory in challenging the notion that the revolution signalled a complete breach with the old regime. The break-up of the big estates, long identified with the revolution, had in fact started 'long before'.[54] The same was true of administrative centralisation. A sub-theme of the book is that, whether before, during or after revolutions, for better or worse, France remains France. Herein lay a danger. Tocqueville was uneasy about the basic character of his countrymen.

> Some nations have freedom in the blood and are ready to face the greatest perils and hardships in its defense ... Other nations, once they have grown prosperous, lose interest in freedom, and let it be snatched from them without lifting a hand to defend it, lest

they should endanger thus the comforts that, in fact, they owe to it alone.[55]

Tocqueville was too tactful to name names, but one can plausibly surmise that the English come into the first category and the French into the second.

Tocqueville was not much given to delineating his sources and acknowledging secondary authorities, yet in *The Old Régime*, Burke is mentioned eight times, more than any other analyst of the revolution.[56] There are, however, some obvious differences between their approaches. For example, Tocqueville's argument for historical continuity is fundamentally different from Burke's belief that in 1789 an adequately functioning society voluntarily plunged into the abyss. Tocqueville noted that for 'Burke the Revolution was not the product of a long development but the sudden outburst of a perfidious emotion'.[57] Similarly, Tocqueville acknowledged lower-class grievances to a degree that Burke never conceded. Yet Tocqueville, like Burke, denied that the nobility and clergy deserved their fate; and like Burke and Paine, he believed that the revolution was caused by a group of literary men who propagated radical ideas. Tocqueville's over-generalised account of them could have come straight from Burke himself:

> ...so many books expounding theories of government in the abstract. Our revolutionaries had the same fondness for broad generalizations, cut-and-dried legislative systems, and a pedantic symmetry; the same contempt for hard facts...the same desire to reconstruct the entire constitution according to the rules of logic and a preconceived system instead of trying to rectify its faulty parts. The result was nothing short of disastrous.[58]

Also, as with Burke, the English set a better example. Their aristocracy had not been drawn away from their estates, nor had they enforced a caste-like separation from the rising middle classes; their writers had not formed a political cabal; and the country's habitual political practice was that of reform rather than revolution. Tocqueville thought that the long-term changes the revolution brought about would have occurred anyway. 'Even if it had not taken place, the old social structure would nonetheless have been shattered everywhere sooner or later.'[59] This is not a point that Burke would have emphasised, but the implication is the Burkeian one that the revolution was unnecessary.

Of Tocqueville's projected second volume, only the first part is fully written up. This deals, once again, with the pre-revolutionary situation. It seems that Tocqueville was more emotionally committed to analysing the aristocracy's loss of power than describing how the revolutionaries enjoyed their use of it. His notes indicate his distaste for events that brought so much suffering to his family. He described the lower classes as 'inclined to license . . . uncouth to an extreme degree' and as having 'barbaric habits'.[60] He also noted the emergence of 'a new kind of revolutionary, a turbulent and destructive type, always ready to demolish and unable to construct. He, however, is not merely violent; he scorns individual rights and persecutes minorities but, what is entirely new, he professes to justify all this.'[61] Finally, we might mention a section which recalls the second volume of *Democracy in America*, where Tocqueville feared that democracy might produce a new version of servitude. His planned section on Napoleonic France describes 'society suppressed and stifled . . . the increasing intellectual sterility of minds, the mental lassitude, the spiritual seclusion, the gradual disappearance of great personalities, the slow unfolding of an immense, flat human landscape in which very little was to stand out except for the colossal figure of the Emperor himself.'[62] The power of this section is surely a product of having been written under the regime of the Emperor's nephew, Louis Napoleon, who, unlike his uncle was certainly no 'colossal figure'.

The French Revolution of 1848

The rise of Louis Napoleon, later Napoleon III, was a consequence of the 1848 revolution. Tocqueville seems to have been the only public figure who saw it coming. From 1839 to 1848, he sat in the Chamber of Deputies, representing Valognes in Normandy. In October 1847, he wrote notes preparatory for the next parliamentary session. In them, we find the acute observation that

> The French Revolution, which abolished all privileges and destroyed all exclusive rights, did leave one, that of property . . . But now that the right to property is the last remnant of a

destroyed aristocratic world, and it alone still stands, an isolated privilege in a levelled society; when it no longer has the cover of other more doubtful or more hated rights, it is in great danger... Soon the political struggle will be between the Haves and the Have-nots; property will be the great battlefield.[63]

These notes were not published at the time, but 3 months later, in January 1848, Tocqueville voiced similar fears in the Chamber of Deputies, describing passions among the working classes which 'bring in their train the most terrifying of revolutions... my profound conviction is that we are lulling ourselves to sleep over an active volcano'. This speech was not well received. Tocqueville noted 'insulting laughter by the majority',[64] but events soon proved him right, for within a month revolution broke out, the king abdicated and the regime fell.

Tocqueville's *Recollections* comprise one of the great eyewitness accounts of this, or any other, revolution and its parliamentary and constitutional aftermath. He vividly portrayed the chaos in the streets, the mob storming the Assembly and, among other things, the doorkeeper who threatened to kill him. Tocqueville described the departed July Monarchy in terms not dissimilar to those of Marx at the same time:

> In 1830 the triumph of the middle class was decisive and so complete that the narrow limits of the bourgeoisie encompassed all political power, franchises, prerogatives, indeed the whole government, to the exclusion, in law, of all beneath it and, in fact, of all that had once been above it. Thus the bourgeoisie became not only the sole director of society, but also, one might say, its cultivator.[65]

The revolution, then, was one of class struggle, in which the propertied bourgeoisie were opposed by the propertyless working classes. Tocqueville took socialism to be the essential feature of the revolution and the one he disliked most. He thought the revolutionaries were motivated by 'greedy, blind, vulgar passions'[66] and, in parliament, Tocqueville had 'no hesitation in voting with' the monarchical parties 'on all measures designed to re-establish order and discipline in society and to strike down the revolutionary and Socialist party'.[67] Panic and emotional distaste coloured his account of French socialism to an extent that badly affected his judgement. He failed, for example, to acknowledge the federalist and decentralist aspects that were so marked in the French socialist tradition and which might actually have rather appealed to him. His description of Louis Auguste Blanqui betrayed an unusual lack of detachment. The revolutionary leader, said Tocqueville, had a 'dirty look like a pallid, mouldy, corpse... he looked as if he had lived in a sewer and only just come out.'[68] Tocqueville regarded socialism as the worst aspect of democracy. It set one class against another, glamorised violence, exalted materialism and, a pervasive concern of Tocqueville's, confirmed state centralisation. On all these counts, it was basically incompatible with the preservation of freedom.

By this time, revolution had come to seem part of the modern order. Men were not merely playing roles first scripted for them in 1789, they were, in terms of the attack on privilege, still taking part in the same revolution, one whose end 'seems ever farther off and hazier'.[69]

Tocqueville, meanwhile, once again became a parliamentarian, elected to the new Constituent Assembly in April 1848 and the Legislative Assembly in May 1849. This did not entirely suit him. He was more of a writer than a speaker and admitted to lacking the 'basic craft for a party leader'.[70] He was happier helping to draft the new constitution, opposing both proposals for a directly elected president and for one who could be eligible for re-election.

These liberal precautions all proved necessary but in vain when President Louis Napoleon, whose term of office was coming to an end, seized power in a *coup d'état*. Tocqueville cannot have been surprised for his previous first impressions of him included visualising 'my country's freedom vanishing under an illegitimate and absurd monarchy'.[71]

Unsurprisingly, then, Tocqueville's last thoughts on his own country were pessimistic. He had travelled to the United States to find out what lay in store for France. The Americans had combined revolution with liberty. Tocqueville's persistent concern was whether the French could do the same. His final reckoning was that they could not, for 'the usual run of French revolutionaries... always mean by "freedom of the people" despotism exercised in the people's name.' Furthermore, in 'France there is only one thing that we cannot make: a free government; and only one that we cannot destroy: centralization'.[72]

Finally, we should note that in his later letters, the gulf between France and America diminishes, and so the 'lot of the Americans' becomes less 'singular'. Their liberty too seems endangered. In a letter of September 1856 to an American friend, Tocqueville remarked that 'Your America itself, to which once turned the dreams of all those who lacked the reality of liberty, has, in my view, given little satisfaction to the friends of liberty for some time.' Two months later, he put it even more strongly, believing that the Americans were no longer the same people they

> were sixty years ago, or even the people that I saw twenty-five years ago, although even then I had already perceived a few distressing changes. But what scares me is, on the one hand, the prodigious number of foreigners that are turning you into a new people; and on the other hand, this race of desperate gamblers that your prosperity, in a land that is still half-empty, has brought forth, a race that combines the passions and instincts of the savage with the tastes, needs, vigor, and vices of civilized men.[73]

Tocqueville's Legacy

Tocqueville enjoyed great prestige during his lifetime. John Stuart Mill wrote a glowing review of *Democracy in America*, and his own thought was much influenced by it. In his own country, Tocqueville, as we have noted, achieved high political office and was elected a member of French Academy and became President of the Academy of Moral and Political Sciences. Tocqueville is now rightly accepted as one of the founders of French sociology, though this was not the accepted view in the nineteenth century, when the influence of Auguste Comte and then Emile Durkheim was very much greater. After his death, then, Tocqueville's writings went out of fashion, though it is clear that his depiction of mass society found strong echoes in the writings of John Stuart Mill, Friedrich Nietzsche and Gustave Le Bon in the nineteenth century, and Ortega y Gasset, C. Wright Mills and Herbert Marcuse in the twentieth. With the rise of totalitarianism, Tocqueville's writings appeared particularly illuminating. His analysis of the social basis of freedom came to provide the means of understanding modern tyranny, particularly through a focus on the significance of 'intermediate powers'.

As these disappear, a mass society emerges and, in the 1950s writings of Hannah Arendt and William Kornhauser, this was taken to be the social base from which both German nazism and Russian communism emerged. We have seen that Tocqueville's concept of a revolution of rising expectations was made in respect of the fall of the Bourbons in 1789, but in the last two decades, this notion has also been applied to the fall of communism. Communism, on this account, partly fell because, with Gorbachev, it sought to mend its ways and so created expectations it could not satisfy. Then, to fortify their newly won freedom, post-communist societies were advised to cultivate a healthy 'civil society'. This term is usually associated with Hegel, but the way it is now used exactly captures Tocqueville's sense of the importance of having powerful, independent social institutions through which the strength of the state can be filtered and countered.

We end here with Tocqueville as social theorist though he is hard to place under modern classificatory labels, whether as between the academic disciplines of sociology, history and politics or between the ideological movements of liberalism and conservatism. In the French Chamber of Deputies, he sat as an independent between government and opposition. He thus remained his own man, an example of the very independence and individuality that it was his life's work to preserve.

8

Karl Marx and Friedrich Engels

Life

Karl Marx was born in the ancient Rhineland city of Trier in May 1818. The area had come under Prussian jurisdiction just a few years earlier, following the defeat of Napoleon. Before that, it had experienced 20 years of French rule. With that had come French ideas and the influence of the early socialist Henri de Saint-Simon was still evident in the years of Marx's youth. One follower of the French reformer was Baron von Westphalen, Marx's neighbour, friend and eventual father-in-law. Just as the Rhineland province achieved its distinctive character through the alternation and integration of German and French influences, so too did the early intellectual development of Karl Marx.

Marx was only 17 when he left home for the University of Bonn, perhaps rather young for the independence he gained, for on one occasion the university imprisoned him for 'disturbing the peace of the night with drunken noise'.[1] His father decided to transfer him to the University of Berlin. Hegel had died in Berlin in 1831. His influence was still considerable when Marx arrived there as a young student 5 years later. At Berlin, Marx became a member of the Young Hegelians, and although his complete attachment to Hegelianism was short-lived, it still had a profound and enduring effect on him. In a situation where censorship restricted free political debate, the Young Hegelian movement and thereby Marxism itself emerged from the context of religious discussion.

By 1841, when he was 22, Marx had finished his doctorate. A stable and rewarding future seemed assured, but the expulsion of liberal academics by the Prussian authorities precluded him from

a university career. A year later, he became editor of the liberal
opposition paper *Rheinische Zeitung* until it was suppressed in 1843.
In the same year, he married Jenny von Westphalen and moved to
Paris. In Berlin, Marx had acquired the sharp cutting edge of radical Hegelianism; now in Paris, he became aware of the plight of
the modern working class. The jigsaw pieces that make up Marxism
were coming together, but in early 1845, Marx was expelled from
Paris at the request of the Prussian government. He moved to
Brussels, where he stayed until the outbreak of the 1848 revolution
in Paris led the Belgian government to deport suspect foreigners.
However, if revolution closed one door, it opened another, for the
provisional government in Paris rescinded the expulsion ordered
by its predecessor. The letter to 'Brave and loyal Marx' explained
that 'Tyranny has banished you, free France opens her doors to you
and all those who fight for the holy cause, the fraternal cause of all
peoples.'[2] In spite of this welcome, Marx only stayed in Paris for
a few months before returning to Cologne as editor of what was
now called the *Neue Rheinische Zeitung*, but this, like its predecessor, did not last long, for the revolutionary tide had turned, and in
May 1849, Marx and the other editors were expelled from Prussian
territory. Marx spent a few months in Paris before being ordered to
leave. So in the wake of the repression that followed the unsuccessful
revolutions of 1848–9, he joined the flight of assorted radicals, revolutionaries and reformers who crossed the Channel to seek refuge
in England. Marx arrived in London in August 1849, at the end of
a decade in which he had been expelled from France, Belgium and
Prussia.

Marx lived in London for the rest of his life, depending primarily on money from Engels. He never had a normal job apart from
some journalism for the *New York Daily Tribune*. It is curious that
with all his prodigious talents, he later applied for a job as a railway
clerk, only to be turned down on account of his poor handwriting.
The family suffered years of financial hardship. 'Never has anyone
written about "money in general" amidst such total lack of money
in particular,'[3] Marx once wrote, though it seems that his financial
troubles were caused less by lack of actual cash than by an inability
to handle it added to his pursuit of a middle-class lifestyle.

Marx was closely linked with the founding of the International Working Men's Association in 1864 but still remained largely
unknown outside of the London political refugee community. He

gained some publicity at the time of the 1871 Paris Commune, of which he was wrongly assumed to be the hidden directing power. The New York *World* correspondent charged Marx with having given secret instructions and even money. The London *Observer* threatened him with prosecution. Marx was thus elevated to notoriety on a somewhat fanciful basis. He neither predicted nor planned the Commune and frequently denied responsibility for it yet seems to have rather enjoyed the attention that came his way. 'I have the honour to be at this moment the most abused and threatened man in London,' he wrote. 'That really does me good after the tedious twenty-year idyll in my den.'[4] Engels too was happy to share the ecstasy of reflected glory. 'The whole of London spoke only of us,'[5] he wrote to a German socialist. Marx died in March 1883 and is buried in Highgate cemetery in north London.

Marx's companion and intellectual partner Friedrich Engels grew up in the manufacturing town of Barmen, now a part of Wuppertal, in the German Rhineland, where his father owned a factory manufacturing lace and ribbon. He was their eldest child of eight, the carrier of his father's first and last names, and also extremely able. Both his seniority and his ability made him a particular focus of attention and hence of disappointment, for the eldest son of a large and strongly Christian, business family became their only rebel as he turned to both atheism and communism. The parental unease was caused not just by shame but by the illiberal Prussian political framework that made all dissent distinctly dangerous. It seemed that young Friedrich would be better off away from undesirable influences. So after a year employed as a clerk for his father's firm, Friedrich was sent to work for his father's export agent in the north German port of Bremen. This might have been designed to keep him away from his radical school friends, but he was more radical than them. Lodgings were arranged with a pietist clergyman, but Engels still enjoyed the freedoms of a large urban centre, including the availability of political pamphlets forbidden in his home area. From Bremen, he wrote to a friend that he was becoming a Hegelian. Berlin remained the centre of radical Hegelianism, and it was there that Engels chose to do his military service. Something of this stayed with him for he cultivated a military image and always looked smart in contrast to the more bohemian Marx. To his father, the army in Berlin must have seemed a bastion of traditional morality, but Engels used his free time to pursue his philosophical interests. His military training was put to practical effect during the 1848–9 uprisings when he supported revolutionary forces in Elberfeld and Baden. Engels later wrote numerous articles on military affairs and became known in the Marx family as 'the General'.

Engels's link with the Young Hegelians brought him into contact with Karl Marx, who had studied at Berlin and had left just a few months before Engels arrived. Marx had become editor of the *Rheinische Zeitung* in October 1842, and when the two met in Cologne a month later, Marx associated Engels with the Berlin radical Young Hegelians from whom he then wished to dissociate himself. So the first meeting was not auspicious, but a year later, Marx read an article by Engels entitled 'Outlines of a Critique of Political Economy'. The effect on him was fundamental. Engels had provided just what the Young Hegelians most lacked, an understanding of political economy from a philosophical perspective. Engels also had the advantage of outstanding journalistic skills and a knowledge of social conditions in England. He next met Marx in Paris in the summer of 1844 when returning to Germany after nearly 2 years in England. This time, his reception was much warmer and so their collaboration began, producing the foundation texts of what became known as Marxism, a label that implicitly designates Engels as the junior partner. However, his contribution was substantial. For the moment, we can note that it was Engels who first directed Marx to the study of economics, who led to his first acquaintance with factory conditions in industrial England, became his closest friend and intellectual collaborator, the advocate and populariser of their joint beliefs and also Marx's major source of financial support during 34 years as a refugee in London. For more than half of these years, Engels continued his work in the Manchester branch of the family firm, Ermen and Engels, leading a strange dual existence as businessman and revolutionary. He was outwardly the very picture of respectability, for he attended the concerts of the Hallé orchestra, rode with the Cheshire Hunt and became Chairman of the prestigious Schiller Institute. Simultaneously, however, he corresponded regularly with Marx in pursuit of their revolutionary aims and, away from the city centre, maintained a second home where he lived with Mary Burns, a working-class Irish woman. She died in 1863, and Engels was happy to be able to retire in 1869 at the age of 49. A year later, he joined Marx in London, where he lived until his death in 1895.

The Historical Process

The Marxist system is the major example of the more general theory of progress that was widely accepted in our period. We have already seen variants of it with Paine, Hegel and Tocqueville. Like Tocqueville, Marx believed that modern society was destined to become more equal; like Hegel, indeed from Hegel, he accepted the idea that development is a product of differences between opposing tendencies. For Hegel, like Plato long before him, the conflict was one of argument and counter-argument at the level of ideas. Marx took up this general structure but gave it a new content. For him, the dynamic behind the historical process was provided not by philosophical argument but by actual clashes between social classes with opposed vested interests; that is, between those, on the one hand, who own the wealth on which productivity depends and those, on the other, who have nothing apart from their ability to labour. In applying this analysis throughout history, Marx and Engels claimed to understand how conflict within feudal society had generated what they called bourgeois or capitalist society. Furthermore, they claimed that this method enabled them to predict how structured antagonism within bourgeois society would inevitably lead to the achievement of communism.

In each instance, the dynamics of social change are powered by a dislocation in what they termed the economic base. This consists of two parts: firstly, the forces of production, that is, the technology, tools, knowledge and skills that a society has at its disposal; and secondly, the appropriate relations of production, that is, the ownership pattern of the workplace. Whereas the forces of production are constantly developing, the relations of production are more static, as the class of owners seeks to fortify its dominance through legal and ideological controls. Thus in time, the ownership pattern curtails society's productive potential. This leads to a period of aggravated class exploitation as the ruling class, who own the means of production, struggle against a rising class seeking to remove constraints that are becoming evermore anachronistic. In this way, Marx and Engels believed that a dynamic logic was written into the structure of the historical process; that feudalism necessarily generated the bourgeois class that would overthrow it and introduce capitalism, and that, at a later stage, capitalism would itself generate the working class destined to battle for the introduction of communism. In each instance, then, in one of the greatest ironies of history, a ruling class necessarily but unwittingly produces its successor.

As an example of this process, Marx and Engels indicated how feudalism had generated capitalism. They believed that the feudal agricultural unit, usually the manor, could not operate without a small market sector. Gradually, both technological developments and the ever more global reach of trade served to develop that sector. As trade expanded, a wider market was created: firstly national, then international, until finally, for the first time ever, the whole world was drawn into the same economic system. In the words of the *Communist Manifesto*: 'The bourgeoisie creates a world after its own image' as all nations are compelled 'on pain of extinction, to adopt the bourgeois mode of production'.[6]

The market stratum, then, clearly had a growth potential which the dominant feudal sector lacked. But the class of rising economic wealth was constrained by traditional law. Feudal law and guild restrictions impeded the free mobility of labour and so operated as a fetter on market expansion. Nevertheless, the conflict between feudal institutions and rising commercial wealth was resolved in favour of the latter. This is, what Marx and Engels called the bourgeois revolution. It brought a new class to political power and resolved the contradiction between the forces and relations of production, for now bourgeois laws were introduced which were, for the time being at least, appropriate for society's technological level. Furthermore, just as the feudal state had sought to defend feudal property relations, so now the bourgeois state did likewise for capitalist property relationships. Marx and Engels regarded the English Civil War as the earliest example of a bourgeois revolution, whose supreme model was the French Revolution of 1789.

This particular and, of course, highly controversial theory of history provided Marx and Engels with a key to understanding their contemporary situation. We can now outline their prediction of how communist society would emerge out of modern capitalism. We now take capitalism as established and dominant, but in order to achieve wealth and develop the industrial resources they own, the bourgeoisie needed a workforce, so they necessarily brought the modern working class into existence. This process is one in which labour is drawn in from the countryside, and thereby a dispersed class of poor, agricultural labourers was transformed into the modern industrial proletariat.

A class aggregated in the cities develops a quite different conception of itself from one that is widely dispersed. In *The Condition of the Working Class in England* (1845), Engels provided a pioneering study of early industrialisation in Manchester, which he regarded as the city where industry was most developed, and where the workers were most numerous and most oppressed. Hence, thought Engels, they were the nearest to socialism. He outlined a developmental scale according to which the workers in the cities were more advanced than those in the countryside, and those in industry more than those in handicraft or agriculture. Within industry too, a gradation was evident, with the factory-hands seeming more enlightened than the miners. In England, the cotton industry was the most mechanised, and so its workers stood at the head of the labour movement and were the most hated by their employers. Engels was certain where this would lead: 'the course of the social disease from which England is suffering is the same as the course of a physical disease; it develops according to certain laws, has its own crises, the last and most violent of which determines the fate of the patient.' Thus 'we can but rejoice over everything which accelerates the course of the disease.'[7] So for Marx and Engels, workers' proximity to each other necessarily leads to awareness of common interests and so greater class-consciousness. It also facilitates organisation. Workers come to feel their exploitation less as a personal grievance and more as a class situation which they organise to oppose. They first attempt to do this by forming trade unions and later, when they have gained the vote, through political parties.

In the 1840s, the formative decade of political Marxism, the sense of party was quite different from what we have now. The age of mass, national parties with membership cards, written constitutions and explicit structures and hierarchies had not yet been born. Unsurprisingly, then, the actual sense of party in the 1848 *Manifesto of the Communist Party* now looks decidedly insubstantial. Anyone coming to Marx and Engels with preconceptions derived from Leninism and Soviet practice is due for a surprise. In the *Manifesto*, we read that the 'Communists do not form a separate party opposed to other working-class parties...They do not set up any sectarian principles of their own, by which to shape and mould the proletarian movement.' From this, we might presume that the communists were just one radical grouping among others, an intellectual think-tank, rather like the Fabian Society in relation to the British labour movement, for their claims were predominantly intellectual: 'they have over the great mass of the proletariat the advantage of clearly understanding the line of march.'[8]

One might suppose the bourgeoisie to be totally opposed to these political developments. This is true in general, but there are important modifications. This is because the bourgeoisie are embattled on all sides. They have to fight against the remnants of feudal and aristocratic privilege; against antagonistic sections of their own class at home, (for economic competition occurs within the bourgeois class as well as between it and the other classes); and against the bourgeois classes abroad. In this situation, it seemed that the bourgeoisie needed the workers not only for economic reasons but also for political ones. The industrial bourgeoisie, then,

> sees itself compelled to appeal to the proletariat, to ask for its help, and thus, to drag it into the political arena. The bourgeoisie, itself, therefore, supplies the proletariat with its own elements of political and general education, in other words, it furnishes the proletariat with weapons for fighting the bourgeoisie.

It was in this sense that Marx wrote of the bourgeoisie producing 'its own grave-diggers'.[9]

Meanwhile, in the economy, some fundamental shifts are occurring; a profound contradiction is re-emerging between the forces and the relations of production. With the further development of industry, society as a whole suffers the consequence of a productive process it is unable to regulate. This predominance of private ownership is also a fetter on society's potential productivity in that there is no overall planning and control. Free trade had earlier been a massive liberating force as compared with the restrictive guild system, but as its productive power was more fully unleashed, its organisational anarchy became ever more apparent. This was the cause of capitalism's recurrent economic crises. Marx drew on Goethe's fable of the sorcerer's apprentice to describe the capitalist economy as dangerously unregulated, 'like the sorcerer, who is no longer able to control the powers of the nether world whom he has called up by his spells'.[10] Consequently, in the depths of the trade cycle, weaker sections of the bourgeoisie go bankrupt and fall into the proletariat. Similarly, in the face of competition from modern industry, the intermediate strata of small tradesmen, shopkeepers, artisans and even the peasantry are no longer able to maintain their distinctive positions. They are reduced to the level of wage labourers. In this way, as Marx once put it, 'the proletariat is recruited from all classes of the population.'[11] This is clearly a process of class polarisation as the working class gets ever larger and other classes diminish. Consequently, the class structure and hence the class struggle become increasingly simplified. Society thus finds itself in a revolutionary situation which is resolved when the workers take over the state machinery and abolish the private ownership of the means of production. This victory of the proletariat is taken to be inevitable.

Revolution

So society changes. Even the most conservative thinkers could acknowledge that and in the nineteenth century, the most powerful and shocking image of such a transformation was the French Revolution of 1789. For Burke, as we saw in Chapter 2, this was absolutely the wrong way to reform, packed with the disadvantages that he was keen to outline. Marx and Engels were also fascinated by historical transformations. If they had followed Burke and chosen England as their model of political development, a quite different theory would have resulted. Instead, however, they chose France, which provided the most dramatic and clear-cut example. The revolution of 1789 had been an uprising in just one country but had spread out and irreversibly transformed the whole European continent. Restoration had been attempted after Napoleon's defeat but had been challenged by the revolutions of 1830. For Marx and Engels, revolution was clearly the form in which social change broke through the crust of conventional established politics.

Revolution, then, moves society forward, but it has its costs. It is clear that Marx and Engels were not discouraged by the mob murders, the Terror, the peasant uprisings in the countryside and all other such excesses of the French Revolution. In fact, the young Engels seems rather to have relished them and imagined a proletarian revolution that was even more bloodthirsty. His fantasy conjured up a forthcoming English Revolution

> with which none hitherto known can be compared... the venge-
> ance of the people will come down with a wrath of which the rage
> of 1793 gives no true idea. The war of the poor against the rich
> will be the bloodiest ever waged... The revolution must come; it
> is already too late to bring about a peaceful solution.[12]

Marx also had the French Revolutionary Terror in mind and was pleased to identify with it. In a speech in Brussels in February 1848, he announced that the 'Jacobin of 1793 has become the Communist of the present day'.[13]

During his first visit to Paris, Marx had drawn up a 'Draft Plan for a Work on the Modern State'. The first of the nine sections is headed: 'The history of the origin of the modern state or the French Revolution'.[14] Unfortunately, this study was never com-pleted. However, shortly after arriving in Paris, Marx wrote 'On the Jewish Question' which contains a stark analysis of liberal politi-cal presuppositions. Drawing on the declarations and constitutional documents of both the French Revolution and some of the North American states, Marx exposed the individualist postulates that underpinned the proclamation of supposedly general rights.

In the name of freedom, the French Revolution had torn asun-der a system that for centuries had bound people to a fixed place within the social order, but in destroying one particular form of society, it seemed, to its opponents, in danger of decimating soci-ety as such. In terms of liberal theory, man was set free, released from onerous communal obligations and left to roam isolated and selfish through the competitive jungle that society had become. But this nominal social anarchy had the state as its support and its con-stitutional guarantees it called 'The Declaration of the Rights of Man and of the Citizen'. Marx immediately recognised the significance of a conceptual duality that he regarded as the expression of a division within bourgeois society itself. Who, he asked 'is *homme* as distinct from *citoyen*?' The latter is universal man conscious of an affinity with his species, but 'the so-called *rights of man* ... are nothing but the rights ... of egoistic man, of man separated from other men and from the community.'[15] The rights of men, then, seemed to be rights for those who want community as little as possible and who view oth-ers less in a spirit of fraternity than one of suspicion and competition.

There is more than a hint of Hegel's analysis of liberalism in Marx's view that the new social freedom is not so much one that people share with each other as one that they use to guard against each other. Any idea of community has disappeared.

'Liberty, Equality, Fraternity' was the appealing battle cry of the French Revolution, but it seemed to Marx and Engels that its definition of liberty precluded the attainment of equality and fraternity. It seemed not so much that people were set free as that capital was liberated from remaining feudal constraints. Equality could not then be achieved in conjunction with freedom of exploitation, nor fraternity from the liberal postulate of natural selfishness. In commenting on the French Revolution of 1848, Marx gave fraternity short shrift as a possibility within a divided and competitive society:

> Fraternité, the brotherhood of antagonistic classes, one of which exploits the other, this *fraternité* ...inscribed in large letters on the facades of Paris, on every prison and every barracks – this *fraternité* found its true, unadulterated and prosaic expression in *civil war*, civil war in its most terrible aspect, the war of labour against capital.[16]

The French Revolution of 1789 had certainly been a mighty liberating force, but it was of its time and stage of development. It was a model in terms of its form rather than its content. At a later stage of development, another revolution would be necessary. That revolution, the communist one, would make real the ideals of liberty, equality and fraternity, that had been proclaimed in 1789 but were only attainable a whole developmental stage later.

Looking back over decades in which too much blood has been spilt for political causes, an insistence on revolution, violence and class war is not attractive. What needs to be said at this stage is that the case for revolution has an intellectual argument behind it. For Marx and Engels, in the 1840s revolution was necessary for the following reasons:

- The workers were subjugated and exploited, as, in one way or another, they always had been.
- What was relatively new was that industrialisation had aggregated workers into factories, and so into cities, thereby, unwittingly and unintentionally, making it easier for them to organise.

- Workers were being homogenised by deskilling and the withering away of intermediate strata.
- Workers either formed the majority or, it was assumed, soon would.
- Workers couldn't vote, so the formal political institutions remained mere instruments of the ruling class.
- Trade unions were either illegal or strictly limited.
- Workers occupied a key location in the production process.
- The ruling class would always defend its material interests by whatever means necessary.
- So workers had the need, the means and no other way forward than revolution.

Some further points needs to be made, all of which serve to differentiate Marx and Engels from the predecessors that they labelled as 'utopian socialists' (Robert Owen, Charles Fourier and Henri de Saint-Simon). These concern the economic pre-requisites of revolution and its necessary agency. One way of designating Marxism is that it provides an economics-based explanation of history. In this, Engels made a major contribution as, in an 1844 article, he first directed Marx to the study of economics. Much that was to become very familiar is already present here: the denunciation of the system of economic competition; the assertion that the gulf between capitalists and workers is antagonistic and bound to deepen and that social polarisation will occur; the tendency of competition to result in economic monopoly; and the belief that regular trade crises are endemic in a system that will reach its destined end in a social revolution.[17] So, as the second section of this chapter has already indicated, revolution has its appropriate placing in the historical process, but its success is possible only when the economic conditions are ripe.

It was on this issue that Marx and Engels drew a clear divide between themselves and other socialist groups. In their account, which was not always accurate, the utopian socialists had a great man theory of social change, one in which the precise moment when the man of genius appears, the saviour with the rational-national plan to rescue society, seems completely arbitrary. He might equally well have arrived a few centuries earlier and so saved humanity many centuries of suffering. Equally arbitrary, consequently, was the precise historical moment at which social justice can be implemented. For Marx and Engels, in contrast, nothing major occurs by chance. Socialism has precise socio-economic (and not merely intellectual) pre-conditions. Before socialism is on the agenda, socio-economic development has to have produced capitalism, then industrialisation, and then the modern urban working class.

A further alleged failure of the utopian socialists was that their theory of social change was not merely false but also paternalistic. The poor had always existed, but what was to be done about them? Both Adam Smith and Hegel had acknowledged that modern commercial society generated a poverty problem that it could not resolve. Hegel had designated the poor as a 'rabble', demoralised, incapable of organisation and generally lacking the advantages that society offered others. He was less optimistic than the utopian socialists, for whom the poor were to be led and then administered. Utopian socialism, said Marx and Engels, was the product of a historical stage at which the workers could not yet be seen as the agents of their own emancipation. Indeed, the message of the utopian socialists was not directed specifically to the poor, for they regarded their theories as appealing equally to all sections of society; 'Hence, they habitually appeal to society at large, without distinction of class',[18] rather than, as Marx and Engels recommended, to the proletariat in particular. As with Thomas Paine, the strength of reason was presumed capable of removing all obstacles in its path. In the utopian socialist view, a true science of society only required reason for its formulation and administration for its implementation. Politics was virtually excluded; revolution definitely so. The utopian socialists assumed that the example of successful small-scale experiments would make the required impression. This echo of the eighteenth century was derided by Marx and Engels as both unrealistic and conservative; unrealistic, as the beneficiaries of a particular social order would not peacefully submit to its planned abolition; conservative, in that a politics of consensus merely causes stagnation in a society riven by deep class divisions.

Finally, with regard to revolution, we must ask what precisely Marx and Engels expected to happen. In the first instance, should the workers storm the factories, the parliament, newspaper offices or all of them? And what then? Fortunately, the *Communist Manifesto* contains a list of recommendations. What is clear is that the proposals considerably strengthen the role of the state. It is expected to take over many of the factories, set up a national bank so as to give it control of credit, and centralise 'the means of communication and transport'. As for the legal changes to be introduced, these include the abolition of land ownership and of the right of inheritance. Child factory labour 'in its present form' would be replaced by free schooling. A progressive income tax would be introduced and the 'gradual abolition of the distinction between town and country' would come about. Marx also proclaimed the 'equal liability of all to labour' in 'an association' where the 'free development of each'[19] would be attained.

The Vision of Communism

A significant part of the appeal of Marxism within European labour movements was that it provided hope for the future, yet the first chapter of the *Communist Manifesto* is basically about the past. It provides a broad historical sweep from ancient Rome through to modern capitalism. This brief survey is less scholastic than might at first appear. Its purpose was to tell the workers that class struggle, as currently experienced, was nothing new; that in the various forms of slavery or feudalism, it had always existed. What is more to the point, all the previous modes of exploitation had – eventually – been defeated. So, the industrial workers were assured that their subservience was part of a long historical pattern in which previously exploited classes had overthrown their masters and created a new and more congenial society. This theory of history was taken to be scientifically ascertained. On that basis, the attainment of communism could be regarded as inevitable.

We are clearly now in the realm of prediction and have in fact been there ever since the presumption of a workers' revolution. The next step was taken to be not full communism but a transitional phase of the 'dictatorship of the proletariat'. In the twentieth century, dictatorship became identified with some particularly gruesome political occurrences. Marx and Engels obviously did not know of these events and so cannot have intended to give the impression that now comes to mind. Dictatorship for them was derived from the usage of the Roman Republic (from where the word derives), where it connoted temporary but still constitutional powers exercised for the duration of a declared emergency. So in the dictatorship of the proletariat class rule continues, but the boot is on the other foot. The majority working class now uses the state to hold down the former bourgeoisie, who are dispossessed by the onset of communal ownership. Bourgeois class existence dissolves with the disappearance of its ownership base. As the state is seen as an instrument of class domination, it becomes redundant when class is overcome. The dictatorship of the proletariat, then, lasts only so long as it has a job to do and has its object its own eventual demise.

We now arrive at communist society. It's worth emphasising that Marx and Engels, the founders of modern communism, wrote comparatively little about it. In some ways, this is just as well, for the science of social prediction is hardly more successful than that of racehorse betting, and the twentieth-century societies that claimed Marxist inspiration were far from providing the characteristics that we shall shortly outline. The Marxist vision of communism can be put together from a scissors-and-paste aggregation of a few comments scattered over various writings. We have already seen that private property is appropriated by the whole community. Consequently, class distinctions disappear as their ownership base is undermined. As antagonism is no longer built into the social structure, its apparatus of control, the state, becomes redundant and gradually 'withers away'. This does not mean that all previous state functions disappear. Those that are legitimate are absorbed back into society. Public order, for example, still has to be maintained. This task is performed not by a specialist, uniformed police force but, in accord with an old radical demand, by the armed people themselves.

In the sphere of production, the previous enforced and excessive division of labour is overcome. Work remains, but within a broader context that facilitates the full diversity of human potential. In a famous youthful outburst of utopian optimism, Marx and Engels wrote that:

in communist society, where nobody has one exclusive sphere of activity but each can become accomplished in any branch he wishes, society regulates the general production and thus makes it possible for me to do one thing today and another tomorrow, to hunt in the morning, fish in the afternoon, rear cattle in the evening, criticise after dinner, just as I have a mind, without ever becoming hunter, fisherman, shepherd or critic.[20]

It was assumed that capitalism had impeded the economy from the full productivity that had become technically feasible. This constraint is overcome once society exerts unified conscious control over the production process. Now, the full development of society's productive forces is achieved, and scarcity is abolished. A communism society is still an industrial one but is directed to meeting the needs of all.

At the more philosophical level, communism is presented as the re-appropriation by society of its own capacities. In 1841, Ludwig Feuerbach, in *The Essence of Christianity*, had argued that the notion of God involved an externalisation of what were actually human powers. In other words, people had created a God which then became a power over them. They had become subordinate to their own product. Marx believed that an analogous alienation occurred in the workplace, where work is not intrinsically satisfying, but merely a means to an end. Workers produce wealth that is not their own, that is expropriated from them by the employer and so fortifies a power that dominates them. All this comes to an end under communism. The production process, based on communal ownership, now augments the workers' powers rather than contributing to their subservience. Consequently, the alienation of the workers from their product has been overcome. We have reached the end of a long journey. From primitive communism through to slavery, feudalism and capitalism, each social formation has unwittingly generated its successor. What now? Would the same apply to communism? Would it, like its predecessors, have its guaranteed historical epoch foredoomed to eventual demise? The answer of Marx and Engels was 'No' because, according to their theory, the inevitable and determined pre-history of humanity gives way to free human history, for with the disappearance of class society there should be no powerful group with a vested interest in blocking potential developments.

Germany

So much for the theory. We now fall back to earth with a bump, and ask where along this long developmental plane did Marx and Engels place their own country? In the second section of Chapter 5, we noted Hegel's concern with German backwardness. This was a common anxiety among his contemporaries, so the issue of belated modernity was part of the intellectual culture in which Marx and Engels grew up. It seemed to them that Germany lay a whole historical stage behind the major states of Western Europe. It was France that had developed the most advanced political movements, and England was clearly the foremost industrial power. In their initial concern for the future of Germany, Marx and Engels looked westward, for the most developed countries show the less developed where they are heading. The indices of advancement included national unification, a republican constitution, extension of the parliamentary franchise, the development of industry and the emergence of the workers' movement. There was, however, one aspect in which Germany could be taken to be advanced. That was in philosophy. In 1844, Marx wrote that 'we Germans... are *philosophical* contemporaries of the present without being its *historical* contemporaries.' Consequently, 'the German proletariat is the *theoretician* of the European proletariat, just as the English proletariat is its *economist*, and the French proletariat its *politician*.'[21]

For the young Marx, Germany was the land of theory, France of practice. Germany had produced, in Hegel, the greatest philosopher of the age, and France, in its great revolution of 1789, and in that of 1830, the foremost political movement; but German philosophy was without political commitment while French politics seemed devoid of adequate theoretical foundations. For the German defenders of Restoration, France was the traditional enemy; its language, culture and revolutionary politics were to be avoided at all costs. Conversely, for many German radicals, France shone brightly as a beacon of modernity. 'And so – to Paris... the new capital of the new world', wrote Marx in September 1843. 'I shall be in Paris by the end of this month, since the atmosphere here makes one a serf, and in Germany I see no scope at all for free activity.'[22] Once in Paris, Marx mixed with both the Germany immigrant community (estimated at 85,000) and the French workers' associations. He thereby discovered the proletariat, the presumed harbingers of a new social order. He also resumed his studies on the French Revolution. No substantial piece of writing resulted, yet the research was far from negligible, for Marx's understanding of that revolution became his basic model not just of bourgeois revolution but of how one social order gives way to its successor.

While Marx first looked to France, Engels was busy in England, but, like Marx, was concerned with comparative levels of development. Also, like Marx, he was particularly impressed with the country he was visiting. Though England had remained constitutionally intact during the decades of revolutionary and Napoleonic turmoil, the development of industry had led to a massive transformation. In consequence, 'England has experienced a greater upheaval than any other country', wrote Engels, and will 'therefore in all probability attain its goal more readily in practice than the political revolution in France or the philosophical revolution in Germany. The revolution in England is a social one and therefore more comprehensive and far-reaching than any other.'[23]

The best-known Marxist consideration of the leading countries' political placing in the 1840s is in the last chapter of the *Communist Manifesto*, where Germany appears as a surprising exception to the general scheme outlined in the first chapter. This opening chapter provides a brief philosophy of history, the purpose of which is to give a class context to historical changes reaching as far back as ancient Rome and forward to the presumed victory of the working class. The account is marked by a high level of generality and abstraction. Industrial Western Europe is taken as a whole in terms of the general process it is undergoing. When Marx and Engels turned their attention from the general to the particular, this simple model was subjected to considerable amendment, and particularly so in respect of their own country. The peculiarity of Germany was that a working class had emerged even before the full victory of the bourgeoisie. In chapter one of the *Manifesto*, it appears that the full capitalist system, from which the proletariat is produced, is a consequence of bourgeois power. Yet capitalism in Germany is acknowledged to have developed without the bourgeois conquest of political power. Economic and political developments, then, seemed to be moving at a different pace, although in the general theory the latter was a product of the former. In the simple, general account, the feudal state placed 'fetters' on the development of capitalism. For the bourgeois productive forces to be fully exploited, it was a necessity that these fetters be 'burst asunder'. Yet in Germany – in spite of its feudal remnants – a bourgeois economic system had developed to the stage of producing a proletariat class that was not merely beginning to organise itself, but was actually and rather amazingly on the verge of assisting in a bourgeois revolution that will be 'but the prelude to an *immediately following* proletarian revolution' (Italics added). For this reason, the 'Communists turn their attention chiefly to Germany',[24] even though France was taken to have had its bourgeois revolution in the previous century and England in the century before that. This notion that Germany could take a shortcut to communism clearly contradicts much of what both Marx and Engels had previously written concerning both German backwardness and the general theory of historical development. It may be partially explained by the *Manifesto*, which was published anonymously and in German, having been commissioned by the German dominated Communist League. The League's members were mainly artisans, rather than factory workers, and industrialisation was threatening their liveli-hood. They would not have welcomed the suggestion of a long period of bourgeois rule and capitalist expansion.

The Revolutions of 1848

The publication of the *Manifesto* and the outbreak of revolution were almost simultaneous, so the prognosis of revolution was instantly confirmed. Actual events would now indicate whether Germany's backwardness could facilitate the expected great leap forward. Marx began 1848 in Brussels, moved to Paris in March but returned to Germany a month later when he received news of uprisings in Berlin. He settled in Cologne and established contacts with various workers' organisations. His main platform was the *Neue Rheinische Zeitung*, in whose pages he campaigned for German unification and a revolutionary war against Russia. He upset some fellow socialists by advocating an alliance of the working class with the lower mid-dle class and the peasantry. His model, here and elsewhere, was the great French Revolution of 1789. In an article published in July 1848, Marx noted that 'The French bourgeoisie of 1789 never left its allies, the peasants, in the lurch. It knew that the abolition of feudalism in the countryside and the creation of a free, landown-ing peasant class was the basis of its rule.' In stark contrast, the 'German bourgeoisie of 1848 unhesitatingly betrays the peasants, who are its *natural allies*, flesh of its own flesh, and without whom it cannot stand up to the aristocracy.' The same article indicates that for Marx a key moment of the 1789 revolution occurred on 4 August when 'the French people, in a *single* day, got the better of the feudal obligations.' In 1848, by contrast, 'feudal obligations got the better of the German people.'[25] So, Germany failed to achieve its 1789 – the unequivocal victory of the rising middle class against aristocratic power – let alone the 'immediately following proletarian revolution' predicted in the *Manifesto*.

Engels, meanwhile, had started the year in Paris, but in April joined Marx in Cologne as one of the editors of the *Neue Rheinische Zeitung*. He went into hiding after the city authorities issued a warrant for his arrest, left for Belgium from where he was expelled, and arrived in Paris in early October. He then set out on a leisurely walk to Switzerland, enjoying wine and women *en route*, before returning to Germany in January 1849. Revolution had not passed him by. He was able to put his military training to use in a democratic uprising in Elberfeld in May 1849, and against Prussian troops in Baden and the Bavarian Palatinate in the following months. This did not provide the glory for which he hoped, for in the end, it was just a matter of organising a withdrawal. The historian W.O. Henderson has noted that the 'Baden insurgents...were completely isolated and could no longer take the offensive. They could only retreat in face of the overwhelmingly superior forces of Prussia and the German Federation massed against them.' Engels did well 'to escape capture for the Prussians took a terrible revenge upon the revolutionaries who fell into their hands'.[26] After the revolutionary movements had been crushed, Engels crossed Switzerland, got a boat from Genoa and arrived in London in November 1849.

Events in Germany, then, had clearly not gone according to plan. The previously suspected weaknesses of the German bourgeoisie were, for Marx and Engels, fully confirmed by the dismal performance of the Frankfurt parliament and the failure to consolidate the gains of 1848. Unification from below – a central aspect of their strategy – had not occurred. Anger was the initial response. Already in August, Engels concluded that 'the Germans demonstrated their vocation as the philistines of world history.' In similar vein, Marx wrote that 'History presents no more *shameful and pitiful spectacle* than that of the *German bourgeoisie*.'[27] The vehemence with which this disappointment was expressed is, from one angle, surprising. The bourgeoisie were doing exactly what Marx's whole analysis should have led him to expect – defending their own class position. Soon, a more analytical understanding came to the fore as the weaknesses of the German bourgeoisie were attributed to its late emergence and consequent possibility of political influence only at a time when it had political enemies on both flanks. The German bourgeoisie, then, was trapped between aristocratic reaction above and the danger of revolutionary anarchy below, a situation that induced paralysis instead of progress. From the perspective of the German middle class, once they had got the vote they were satisfied, and felt no concern to further the claims of their former allies among the working class and peasantry. By March 1850, rather than being described as on the verge of a communist revolution, Germany was downgraded to a country 'where there are still so many remnants of the Middle Ages to be abolished'.[28] A year later, Engels described the German working class as being 'in its social and political development as far behind that of England and France as the German bourgeoisie is behind the bourgeoisie of those countries'.[29]

What, then, of France, the classic land of political revolution? France, declared Friedrich Engels in 1885, is the country where the class struggle always appears in the sharpest outline. This was anything but apparent in the early 1850s, for what then appeared more obvious was the complexity of the class situation. In 1851, Marx saw French society as divided into at least seven layers, which seems far from the assimilation into two great antagonistic classes that the *Manifesto* had described. The *three* major classes – the bourgeoisie, proletariat and peasantry – were all internally divided. The bourgeoisie divided politically into Bourbon legitimists, representing the big landowners, and Orleanists, representing high finance and industry, the declared adherence to a particular royal house veiling the different material interests that were their prime concern. Beneath them was a petty-bourgeoisie of small traders and shopkeepers. The proletariat are distinguished from the 'lumpenproletariat',[30] while the most numerous class of all, the peasantry, was divided into progressive and reactionary elements, but in any case was said to be 'absolutely incapable of any revolutionary initiative'.[31]

Marx treated France as a bourgeois society in spite of the peasantry being the largest single class, for he defined a society by its dominant mode of economic production. Even so the political advances and setbacks in that country belied the idea of history moving in a simple incremental progression. Marx's analysis of the period separating the downfall of the monarchy in 1848 from the establishment of the Second Empire in 1851 suggests that France, the land of revolutions, was travelling backwards. The mimicry of 1789 is marked by at least one important difference. In 1789, events moved in an increasingly progressive direction, whereas between 1848 and 1851 the reverse occurred. The workers set off the 1848 revolution but were not able to consolidate their position, so power first passed from them to the petty-bourgeois democrats, then to the bourgeois 'Party of Order' until, finally, the 'grotesque mediocrity', Louis Bonaparte, representing the conservative peasantry, in December 1851 staged the coup that was to keep him as President for nearly two decades.[32] Had, then, Marx's studies of France undermined his general theory of historical progress? This Marx did not concede. The conservatism of the peasantry was taken to be a merely provisional characteristic. The peasantry, so recently freed from the power of the feudal lords, were increasingly coming under the control of 'urban usurers', and so would eventually develop an opposition to capital. 'Hence the peasants find their natural ally and leader in the *urban proletariat*, whose task is the overthrow of the bourgeois order.'[33] This was an alliance of which as yet there was no evidence but was, thought Marx, inevitable given the logic of the class situation.

What, then, of England, the country with the most developed industrial economy, the one in which Engels in particular had focused his hopes? The Chartist demonstration of 10 April 1848 had caused considerable alarm, but in the end the throne, parliament and the economic system all survived the year. According to Marxist theory, the country that was most developed economically ought to be the one nearest to a communist revolution. In fact, nothing of the sort happened. In contrast with so many other European countries, there was no major uprising in England let alone anything worth calling a revolution. A Marxist explanation for this was not hard to find; it lay in economic prosperity. Continental revolution had in fact aided British prosperity in that it brought 'industry to an almost complete standstill' among her competitors and 'helped the English to weather a year of crisis in a quite tolerable fashion, contributed substantially to clearing away the piled-up stocks of goods in the overseas markets, and made a new industrial upswing possible in the spring of 1849'. However, patterns of trade were cyclical and on this Marx and Engels based their hopes. The 'only question' about British prosperity was 'how long this intoxication will last'.[34]

The failures of the 1848–9 revolutions led Marx and Engels to a definite political shift. There was now less emphasis on political will and more on socio-economic processes. It seemed that a long, hard road had to be travelled before the final overthrow of capital. In a speech of September 1850, in what was hopefully a conscious act of self-criticism, Marx complained of those who had pandered to German artisan impatience. In contrast, 'we say to the workers: You have 15, 20, 50 years of civil war to go through in order to alter the situation and train yourselves for the exercise of power.' Marx and Engels now broke with other members of the Communist League who saw revolution merely 'as the result of an effort of *will*'.[35] The task now was educational. Marx turned to the economic studies that eventually resulted in *Capital* volume one being published in 1867, and Engels returned to Manchester to earn the living on which both he and the Marx family depended.

In summary, Marx and Engels read the 1848–9 evidence as indicating that they had initially been too optimistic. The revolution would come later. A plausible alternative reading was that the age of revolution was at an end so far as western and central Europe were concerned; that is, in the more advanced countries in which they had originally placed their main hopes.

Legacy

It will hardly need saying that the legacy of Marx and Engels's writings is more significant than that of any of our other thinkers. For much of the twentieth-century communist system based on professed allegiance to Marxism were operative first in the Soviet Union after 1917, then in most of Eastern Europe after the Second World War and also in some Asian countries, still surviving in China and North Korea.

This all looks like Marx and Engels being right about the likelihood of communist revolution but wrong about its manner and place. Yet during the later years of his life, Marx (more than Engels) looked to the periphery rather than the centre of capitalism for the outbreak that would signal the collapse of the whole system. Russia had long been dismissed as 'the unbroken bulwark and reserve army of counter-revolution', but the freeing of the serfs in 1861 and the social conflicts of the 1870s led to a complete change of attitude. 'This time the revolution will begin in the East, hitherto the impregnable bastion and reserve army of counter-revolution,' wrote Marx in September 1877. 'All sections of Russian society are in full decomposition economically, morally and intellectually.'[36] Marx's attention was drawn to Russia again when in 1881 he received what turned out to be a significant letter from Vera Zasulich, a Russian Marxist living safely in Geneva. She had achieved notoriety 3 years earlier when she shot the governor of St. Petersburg for flogging a prisoner. Her letter began as follows:

> Honoured Citizen,
>   You are not aware that your *Capital* enjoys great popularity in Russia. Although the edition has been confiscated, the few remaining copies are read and re-read by the mass of more or less educated people in our country; serious men are studying it. What you probably do not realise is the role which your *Capital* plays in our discussions on the agrarian question in Russia and our rural commune.[37]

At issue here was whether Russia had to go through the full industrial capitalist phase to reach socialism or whether the survival of the rural commune provided an alternate path. This involved, even more significantly, the question of whether the general Marxist theory of development was of global application. This was a troubling problem for Marx as the many drafts of his reply clearly indicate. In the end, he conceded, what had not been explicit before, that his notion of historical inevitability applied only to Western Europe.[38]

The following year, a Russian translation of the *Communist Manifesto* was published. In the Preface, Russia was described as forming 'the vanguard of revolutionary action in Europe'. Given their low level of economic development, the Russians were not deemed capable of sustaining communism on their own, but if their revolution became 'the signal for a proletarian revolution in the West, so that both complement each other', then 'the present Russian common ownership of land may serve as the starting-point for a communist development.'[39] So in spite of its relative backwardness, Marx held out the hope that particular circumstances might allow Russia to skip the full development of the capitalist stage and leap forward to communism. This is, in some ways, an echo of the *Communist Manifesto* statement on Germany, which, to an extent, opens up the divide between Russian Mensheviks and Bolsheviks in the early twentieth century. The Mensheviks inclined more to the view that each society must go through the full capitalist stage of development according to the logic of chapter one of the *Manifesto*, whereas the Bolsheviks followed the argument of chapter four, that certain situations can facilitate a shortcut.

At the end of his life, Marx was hardly known outside of socialist circles. Though he died in London, the short obituary in *The Times* was compiled from a report by their Paris correspondent. Marx only became known, famous and infamous, because of the 1917 Bolshevik Revolution and the spread of communism out from Russia and into Eastern Europe and China after the Second World War. The Cold War, fortunately, remained mostly a war of ideas and the ideas of the communist bloc were held to derive from Marx and Engels. So, whether fairly or not, our two advocates of liberation and egalitarianism became associated with bureaucracy and dictatorship. Over the twentieth century, this linkage produced a vast literature. For some, Marx and Engels were both directly responsible for Soviet totalitarianism, and for some, only Engels took the blame; for others, communism went wrong through an adherence to Marxism that was formal rather than genuine. A lesser strand took the view that communist societies failed because Marx and Engels gave insufficient guidance on how they should be organised. The Cold War context meant that this whole debate occurred in a constricting and heightened emotional atmosphere, for the analysis of Marxism and communism was no trivial matter. It was, after all, concerned with fundamental existential issues, not just for the communist countries themselves, but for the whole world, for the Soviet bloc constituted one of the two global superpowers which, like its western opponents, was heavily armed with an array of nuclear weaponry.

That, fortunately, is now all in the past. Marxism has been returned from the Soviet politburo to the academic context from which it originally emerged. It will not, however, easily sink back into neutrality, for just about anything political can be controversial, and Marxism will always remain associated with its own history. It should, though, now be easier to study Marx and Engels in the same relatively dispassionate way that we treat the other thinkers covered in this book.

Marx and Engels developed a whole social science, integrating economics, history, sociology, politics, philosophy and culture,[40] yet at the very core of their approach is the injunction to look to the material interest. As Marx once put it: 'The Tories in England long imagined that they were enthusiastic about monarchy, the church and the beauties of the old English Constitution, until the day of danger wrung from them the confession that they are enthusiastic only about ground rent.'[41]

Lastly, intellectual fashions are immensely persuasive, but they come and go. In the 1960s, among students, it was very fashionable to read Marx; now, it is very unfashionable. Part of the appeal of the *history* of political thought is that it takes seriously thinkers whose basic presuppositions are no longer acceptable. It remembers John Stuart Mill's injunction that ages are no more infallible than individuals. With that in mind, let's close with the words of a writer certainly not sharing Marx's theories yet acknowledging that he 'produced the most powerful, coherent, and influential secular system of ideas ever devised to explain man's past, analyze his present, and predict his future'.[42]

9
Epilogue

The American Declaration of Independence can be seen, with hindsight, as the start of a long process of decolonisation that was most pronounced only after the Second World War. For Europe, its effect on the collective consciousness was less than that of the 1789 French Revolution. What happened, or threatened to happen, in the home country struck deeper than events, however disastrous, in the colonies. The excesses, perhaps more than the successes, of the French Revolution have been a constant source of fascination for both opponents and supporters. Dominic Lieven once noted that the 'shadow of 1789 lay over Europe's nineteenth-century aristocracy. Never again would aristocratic politics be quite so carefree.' As just one instance, he mentions that 'Alexander II of Russia, contemplating cautious constitutional reform in 1881, could terrify himself by memories of Louis XVI and the Estates General.'[1]

What for one side was a disaster, the other saw as grounds for celebration and identification. For example, in 1939 the French Communist Party marked the 150th anniversary of the French Revolution with a series of essays congratulating themselves on being 'the authorized continuator of the work of the first French revolutionaries'.[2] This was no isolated instance. Noel O'Sullivan has pointed out that 'Ever since 1917, French Marxists had embraced Soviet Communism as a legitimate continuation of the revolutionary tradition they themselves [i.e. the French] had begun with the French Revolution... The torch of freedom previously carried by the French Jacobins, in other words, had for the time being passed into Soviet hands.'[3]

The implication of this is that Paris and France no longer formed the storm centre of revolutionary endeavour. In fact, the age of

revolution had come to an end, at least as far as central and Western
Europe were concerned. If Paris was the epicentre, then nothing
after 1848 matches what went before. That, of course, was not, nor
could have been, obvious at the time. One of the German revolutionaries of 1848, Joseph Weydemeyer, fled to the United States to
escape the counter-revolution. In May 1852, writing from the 'New
World' he reiterated the old view: 'France is and remains the land
of revolutionary energy, and, although our Germany has wrested
first place from France in intellectual and theoretical development,
the latter country remains the center of gravity of revolutionary
development.'[4] At least in respect of France, the aristocrat might
have agreed with the revolutionary, for right to the end of his
life in 1859 Alexis de Tocqueville regarded the French Revolution
as ongoing: 'that strange drama whose end is not yet in sight'.
On the last page of his notes for the intended second volume on
the French Revolution, he wrote of 'the endurance of the revolutionary illness in our times'.[5] However, no such outbreak occurred
again, for the Paris Commune of 1871 was an uprising in the capital alone. It did not stimulate wider French, let along European,
equivalents.

What, then, had changed? How had central and western Europe
managed to stablise after decades of turmoil? Eugene Weber has
supplied one part of the answer: 'All the French revolutions had
a background of economic crisis, hunger, misery. On 14 July 1789
the price of bread in Paris was higher than on any other day in the
eighteenth century... after the 1850s there are no more bread riots
in France.'[6]

What had also changed was that working-class men were getting
the vote. Of all the major thinkers covered in this book, Friedrich
Engels is the one who lived furthest into the nineteenth century.
He died in August 1895. In March of that year, in the last publication of his life, Engels provided an introduction to Marx's 'The
Class Struggles in France 1848 to 1850'. He looked back over more
than four decades to an earlier world with different assumptions and
confessed that

> history has shown us too to have been wrong, has revealed our
> point of view at that time as an illusion. It has done even more:
> it has not merely dispelled the erroneous notions we then held; it
> has also completely transformed the conditions under which the

proletariat has to fight. The mode of struggle of 1848 is today obsolete in every respect.[7]

And even more explicitly: 'Rebellion in the old style, street fighting with barricades, which decided the issue everywhere up to 1848, had become largely outdated.'[8]

In the new situation, the electoral process supplied a platform from which workers' demands could be articulated and an accurate measure of party strength ascertained. For the German Social Democrats, said Engels, 'Slow propaganda work and parliamentary activity are...the immediate tasks of the party.' He clearly enjoyed the irony of the change. 'We, the "revolutionaries", the "overthrowers" – we are thriving far better on legal methods than on illegal methods and overthrow.' He saw that once numbers weighed in the balance, the boot was on the other foot. 'The parties of Order, as they call themselves, are perishing under the legal conditions created by themselves. They cry despairingly...legality is the death of us; whereas we, under this legality, get firm muscles and rosy cheeks and look like life eternal.'[9]

That democracy could appear as a threat serves as a reminder that the 1848–51 period in Europe was not just one of revolution but also of counter-revolution. Here, we see a precursor of fascism, for the fear of socialism that contributed to the rise of Louis Bonaparte's authoritarian regime contains intimations of the ascent of Mussolini, Hitler and Franco in countries where democracy had only recently been achieved.

The counter-revolutionary use of military force, made easier by the development of the railways, was another of the factors that tilted the balance against revolution. Engels's introduction included the following:

In addition, the military have at their disposal artillery and fully equipped corps of trained engineers, means of warfare which, in nearly every case, the insurgents entirely lack. No wonder, then, that even the barricade fighting conducted with the greatest heroism – Paris, June 1848; Vienna, October 1848; Dresden, May 1849 – ended in the defeat of the insurrection as soon as the leaders of the attack, unhampered by political considerations, acted according to purely military criteria, and their soldiers remained reliable.[10]

It can, then, seem that affluence renders revolution unlikely, democracy makes it unnecessary, and military power makes it impossible. However, these factors did not always prevail concurrently, and where they didn't, revolution remained a possibility. Following Martin Malia,[11] we can say that the revolutions of our period were part of the transition to modernity. Revolution since then has usually had the same function. This can be applied to the communist revolutions in Russia and China as well as the anti-colonial revolutions after the Second World War. If, as we have earlier stipulated, modernity includes the move towards political democracy, then the revolutions that overthrew European communism can be seen in the same light. The evidence so far suggests that modern democratic societies are not subject to revolutionary overthrow. They are, however, entering an era of immense stress and transformation occasioned by the incipient ecological challenge. Precisely, how this period will be managed politically cannot be predicted. We can merely assert that, contrary to one famous account,[12] the end of history is not in sight.

Notes

Preface

1. Jay Winik has described the late eighteenth century as having produced 'a galaxy of humankind's greatest thinkers and doers'. *The Great Upheaval: America and the Birth of the Modern World, 1778–1800* (New York: Harper Collins, 2007), p. xi.

Chapter 1: The Historical Context

1. E.J. Hobsbawm, *The Age of Revolution 1789–1848* (New York: Mentor, 1964). Tony Judt began a chapter on Eric Hobsbawm by calling him 'the best-known historian in the world.' *Reappraisals: Reflections on the Forgotten Twentieth Century* (London: Heinemann, 2008), p. 116.
2. E.J. Hobsbawm, *The Age of Revolution*, pp. 17, xv.
3. J. Winik, *The Great Upheaval: America and the Birth of the Modern World, 1778–1800* (New York: Harper Collins, 2007), p. xi.
4. I. Hampsher-Monk, *The Impact of the French Revolution: Texts from Britain in the 1790s* (Cambridge: Cambridge University Press, 2005), p. 1.
5. J. Waldron, *'Nonsense Upon Stilts': Bentham, Burke and Marx on the Rights of Man* (London: Methuen, 1987), p. 21.
6. S.M. Lipset, *The First New Nation: The United States in Historical and Comparative Perspective* (New York: Norton, 1979).
7. M. Malia, *History's Locomotives: Revolutions and the Making of the Modern World* (New Haven, CT: Yale University Press, 2006), p. 6.
8. T. Paine, *Common Sense* in M. Foot and I. Kramnick, eds, *The Thomas Paine Reader* (Harmondsworth: Penguin Books, 1987), p. 81.
9. T. Paine, *Rights of Man* in *The Thomas Paine Reader*, p. 240.
10. Quoted in R.R. Palmer, 'Social and Psychological Foundations of the Revolutionary Era' in A. Goodwin, ed., *The New Cambridge Modern History*, vol. viii, *The American and French Revolutions 1763–93* (Cambridge: Cambridge University Press, 1965), p. 440.
11. From Condorcet, 'The Influence of the American Revolution on Europe', 1786, quoted in J. Salwyn Schapiro, *Condorcet and the Rise of Liberalism* (New York: Harcourt, Brace and Co., 1934), p. 222.

189

12. A. de Tocqueville, *The Old Régime and the French Revolution* (Garden City, NY: Doubleday Anchor, 1955), p. 146.
13. J. Godechot, *France and the Atlantic Revolution of the Eighteenth Century* (New York: The Free Press, 1965), pp. 3, 7. Godechot expressed the same view a few years later in *The Counter-Revolution. Doctrine and Action 1789–1804* (London: Routledge and Kegan Paul, 1972), p. 50.
14. R.R. Palmer, *The Age of the Democratic Revolution: A Political History of Europe and America, 1760–1800* [1959] (Princeton, NJ: Princeton University Press, 1974), p. 7. See also R.R. Palmer, *The World of the French Revolution* (London: Allen and Unwin, 1971), pp. 4, 265, 269 and J. Winik, *The Great Upheaval*, pp. xiv, 113.
15. E. Hobsbawm, *Age of Revolution*, p. 56.
16. E.J. Evans, *The Forging of the Modern State: Early Industrial Britain 1783–1870* (London: Longman, 1991), p. 412.
17. P.H. Beik, *Louis Philippe and the July Monarchy* (Princeton, NJ: Van Nostrand, 1965), p. 57.
18. Quoted in P.N. Carroll and David W. Noble, *The Free and the Unfree: A New History of the United States* (Harmondsworth: Penguin Books, 1985), p. 128.
19. A. De Tocqueville, *Democracy in America* (New York: Vintage Books, n.d.), vol. 2, p. 171.
20. B. Moore, Jr., *Social Origins of Dictatorship and Democracy: Lord and Peasant in the Making of the Modern World* (Harmondsworth: Penguin Books, 1969), p. 121.
21. M. Rapport, *1848: Year of Revolution* (London: Abacus, 2009), p. 16.
22. E. Hobsbawm, *Age of Revolution*, p. xv.
23. L. Colley, *Britons: Forging the Nation 1707–1837* (London: Pimlico, 1992), p. 332 and see pp. 337, 345, 349.
24. On this and related issues, see E. Royle, *Revolutionary Britannia? Reflections on the Threat of Revolution in Britain, 1789–1848* (Manchester: Manchester University Press, 2000), pp. 52–3.
25. G.O. Trevelyan, *The Life and Letters of Lord Macaulay* (Oxford: Oxford University Press, 1978), p. 160.
26. E.P. Thompson, *The Making of the English Working Class* (Harmondsworth: Penguin Books, 1968), p. 898. E. Royle, 'There was clearly a revolutionary situation in 1830–32', *Revolutionary Britannia?*, p. 88. But note the question mark in the book's title.
27. R. Jahanbegloo, *Conversations with Isaiah Berlin* (Oxford: Clarendon Press, 1991), p. 126.
28. Italics in original. *The Letters of Queen Victoria: A Selection from Her Majesty's Correspondence Between the Years 1837 and 1861*, A.C. Benson and Viscount Esher, eds, 3 vols (London: John Murray,1907), vol. ii, p. 218.
29. W.E. Houghton, *The Victorian Frame of Mind, 1830–1870* (New Haven, CT: Yale University Press, 1985), pp. 54–5. I have discussed the tensions of the 1840s in *The Condition of England Question. Carlyle, Mill, Engels* (Basingstoke: Palgrave Macmillan, 1998). See esp. pp. 16–29, 157–60.

30. L. Namier, *1848: The Revolution of the Intellectuals* (Oxford: Oxford University Press, 1950).
31. N. Davies, *Europe: A History* (London: Pimlico, 1997), p. 805.
32. M. Rapport, *1848: Year of Revolution* (London: Abacus, 2009), p. 400.
33. K. Stephen Vincent (2008), 'Martin Malia and the European Revolutionary Tradition', *Political Theory*, 7.4, p. 504.
34. M. Malia, *History's Locomotives*, p. 217.
35. See M. Levin, *The Spectre of Democracy: The Rise of Modern Democracy as Seen by Its Critics* (Basingstoke: Palgrave Macmillan, 1992), ch. 1.
36. 'Sometimes' because 'serfdom meant many different things in different regions'. D. Lieven, *The Aristocracy in Europe 1815–1914* (Basingstoke: Palgrave Macmillan, 1992), p. 78. According to one estimate, in 1848 there were still 20 million serfs in Russia. M. Rapport, *1848: Year of Revolution*, p. 10.

Chapter 2: Modern Society and Modern Thought

1. A. de Tocqueville, *The Old Régime and the French Revolution* (New York: Doubleday, 1955), p. 139.
2. Quoted in R.R. Palmer, *The Age of the Democratic Revolution: A Political History of Europe and America, 1760–1800* (Princeton, NJ: Princeton University Press, 1974), p. 517.
3. T. Paine, *The Rights of Man* in *The Thomas Paine Reader*, M. Foot and I. Kramnick, eds (Harmondsworth: Penguin Books, 1987), p. 250.
4. E. Burke, *Reflections on the Revolution in France* (London: Dent, 1964), p. 73.
5. Quoted in R. Porter, *Enlightenment: Britain and the Creation of the Modern World* (London: Penguin Books, 2001), p. 399.
6. G. Best, *Mid-Victorian Britain 1851–75* (Glasgow: Fontana/Collins, 1982), p. 24.
7. C. Kingsley, *Alton Locke, Tailor and Poet: An Autobiography* [1850] (Oxford: Oxford University Press, 1983), p. 303.
8. A. de Tocqueville, *The Old Régime and the French Revolution*, p. 96.
9. Voltaire, *Letters on England* [1734] (Harmondsworth: Penguin, 1980), pp. 57, 62.
10. See D. Edmonds and J. Eidenow, *Rousseau's Dog: Two Great Thinkers at War in the Age of Enlightenment* (London: Faber and Faber, 2006).
11. 'For during the Enlightenment every important thinker and commentator centrally engaged with Spinoza, if only silently, as in the case of Locke'. J. Israel intro. to B. de Spinoza, *Theological-Political Treatise* [1669–70] (Cambridge: Cambridge University Press, 2007), p. xxxiii.
12. T. Munck, *The Enlightenment: A Comparative Social History* (London: Arnold, 2000), p. 7.
13. Voltaire, *Zadig: L'Ingénu* (Harmondsworth: Penguin Books, 1964), p. 61.

14. R. Descartes, *Discourse on Method and Other Writings* (Harmondsworth: Penguin Books, 1966), p. 46.
15. B. de Spinoza, *Theological-Political Treatise*, pp. 8–9.
16. I. Kant, *Critique of Pure Reason* [1781] (New York: Anchor, 1966), p. xxiv.
17. I. Kant, *An Answer to the Question: 'What is Enlightenment?'* (London: Penguin Books, 2009), p. 3.
18. I. Kant, 'What is Orientation in thinking?' Quoted from J. Schmidt, ed., *What is Enlightenment? Eighteenth Century Answers and Twentieth Century Questions* (Berkeley, CA: University of California Press, 1996), p. 30.
19. R. Porter, *Enlightenment*, p. 72. A further indication of the urge to control is that, at the same time, '40,000 people in the city of Paris were under surveillance for "immorality"'. A. Hussey, *Paris. The Secret History* (London: Penguin Books, 2007), p. 203.
20. D. Outram, *The Enlightenment* (Cambridge: Cambridge University Press, 2003), p. 38.
21. Quoted by J.C.D. Clark in his introduction to Burke's *Reflections on the Revolution in France* (Stanford, CA: Stanford University Press, 2001), pp. 44–5.
22. T. Todorov, *In Defence of Enlightenment*, p. 6.
23. Quoted in M. Neocleous, *The Monstrous and the Dead: Burke, Marx, Fascism* (Cardiff: University of Wales Press, 2005), p. 46.
24. J.Y.T. Greig, ed., *The Letters of David Hume* (Oxford: Clarendon, 1932), vol. 2, p. 197; T.H. Green and T.H. Grose, ed., *David Hume. Essays: Moral, Political and Literary* (London: Longmans, 1875), vol. 1, p. 135.
25. R. Porter, *Enlightenment*, pp. 35–6.
26. Quoted in R.B. Morris, *Basic Documents in American History* (Princeton, NJ: Van Nostrand, 1956), pp. 40, 62, 63.
27. D. Hume, *Enquiries Concerning the Human Understanding and Concerning the Principles of Morals* [1751] (Oxford: Clarendon Press, 1966), p. 83.
28. Kant, *An Answer to the Question: 'What is Enlightenment?'* p. 1.
29. Helvetius, *De l'homme*, 1772, quoted in F. Copleston, *A History of Philosophy*, vol. 6, part 1 (New York: Doubleday, 1964), p. 51.
30. Quoted in A. de Tocqueville, *The Old Régime and the French Revolution*, p. 160.
31. M. de Condorcet, *Outlines of an Historical View of the Progress of the Human Mind* (London: J. Johnson, 1795), p. 14.
32. Quoted in H. Marcuse, *Reason and Revolution* (London: Routledge and Kegan Paul), 1969, p. 7.
33. A. Ferguson, *An Essay on the History of Civil Society* [1767] (Cambridge: Cambridge University Press, 1995), p. 75.
34. Quoted in R. Nisbet, *The Making of Modern Society* (Brighton: Wheatsheaf, 1986), p. 102.
35. J.J. Rousseau, *The Social Contract: Discourses*, G.D.H. Cole, ed. (London: Dent, 1961), p. 73.
36. Voltaire, *Zadig: L'Ingénu*, p. 52.

37. Quoted in P. Hazard, *European Thought in the Eighteenth Century* (Harmondsworth: Penguin Books, 1965), p. 394.
38. Quoted in T. Munck, *The Enlightenment: A Comparative Social History* (London: Arnold, 2000), p. 196.
39. Voltaire, *Political Writings*, D. Williams, ed. (Cambridge: Cambridge University Press, 1994), p. 281. On Diderot's contempt for the masses, see G. Himmelfarb, *The Roads to Modernity. The British, French and American Enlightenments* (London: Vintage Books, 2008), pp. 154–5, 177.
40. A. de Tocqueville, *The Old Régime and the French Revolution*, p. 281.
41. Voltaire, *Letters on England*, p. 67.
42. Dedication to 'A Discourse on the Origin of Inequality' in J.J. Rousseau, *The Social Contract: Discourses*, p. 145.
43. I. Kant, *An Answer to the Question 'What is Enlightenment?'*, p. 3.
44. A. Cobban, *Aspects of the French Revolution* (London: Cape, 1968), p. 21. See also a much more recent publication, Todorov, *In Defence of the Enlightenment*.
45. Quoted in G. Himmelfarb, *The Roads to Modernity*, p. 191.
46. R.R. Palmer in M. Williams, eds, *1775–1830 Revolutions* (Harmondsworth: Penguin Books, 1971), p. 21.
47. C.L.R. James, *The Black Jacobins: Toussaint L'Ouverture and the San Domingo Revolution* (London: Penguin Books, 1980), p. 55.
48. J.H. Plumb, *Men and Places* (Harmondsworth: Penguin Books), 1966, p. 15. 'When Voltaire went to Berlin, and Diderot to St. Petersburg, they did not have to learn a foreign language or adapt to a foreign culture. The language of both courts was French.' C.C. O'Brien, 'Nationalism and the French Revolution' in G. Best, *The Permanent Revolution*, p. 19.
49. G. Rudé, *Revolutionary Europe 1783–1815* (London: Collins, 1966), p. 185.
50. M. Wollstonecraft, *A Vindication of the Rights of Woman* [1792] (Harmondsworth: Penguin Books, 1975), p. 79.
51. Hobsbawm, *The Age of Revolution 1789–1848*, p. 17.
52. F. Oz-Salzberger's introduction to Adam Ferguson, *An Essay on the History of Civil Society* [1767] (Cambridge: Cambridge University Press, 1995), p. xxv.
53. R. Porter, *Enlightenment*, p. 517, fn. 60.
54. See N. Hampson, *The Enlightenment* (Harmondsworth: Penguin Books, 1968), pp. 140, 151, 152.
55. Strikes remained illegal in France until 1864 and trades unions until 1884.
56. See A. de Tocqueville, *Ancien Régime*, p. 226.
57. D. Lieven, *The Aristocracy in Europe*, p. 78.
58. 'The Prelude', Book XI, from H. Davies, ed., *A Wordsworth Anthology* (London: Collins, n.d.), p. 95. Also see S.T. Coleridge, 'Destruction of the Bastille', in Coleridge, *Poems* (London: Dent, 1966), pp. 4–5.
59. Quoted in E. Burke, *Reflections on the Revolution in France*, pp. 62–3.

Chapter 3: Edmund Burke

1. For an account of the significance of the Catholic element of Burke's background, see C.C. O'Brien, *Edmund Burke* (Dublin: New Island Books, 1997), ch. 1 and his introduction to E. Burke, *Reflections on the Revolution in France* (Harmondsworth: Penguin Books, 1968).
2. E. Burke, *Speeches and Letters on American Affairs* (London: Dent, 1961), p. 73.
3. Ibid., p. 279.
4. Ibid., p. 65.
5. Ibid., p. 278.
6. Ibid., pp. 277–8.
7. Ibid., p. 279.
8. Ibid., p. 106.
9. R.W. Harris, *England in the Eighteenth Century* (London: Blandford Press, 1966), p. 137.
10. Ibid., p. 141.
11. E. Burke, *American Affairs*, p. 184.
12. 'Appeal from the New to the Old Whigs', 1791, in *Works* in 12 volumes (London: John C. Nimmo, 1899), vol. 4, p. 101. This edition is the most recent *full* publication that I can trace!
13. James Wilson, 'On the Authority of Parliament' in B.E. Brown, ed., *Great American Political Thinkers* (New York: Avon Books, 1983), vol. 1, p. 90.
14. E. Burke, *American Affairs*, p. 180.
15. E. Burke, From 'Speech on Mr. Fox's East India Bill, Dec. 1783' in *Writings and Speeches*, vol. 5, p. 430.
16. E. Burke, *The Writings and Speeches of Edmund Burke*, 9 vols (Oxford: Clarendon Press, 1981–2000), vol. 9, p. 357.
17. Ibid., vol. 5, p. 389.
18. C.C. O'Brien, *Edmund Burke*, p. 176, and see p. 182.
19. U.S. Mehta, *Liberalism and Empire: A Study in Nineteenth-Century British Liberal Thought* (Chicago, IL: University of Chicago Press, 1999), p. 155.
20. Quoted in O'Brien, *Edmund Burke*, p. 196.
21. E. Burke, *Reflections on the Revolution in France* (London: Dent, 1964), p. 160.
22. See E. Burke, *The Correspondence of Edmund Burke*, 10 vols (Cambridge: Cambridge University Press, 1958–78), vol. vi, pp. 39–50.
23. E. Burke, *Reflections*, p. 2.
24. Ibid., p. 8.
25. G. Claeys, *Thomas Paine: Social and Political Thought* (Boston, MA: Unwin Hyman, 1989), p. 66.
26. See R.R. Fennessy, *Burke, Paine and the Rights of Man* (The Hague: Martinus Nijhoff, 1963); G. Claeys, ed., *Political Writings of the 1790s*, 8 vols (London: William Pickering, 1995). Volumes 1 and 2 contain responses to Burke; G. Claeys, *The French Revolution Debate in Britain*.

The Origin of Modern Politics (Harmondsworth: Palgrave Macmillan, 2007).

27. Philip Magnus, *Edmund Burke* (London: John Murray, 1939), p. 195.
28. E. Burke, *Correspondence*, vol. vi, p. 160, fn 1.
29. T. Paine, *The Rights of Man* (London: Dent, 1958), p. 4.
30. On Cobbett, see R. Williams, *Culture and Society 1780–1950* (Harmondsworth: Penguin Books, 1968), p. 38. Marx described Burke as 'this sycophant, who, in the pay of the English oligarchy, played the part of romantic opponent of the French Revolution, just as, in the pay of the North American colonies at the beginning of the troubles in America, he had played the liberal against the English oligarchy, was a vulgar bourgeois through and through'. *Capital* [1867] (Harmondsworth: Penguin Books, 1976), vol. 1, pp. 925–6.
31. E. Burke, *Reflections*, p. 8.
32. Quoted in ibid., pp. 62–3.
33. E. Burke, 'First Letter on a Regicide Peace', 1796, in *Writings and Speeches*, vol. ix, p. 199.
34. *Works*, vol. vi, p. 99. 'It is now obvious to the world, that a theory concerning government may become as much a cause of fanaticism as a dogma in religion', 'Appeal from the New to the Old Whigs' in I. Hampsher-Monk, ed., *The Political Philosophy of Edmund Burke* (London: Longman, 1987), p. 254.
35. E. Burke, *Reflections*, pp. 107–8.
36. 'A Letter from Mr. Burke to a Member of the National Assembly in Answer to some objections to his book on French Affairs', 1791, in same edition as *Reflections*, pp. 262, 65.
37. E. Burke, *Reflections*, pp. 52, 55, 103, 153.
38. E. Burke, 'Speech on Conciliation with America', 22 March 1775 in *American Affairs*, p. 121.
39. E. Burke, *Reflections*, p. 84.
40. Ibid., p. 83.
41. Ibid., p. 83. Also: 'It were better to forget once for all, the *Encyclopedie* and the whole body of Economists and to revert to those old rules and principles which have hitherto made princes great and nations happy.' Letter of 1 June 1791 to Claude-Francois de Rivarol. E. Burke, *Correspondence*, vol. vi, p. 267.
42. E. Burke, *Correspondence*, vol. vi, p. 42.
43. E. Burke, 'An Appeal from the New to the Old Whigs' in Hampsher-Monk, *The Political Philosophy of Edmund Burke*, p. 235.
44. E. Burke, *Reflections*, p. 46.
45. Ibid., pp. 40, 41, 43.
46. Burke did admit that most of them came from the legal profession, of which he clearly had a low opinion. See ibid., p. 40.
47. Ibid., p. 40.
48. Ibid., p. 73.
49. Ibid., p. 66.

50. Quoted in Hampsher-Monk, *The Political Philosophy of Edmund Burke*, p. 243. Note the consistent tendency of the key words: duties, subjection, obligation, binding.
51. E. Burke, *Reflections*, p. 93.
52. Ibid., p. 161.
53. 'Against Price, too, Burke thus contended that the king owed his crown to a fixed rule of succession, not the choice of his people.' G. Claeys, *The French Revolution Debate in Britain*, p. 15.
54. E. Burke, *Reflections*, p. 93.
55. C.B. Macpherson, *Burke* (Oxford: Oxford University Press, 1980), p. 45.
56. E. Burke, *Reflections*, p. 76.
57. Ibid., pp. 240–1.
58. Ibid., p. 157.
59. Quoted in Hampsher-Monk, *The Political Philosophy of Edmund Burke*, p. 237.
60. Ibid., p. 236.
61. Ibid., p. 237.
62. E. Burke, *American Affairs*, pp. 57–8.
63. E. Burke, *Works*, 1899, vol. 4, p. 137.
64. E. Burke, *Reflections*, p. 23.
65. Ibid., p. 29.
66. Ibid., pp. 73, 82.
67. E. Burke, *Correspondence*, vol. vi, p. 459.
68. See D. Herzog, *Poisoning the Minds of the Lower Orders* (Princeton, NJ: Princeton University Press, 1998), ch. 12 and E.P. Thompson, *The Making of the English Working Class* (Harmondsworth: Penguin, 1968), p. 98.
69. On the latter see 'Thoughts and Details on Scarcity', 1795, in E. Burke, *Writings and Speeches*, vol. 9, pp. 119–45. A selection is available in Hampsher-Monk, *The Political Philosophy of Edmund Burke*, pp. 269–80. Also see Macpherson, *Burke*, ch. 5 and pp. 3–4 on Burke as a liberal.
70. R. Kirk, *The Conservative Mind* (London: Faber, 1954), p. 79. Kirk is also the author of *Edmund Burke: A Genius Reconsidered* (Wilmington, DE: Intercollegiate Studies Institute, 1997).
71. S.P. Huntington (1957) 'Conservatism as an Ideology', *American Political Science Review*, LI, 463.

Chapter 4: Thomas Paine

1. N. Davies, *Europe: A History* (London: Pimlico, 1997), p. 679.
2. M. Foot and I. Kramnick, eds, *Thomas Paine Reader* (Harmondsworth: Penguin Books, 1987), p. 323. Where possible reference will be given to this easily available edition.
3. Anyone leaving school at that age now, which would be illegal, might hardly have basic literacy. Paine, and Engels, are the only ones of our thinkers not to have attended a university. Burke-Trinity College,

Dublin; Bentham – Oxford University; Hegel – Tübingen University; Tocqueville – University of Paris; Marx-Bonn and Berlin Universities. Engels, though not an official student, seems to have attended lectures at the University of Berlin

4. See M. Foot and I. Kramnick, *Thomas Paine Reader*, pp. 39–51.
5. As it happens it was precisely 37, according to John Keane, *Tom Paine: A Political Life* (London: Bloomsbury, 1995), p. 32.
6. G. Claeys, *Thomas Paine: Social and Political Thought* (Boston: Unwin Hyman, 1989), p. 51.
7. Quoted in A.O. Aldridge, *Man of Reason: The Life of Thomas Paine* (London: The Cresset Press, 1960), pp. 42–3.
8. See E. Burke, *Correspondence*, vol. v, p. 412.
9. M. Foot and I. Kramnick, *Thomas Paine Reader*, pp. 66–7.
10. Ibid., p. 67.
11. Ibid., p. 72.
12. Ibid., p. 79.
13. Ibid., pp. 92 and 104, which omit the bracketed words which other editions contain.
14. Gregory. Claeys notes that 'about a quarter of the poor's wages disappeared through taxes upon consumption'. *Thomas Paine: Social and Political Thought*, p. 80.
15. See M. Levin, *The Spectre of Democracy, the Rise of Modern Democracy as seen by its Critics* (Basingstoke: Palgrave Macmillan, 1992), ch. 3.
16. 'The Crisis' from T. Paine, *Common Sense and the Crisis* (Garden City, New York: Dolphin Books, 1960), pp. 93, 224.
17. T. Paine, 'Dissertations on Government' etc., 1786. *The Writings of Thomas Paine*, 4. vols, M.D. Conway, ed. [1894–6] (London: Routledge, Thoemmes, 1996), vol. 2, p. 134.
18. M. Foot and I. Kramnick, 'Common Sense' in *Thomas Paine Reader*, pp. 80, 65.
19. T. Paine, 'The Crisis' in *Common Sense and the Crisis*, p. 225.
20. T. Paine, *The Writings of Thomas Paine*, vol. 2, pp. 193, 206.
21. M. Foot and I. Kramnick, *Thomas Paine Reader*, pp. 360, 265.
22. Ibid., p. 259.
23. John Keane notes that 'At the time, there were around ten million people living on mainland Britain, of whom perhaps a maximum of four million were able to read.' *Tom Paine*, p. 307. The *Rights of Man* has been described as 'the single most influential and widely read political text of the 18th century'. Christopher Hobson (2008) 'Revolution, Representation and the Foundations of Modern Democracy', *European Journal of Political Theory*, 7.4, p. 455.
24. M. Foot and I. Kramnick, *Thomas Paine Reader*, p. 220.
25. Ibid., p. 219.
26. Ibid., p. 220.
27. Ibid., p. 267.
28. Ibid., p. 285.
29. Ibid., p. 271.
30. Ibid., p. 314.

31. T. Paine, *Rights of Man* (London: Dent, 1958), p. 104. Note that Paine always referred to 'English' rather than 'British' government.
32. Ibid., p. 57.
33. M. Foot and I. Kramnick, *Thomas Paine Reader*, pp. 302, 285.
34. Ibid., p. 250.
35. Ibid., p. 228.
36. Ibid., p. 230.
37. Ibid., p. 226.
38. Ibid., p. 242.
39. Ibid., pp. 278, 281.
40. Ibid., p. 255.
41. Ibid., p. 333.
42. Quoted in E.P. Thompson, *The Making of the English Working Class* (Harmondsworth: Penguin Books, 1968), p. 19.
43. Ibid., pp. 460, 472.
44. Ibid., p. 357. 'Paine never went so far as to advocate votes for women', A.J. Ayer, *Thomas Paine* (London: Secker and Warburg, 1988), p. 81 and see Keane, *Tom Paine*, p. 127.
45. M. Foot and I. Kramnick, *Thomas Paine Reader*, p. 350.
46. Ibid., p. 347.
47. Ibid., p. 341.
48. Ibid., p. 306.
49. Ibid., p. 273.
50. Ibid., p. 267.
51. Ibid., p. 240.
52. Ibid., pp. 260, 265.
53. T. Paine, *Rights of Man*, p. 147.
54. M. Foot and I. Kramnick, *Thomas Paine Reader*, pp. 313, 359.
55. Ibid., p. 359.
56. Ibid., p. 229.
57. Ibid., pp. 228–9.
58. Paine was wrong to assume that Burke regarded the 1688 revolution as one of constitutional innovation. On the contrary Burke regarded that event as actually a revolution *prevented*. 'The Revolution was made to preserve our *ancient* indisputable laws and liberties, and that *ancient* constitution of government which is our only security for law and liberty.' Burke, *Reflections on the Revolution in France* (London: Dent, 1964), p. 29.
59. M. Foot and I. Kramnick, *Thomas Paine Reader*, p. 204.
60. See G. Claeys, ed., *Political Writings of the 1790s*, 8 volumes (London: William Pickering, 1995). Volumes 5 and 6, totalling over 800 pages, consist of responses to Paine written between 1790 and 1792. These include what purports to be 'Intercepted Correspondence from Satan to Citizen Paine'.
61. E. Burke, *The Correspondence of Edmund Burke*, 10 vols. (Cambridge: Cambridge University Press, 1958–78), vol. vi, p. 303.
62. Ibid., vol. v, p. 412.

63. T. Paine, *Rights of Man*, p. 148.
64. T. Paine, *The Writings of Thomas Paine*, vol. 4, p. 451.
65. M. Foot and I. Kramnick, *Thomas Paine Reader*, p. 213.
66. T. Paine, *The Writings of Thomas Paine*, vol. 3, p. 133.
67. Ibid., vol. 4, p. 85.
68. Quoted in J.T. Boulton, *The Language of Politics in the Age of Wilkes and Burke* (London: Routledge and Kegan Paul, 1963), p. 138.
69. E.P. Thompson, *The Making of the English Working Class* (Harmondsworth: Penguin Books, 1968), p. 99.
70. Ibid., p. 125.
71. F. O'Gorman (2006) 'The Paine Burnings of 1792–1793', *Past and Present*, no. 193, 111–155, 121.
72. M. Foot and I. Kramnick, *Thomas Paine Reader*, p. 117.
73. 'Answer to Four Questions on the Legislative and Executive Powers', 1791, T. Paine, *The Writings of Thomas Paine*, vol. 2, p. 248.
74. M. Foot and I. Kramnick, *Thomas Paine Reader*, p. 400.
75. T. Paine, *The Writings of Thomas Paine*, vol. 4, p. 151.
76. M. Foot and I. Kramnick, *Thomas Paine Reader*, p. 403.
77. T. Paine, *The Writings of Thomas Paine*, vol. 4, p. 157.
78. Ibid., vol. 4, p. 169.
79. M. Foot and I. Kramnick, *Thomas Paine Reader*, p. 411.
80. T. Paine, *The Writings of Thomas Paine*, vol. 4, p. 88.
81. M. Foot and I. Kramnick, *Thomas Paine Reader*, p. 430.
82. Ibid., pp. 431, 432.
83. Letter to Camille Jourdan, 1797, T. Paine, *The Writings of Thomas Paine*, vol. 4, pp. 249, 252.
84. M. Foot and I. Kramnick, *Thomas Paine Reader*, p. 400.
85. T. Paine, *The Writings of Thomas Paine*, vol. 4, pp. 188–9.
86. M. Foot and I. Kramnick, *Thomas Paine Reader*, p. 451.
87. Ibid., p. 400.
88. Bishop Beilby Porteous, 'A Charge Delivered to the Clergy of the Diocese of London in 1798 and 1799', 1799, in M. Williams, ed., *Revolutions 1775–1830* (Harmondsworth: Penguin Books, 1971), pp. 524–5.
89. R.R. Fennessy, *Burke, Paine and The Rights of Man* (The Hague: Martinus Nijhoff, 1963), p. 41.

Chapter 5: Jeremy Bentham

1. Quoted in E. Halévy, *The Growth of Philosophic Radicalism* (London: Faber and Faber, 1952), p. 298.
2. J. Bentham, *The Correspondence of Jeremy Bentham* (London: Athlone Press and Clarendon Press), 12 vols, 1968–2005, vol. viii, p. 400.
3. J. Bentham, *A Fragment on Government* [1776] (Cambridge: Cambridge University Press, 1988), p. 8.

4. J. Bentham, *Correspondence*, vol. v, p. 306 and W. Twining, ed., *Bentham: Selected Writings of John Dinwiddy* (Stanford, CA: Stanford University Press, 2004), p. 97.

5. C. Blamires, *The French Revolution and the Creation of Benthamism* (Basingstoke: Palgrave Macmillan, 2008), pp. 13, 295. This book provides the best and fullest account in English of Dumont's life and his association with Bentham.

6. John Stuart Mill once referred to Bentham's 'interminable classifications'. J.S. Mill, 'Bentham' in A. Ryan ed., *Utilitarianism and Other Essays: J.S. Mill and Jeremy Bentham* (London: Penguin Books, 1987), p. 13.

7. R. Layard, *Happiness: Lessons from a New Science* (London: Penguin Books, 2006), p. 5.

8. 'The day *may* come, when the rest of the animal creation may acquire those rights which never could have been withholden from them but by the hand of tyranny.' J. Bentham, *Introduction to the Principles of Morals and Legislation* [1789], (New York: Hafner, 1965), p. 311, fn.

9. J. Bentham, *Correspondence*, vol. vii, p. 542; vol. viii, p. 401; vol. viii, 216 fn.

10. Quoted in J. Rawls, *A Theory of Justice* (Oxford: Oxford University Press, 1978), p. 22n.

11. J. Bentham, 'Essay on the Influence of Time and Place in Matters of Legislation' (1782) in *The Works of Jeremy Bentham*, vol. 1, J. Bowring, ed. (Edinburgh: Tait, 1838), p. 185.

12. J. Bentham, *Morals and Legislation*, p. 335.

13. J. Bentham, *Fragment on Government*, p. 4.

14. Ibid., p. 10.

15. Ibid., p. 56. There is another formulation of this on p. 96.

16. Ibid., p. 98.

17. Ibid., p. 105.

18. J. Bentham, *Morals and Legislation*, p. 1.

19. Ibid., p. 31.

20. Ibid., pp. 9, 10, 11.

21. 'Though the number of *inhabitants* be 2000, the *House* is but *one*; and that one House is capable of being pervaded in all directions, – pervaded by a single glance, and without so much as a change of posture.' J. Bentham, *Correspondence*, vol. viii, p. 146.

22. See M. Foucault, *Discipline and Punish: The Birth of the Prison* (London: Allen Lane, 1977), Part III, ch. 3, 'Panopticism'.

23. M. Horkheimer and T. Adorno, *Dialectic of Enlightenment* [1944] (London: Verso, 1992).

24. See C. Blamires, *The French Revolution and the Creation of Benthamism*, p. 32, where we are reminded that Bentham regarded the panopticon as 'an architectural technique applicable to any establishment which involved the supervision of numbers of persons – hospital, school, poorhouse, asylum, factory'. Also see ch. 2. 'Panopticon Dominates Bentham's Existence'.

25. J. Bentham, *The Theory of Legislation*, ed., and intro. by C.K. Ogden (London: Kegan Paul, Trench, Trubner & Co., 1931), p. 109.
26. Ibid., p. 84.
27. J. Bentham, *Morals and Legislation*, pp. 335, 336.
28. J. Bentham, *Correspondence*, vol. xii, p. 308.
29. Ibid., vol. iv, p. 84.
30. J. Bentham, *Correspondence*, vol. iv, p. 484.
31. 'Anarchical Fallacies; being an examination of the Declaration of Rights issued during the French Revolution' in J. Waldron, *'Nonsense upon Stilts': Bentham, Burke and Marx on the Rights of Man* (London: Methuen, 1987), p. 74.
32. Quoted in J. Waldron, *'Nonsense upon Stilts'*, p. 66.
33. The origin of this famous phrase is obscure. It became known through J.S. Mill, who quoted it in his 1838 'Bentham' essay. See A. Ryan ed., *Utilitarianism and Other Essays*, pp. 173–4. Also see R. Harrison introduction to Bentham, *Fragment*, p. xvii.
34. J. Bentham, *Morals and Legislation*, p. 5.
35. J. Bentham, *Theory of Legislation*, p. 81. Also see p. 39.
36. B. Parekh ed., *Bentham's Political Thought* (London: Croom Helm, 1973), p. 208.
37. J. Bentham, *Works*, ed., Bowring, vol. 1, pp. 178–9, 187.
38. J. Bentham, 'Emancipate Your Colonies! Address to the National Convention of France, 1793, Shewing the Uselessness and Mischievousness of Distant Dependencies to an European State', in *The Collected Works of Jeremy Bentham: Rights, Representation, and Reform. Nonsense Upon Stilts and Other Writings on the French Revolution*, P. Schofield, C. Pease Watkin and C. Blamires, eds (Oxford: Clarendon Press, 2002).
39. E. Halévy, *Growth of Philosophic Radicalism*, p. 510.
40. J. Bentham, *Works*, Bowring ed., vol. 1, p. 188.
41. E. Halévy, *Growth of Philosophic Radicalism*, p. 511.
42. Ibid., p. 510.
43. J. Bentham, *Works*, Bowring, ed., vol. 1, p. 180.
44. Quoted in E. Halévy, *Growth of Philosophic Radicalism*, p. 510.
45. J. Bentham, *'Legislator of the World': Writings on Codification, Law and Education*, P. Schofield and J. Harris, eds (Oxford: Clarendon Press, 1998), p. 5.
46. Ibid., p. 36.
47. Ibid., p. 48.
48. Venezuelan revolutionary, 1750–1816.
49. President of Argentina 1826–7.
50. President of Colombia 1821–30.
51. Vice-President of Colombia from 1821–8 and President from 1832–7.
52. C.K. Ogden, ed., Bentham, *Theory of Legislation*, intro. p. xx.
53. J. Bentham, *Morals and Legislation*, p. 267.
54. J. Bentham, *Theory of Legislation*, p. 18.
55. John Stuart Mill acknowledged this point in *Principles of Political Economy* [1848] *Mill Collected Works*, vol. III (Toronto: University of Toronto

Press, 1965), pp. 959–60. Also see E. Halévy, *Growth of Philosophic Radicalism*, p. 506.

56. J. Bentham, *Theory of Legislation*, p. 74. Also see p. 109.
57. J. Bentham, *Morals and Legislation*, pp. 58–9, but see p. 268, fn., which takes a quite different approach. Also see *The Theory of Legislation*, pp. 39, 81.
58. J. Bentham, *Theory of Legislation*, p. 64. Emphasis added.
59. Ibid., pp. 368–9.
60. I take this term from B. Parekh. See his 'Superior People: the narrowness of liberalism from Mill to Rawls', *Times Literary Supplement*, 25 February 1994.
61. J. Bentham, *Theory of Legislation*, p. 53.
62. E. Halévy, *Growth of Philosophic Radicalism*, p. 489.
63. 'It was undoubtedly the principle of the natural identity of interests which was the basis of the optimism of the classical economists, and these have been recognised to be the masters of the Utilitarian Radicals.' E. Halévy, *Growth of Philosophic Radicalism*, p. 489.
64. Quoted in Waldron, *'Nonsense Upon Stilts'*, p. 44. Also see Parekh ed., *Bentham's Political Thought*, p. 251.
65. J. Bentham, *Theory of Legislation*, p. 64.
66. Ibid., p. 86.
67. Ibid., p. 64.
68. J. Riley, *Mill on Liberty* (London: Routledge, 1998), p. 189.
69. Richard Layard, *Happiness: Lessons from a New Science*, p. 12 and see p. 20. Emphasis added.
70. Quoted in J.S. Mill, *Collected Works*, vol. x (Toronto, ON: University of Toronto Press, 1969), p. 67.
71. J. Bentham, *Fragment on Government*, p. 104.
72. Henry Sidgwick, *The Method of Ethics* quoted in J.R. Mozley, 'Utilitarianism and Morality', *The Quarterly Review*, vol. 141, April 1876, reprinted in A. Pyle, ed., *Utilitarianism*, vol. 4, *1876–1900* (London: Routledge/Thoemmes Press, 1998), p. 13.
73. Jonathan Wolff, *An Introduction to Political Philosophy* (Oxford: Oxford University Press, 2006), p. 53.
74. This is the main factor in John Rawls' rejection of Utilitarianism in his celebrated *A Theory of Justice*. See pp. 26–31, 156.
75. J. Bentham, *Theory of Legislation*, p. 203.
76. See J. Rawls, *A Theory of Justice*, pp. 136–42.
77. J. Bentham, *Deontology Together with a Table of the Springs of Action and the Article on Utilitarianism*, ed., A. Goldworth (Oxford: Clarendon Press, 1983), p. 309.
78. Bentham's secretary in 1831 and, later, author of the famous *Report on the Sanitary Condition of the Labouring Population of Great Britain*, 1842.
79. See E. Stokes, *The English Utilitarians and India* (Delhi: Oxford University Press, 1992).
80. Quoted in C. Blamires, *The French Revolution and the Creation of Benthamism*, p. 285.

81. A.V. Dicey, *Law and Public Opinion in England during the Nineteenth Century* [1905] (London: Macmillan, 1963), pp. 187, 310.
82. G.D.H. Cole and R. Postgate quoted in B. Pimlott ed., *Fabian Essays in Socialist Thought* (London: Heinemann, 1984), p. 23.

Chapter 6: Georg Hegel

1. J. Toews, *Hegelianism: The Path Towards Dialectical Humanism, 1805–1841* (Cambridge: Cambridge University Press, 1980), p. 19.
2. G.W.F. Hegel, *Introduction to the Lectures on the History of Philosophy* (Oxford: Clarendon Press, 1988), pp. 62, 142.
3. Letter of 4 November 1867, *Mill Collected Works*, vol. 16 (Toronto, ON: University of Toronto Press, 1972), p. 1324.
4. W. Kaufmann, *Hegel: A Reinterpretation* (New York: Anchor Books, 1966), p. 228.
5. S. Avineri, *Hegel's Theory of the Modern State* (Cambridge: Cambridge University Press, 1974), p. 64.
6. G.W.F. Hegel, *Philosophy of History*, intro. C.J. Friedrich (New York: Dover Publications, 1956), p. 86.
7. G.W.F. Hegel, *Hegel's Political Writings*, intro. Z.A. Pelczynski (Oxford: Clarendon Press, 1969), p. 143.
8. Ibid., p. 190.
9. T.M. Knox, 'Hegel and Prussianism' in W. Kaufmann, ed., *Hegel's Political Philosophy* (New York: Atherton Press, 1970), p. 16.
10. F.C. Beiser ed., *The Early Political Writings of the German Romantics* (Cambridge: Cambridge University Press, 2005), p. xxix.
11. T.M. Knox notes to *Hegel's Philosophy of Right* (London: Oxford University Press, 1971), p. 307.
12. Ibid., §274a. I have followed the convention of referencing quotations by their paragraph number.
13. Quoted in S. Avineri, *Hegel's Theory of the Modern State*, p. 71.
14. G.W.F. Hegel's Preface to *Philosophy of Right*, p. 15.
15. R. Plant, *Hegel* (London: Allen and Unwin, 1973), p. 186.
16. G.W.F. Hegel, *Philosophy of Right*, §209.
17. R. Plant, *Hegel*, p. 72.
18. *Philosophy of History* in G.W.F. Hegel, *Political Writings*, L. Dickey and H.B. Nisbet, eds (Cambridge: Cambridge University Press, 2007), pp. 214–5.
19. Ibid., p. 212.
20. *Philosophy of History* (New York: Dover Publications, 1956), p. 255. I use this edition for quotations not included in the selections of Dickey and Nisbet, see fn 18.
21. Ibid., pp. 252, 253, 255.
22. Ibid., p. 256.
23. G.W.F. Hegel, *Philosophy of Right*, §308.
24. Ibid., §317.

25. G.W.F. Hegel, *The Phenomenology of Mind*, quoted in C. Heiman, 'The Sources and Significance of Hegel's Corporate Doctrine' in Z.A. Pelczynski, ed., *Hegel's Political Philosophy. Problems and Perspectives* (Cambridge: Cambridge University Press, 1971), p. 117.

26. G.W.F. Hegel, *Hegel's Political Writings*, intro. Pelczynski, pp. 262–3.

27. G.W.F. Hegel, *Philosophy of Right*, §308.

28. G.W.F.Hegel, *Philosophy of History*, Friedrich ed., pp. 18, 19, 103.

29. G.W.F. Hegel, *Introduction to the Lectures on the History of Philosophy*, p. 169.

30. G.W.F. Hegel, *Philosophy of History*, Friedrich ed., p. 18.

31. Given his notion of German relative backwardness, it seems distinctly partisan of Hegel to adopt the term 'Germanic' for the highest development of the world spirit within European Christendom. Avineri regards it as a 'gross mistranslation' to render *die germanische Welt* as 'The German World', *Hegel's Theory of the Modern State*, p. 222, fn. 4. He implies that there is a difference between '*Germanisch*' and '*deutsch*', with only the latter indicating 'German'. See ibid., p. 228. In an earlier work, Avineri argued that 'the only meaning behind the term "Germanic World" in Hegel implies that Hegel saw in Western Civilization the highlight of mankind's spiritual development. The values of this Germanic world are Christian values.' 'Hegel and Nationalism', *Review of Politics*, xxiv, 1962, pp. 461–484, 481. Also see Allen Wood's editorial notes in *Elements of the Philosophy of Right* (Cambridge: Cambridge University Press, 1991), pp. 479–80.

32. G.W.F. Hegel, *Philosophy of Right*, addition to §339.

33. Quoted in S. Avineri, *Hegel's Theory of the Modern State*, p. 68.

34. Ibid., p. x.

35. A succinct presentation and refutation of this claim is made in D. Leopold, *The Young Marx: German Philosophy, Modern Politics, and Human Flourishing* (Cambridge: Cambridge University Press, 2007), pp. 57–9.

36. G.W.F. Hegel, *Philosophy of Right*, §258.

37. Ibid., addition to §258.

38. Ibid., §272a.

39. Ibid., §255.

40. Ibid., §267.

41. Ibid., §280.

42. Ibid., §306.

43. G.W.F. Hegel, *Hegel's Political Writings*, intro. Pelczynski, p. 93.

44. G.W.F. Hegel, *Philosophy of Right*, §309.

45. G.W.F. Hegel, *Hegel's Political Writings*, intro. Pelczynski, pp. 73, 257.

46. Ibid., p. 95, fn. 1.

47. Ibid., p. 262.

48. Ibid., p. 264.

49. G.W.F. Hegel, *Philosophy of Right*, §241.

50. Ibid., §317.

51. Ibid., §301.

52. G.W.F. Hegel, *Hegel's Political Writings*, intro. Pelczynski, p. 78.

53. K.-H. Ilting, 'The Structure of Hegel's *Philosophy of Right*' in Z.A. Pelczynski, ed., *Hegel's Political Philosophy: Problems and Perspectives* (Cambridge: Cambridge University Press, 1976), p. 108.
54. G.W.F. Hegel, *Philosophy of Right*, §166. Also see §145.
55. Ibid., addition §329.
56. G.W.F. Hegel, *Philosophy of History*, intro. Friedrich, pp. 46–7.
57. G.W.F. Hegel, *Hegel's Political Writings*, intro. Pelczynski, p. 234.
58. G.W.F. Hegel, *Philosophy of Right*, §313.
59. G.W.F. Hegel, *Philosophy of History*, intro. Friedrich, p. 45.
60. K. Marx and F. Engels, *Marx Engels Collected Works*, vol. 26 (London: Lawrence and Wishart, 1990), p. 363.
61. G.W.F. Hegel, *Philosophy of Right*, §57.
62. G.W.F. Hegel, Introduction to the Lectures on the History of Philosophy, pp. 43, 183.
63. K. Löwith, *From Hegel to Nietzsche, The Revolution in Nineteenth-Century Thought* (New York: Anchor Books, 1967), p. 59.

Chapter 7: Alexis de Tocqueville

1. H. Brogan, *Tocqueville* (Bungay, Suffolk: Collinns/Fontana, 1973), p. 14.
2. A. de Tocqueville, *Journeys to England and Ireland*, J.P. Mayer, ed. (New Brunswick: Transaction Books, 1988), pp. 107–8.
3. A. de Tocqueville, *Democracy in America*, 2 vols (New York: Vintage Books, n.d.), vol. 1, p. 4.
4. Ibid., vol. 1, pp. 15, 14.
5. Ibid., vol. 1, pp. 235–6.
6. Ibid., vol. 1, p. 338.
7. Ibid., vol. 1, p. 14.
8. Ibid., vol. 1, p. 21.
9. Ibid., vol. 2, p. 4.
10. Tocqueville's Ideal Types in A.S. Eisenstadt ed., *Reconsidering Tocqueville's Democracy in America* (London: Rutgers University Press, 1988), p. 188.
11. A. de Tocqueville, *Democracy in America*, vol. 1, p. 9.
12. Ibid., vol. 2, p. 223.
13. Ibid., vol. 1, p. 8.
14. Ibid., vol. 1, p. 4.
15. Ibid., vol. 1, p. 5.
16. Ibid., vol. 1, p. 6.
17. Ibid., vol. 1, p. 6, and see vol. 2, p. 340.
18. Ibid., vol. 1, pp. 7, 6.
19. Ibid., vol. 2, p. vi.
20. Ibid., vol. 1, p. 7.
21. Ibid., vol. 1, p. 435.
22. Ibid., vol. 2, p. 6.
23. Ibid., vol. 2, p. 342.

24. Ibid., vol. 1, pp. 223–4.
25. Ibid., vol. 1, pp. 258, 259.
26. Ibid., vol. 1, p. 323.
27. Ibid., vol. 1, p. 307.
28. Ibid., vol. 2, p. 198.
29. Ibid., vol. 2, p. 341.
30. Ibid., vol. 2, p. 342.
31. Ibid., vol. 1, p. 95.
32. Ibid., vol. 2, pp. 318, 336.
33. Ibid., vol. 2, p. 337.
34. Ibid., vol. 2, pp. 3, 36, 59, 78.
35. Ibid., vol. 2, pp. 11, 12, 13.
36. Ibid., vol. 2, p. 240.
37. Ibid., vol. 1, p. 256.
38. Ibid., vol. 1, p. 266.
39. Ibid., vol. 1, p. 7.
40. Ibid., vol. 2, p. 114.
41. Ibid., vol. 1, p. 316.
42. Ibid., vol. 2, p. 316.
43. *The Old Régime and the French Revolution* (Garden City, NY: Doubleday, 1955), pp. 143, 294–5. For contemporary responses to this book and discussion of its accuracy, see Richard Herr, *Tocqueville and the Old Regime* (Princeton, NJ: Princeton University Press, 1962), especially chs. 9 and 10. Jon Elster has recently stated that 'Tocqueville's writings on the *ancien régime* and the revolution may constitute the most theoretically informed historical analyses ever written.' J. Elster, *Alexis de Tocqueville. The First Social Scientist* (Cambridge: Cambridge University Press, 2009), p. 191.
44. Tocqueville, *The Old Régime*, p. 93.
45. Ibid., pp. 120, 123.
46. Ibid., p. 130.
47. Ibid., p. 117.
48. Ibid., p. 187.
49. Ibid., p. 135.
50. Ibid., p. 179.
51. Ibid., p. 274.
52. T. Carlyle, *The French Revolution: A History* [1837] (London: Chapman and Hall, 1891).
53. A. de Tocqueville, *Old Régime*, p. 177.
54. Ibid., p. 25.
55. Ibid., p. 169.
56. 'During the spring or early summer of 1853, Tocqueville read in their original English the complete corpus of Burke's speeches, public letters, and private correspondence on the French Revolution.' R.T. Gannett, Jr., *Tocqueville Unveiled: The Historian and His Sources for 'The Old Regime and the Revolution'* (Chicago, IL: University of Chicago Press, 2003), p. 61.

57. A. de Tocqueville, '*The European Revolution*' *and Correspondence with Gobineau* (Westport, CT: Greenwood Press, 1974), p. 164.
58. A. de Tocqueville, *Old Régime*, p. 147.
59. Ibid., p. 20.
60. A. de Tocqueville, *European Revolution*, pp. 159, 161.
61. Ibid., p. 162.
62. Ibid., p. 144.
63. A. de Tocqueville, *Recollections* (Garden City, NY: Anchor Books, 1975), p. 15.
64. Ibid., pp. 17, 20.
65. Ibid., p. 5.
66. Ibid., p. 180.
67. Ibid., p. 348.
68. Ibid., pp. 147–8.
69. Ibid., p. 83.
70. Ibid., p. 103.
71. Ibid., p. 349.
72. Ibid., p. 211.
73. A. Craiutu and J. Jennings, eds., *Tocqueville on America after 1840. Letters and Other Writings* (Cambridge: Cambridge University Press, 2009), pp. 184, 188–9. see also pp. 21–33.

Chapter 8: Karl Marx and Friedrich Engels

1. Quoted in D. McLellan, *Karl Marx. His Life and Thought* (London: Palgrave Macmillan, 2008), p. 17.
2. Ibid., p. 190.
3. Quoted in M. Nicolaus foreword to K. Marx, *Grundrisse: Foundations of the Critique of Political Economy* (Harmondsworth: Penguin Books, 1973), p. 11.
4. Quoted in D. McLellan, *Karl Marx: His Life and Thought*, p. 402.
5. *Karl Marx. Friedrich Engels. Collected Works*, 50 vols (London: Lawrence and Wishart, 1975–2005), hereafter abbreviated to MECW, vol. 4, p. 159.
6. MECW, vol. 6, p. 488.
7. MECW, vol. 4, p. 419.
8. MECW, vol. 6, p. 497.
9. Ibid., pp. 493, 496.
10. Ibid., p. 489.
11. Ibid., p. 492.
12. MECW, vol. 4, p. 581.
13. MECW 6,545. Also see D. McLellan, ed., *Karl Marx Interviews and Recollections* (London: Palgrave Macmillan, 1981), p. 138.
14. MECW, vol. 4, p. 666.
15. MECW, vol. 3, p. 162.

16. MECW, vol. 10, p. 68.
17. See MECW, vol. 3, pp. 418–43.
18. MECW, vol. 6, p. 515.
19. Ibid., pp. 504–5.
20. MECW, vol. 5, p. 47. Nothing like this resurfaces in the later writings.
21. MECW, vol. 3, pp. 180, 202.
22. Ibid., p. 142.
23. Ibid., p. 469.
24. MECW, vol. 6, p. 519.
25. MECW, vol. 7, p. 295. Marx's presentation of the 1789 French Revolution is analysed in F. Furet, *Marx and the French Revolution* (Chicago, IL: University of Chicago Press, 1988).
26. W. O. Henderson, *The Life of Friedrich Engels* (London: Cass, 1976), vol. 1, pp. 162–3.
27. MECW, vol. 7, pp. 339, 504.
28. MECW, vol. 10, p. 285.
29. MECW, vol. 11, p. 10.
30. A group of the poor who have become separated from their class, described in the *Communist Manifesto* as liable to become 'a bribed tool of reactionary intrigue'. MECW, vol. 6, p. 494.
31. Ibid., p. 134. In the *Communist Manifesto*, Marx had also referred to 'the idiocy of rural life'. Ibid., p. 488.
32. Marx seems not to have known of the level of working class support for Louis Bonaparte. See M. Rapport, *1848. Year of Revolution* (London: Abacus, 2009), pp. 328–9, 333.
33. MECW, vol. 11, pp. 190–1.
34. MECW, vol. 10, p. 264.
35. Ibid., p. 626.
36. MECW, vol. 45, p. 278.
37. Quoted in T. Shanin, *Late Marx and the Russian Road. Marx and 'the peripheries of capitalism'* (London: Routledge and Kegan Paul, 1984), p. 98.
38. Ibid., p. 124.
39. MECW, vol. 24, p. 426.
40. See D. McLellan, ed., *Marx: The First 100 Years* (Oxford: Fontana, 1983).
41. MECW, vol. 11, p. 128.
42. Robert Skidelsky, 'What's Left of Marx?' *New York Review of Books*, 16 November 2000, p. 24.

Chapter 9: Epilogue

1. D. Lieven, *The Aristocracy in Europe 1815–1914* (Basingstoke: Palgrave Macmillan, 1992), pp. 2–3.
2. 'Authorized' by whom? *Cahiers du Communisme*, 1939, appeared in English translation as T.A. Jackson ed., *Essays on the French Revolution* (London: Lawrence and Wishart, 1945), p. 208. The communists of

1939 would have assumed that the future was on their side. They could hardly have imagined what was happening politically around the time of the 200th anniversary of the French Revolution.

3. N'O Sullivan, *European Political Thought since 1945* (Basingstoke: Palgrave Macmillan, 2004), pp. 70, 65.

4. K. Obermann, *Joseph Weydemeyer: Pioneer of American Socialism* (New York: International Publishers, 1947), p. 141.

5. A. de Tocqueville, *"The European Revolution" and Correspondence with Gobineau* (Westport, CN: Greenwood Press, 1974), pp. 144, 172.

6. E. Weber, 'The Nineteenth-century Fallout' in G. Best, ed., *The Permanent Revolution: The French Revolution and its Legacy* (London: Fontana Press, 1988), p. 164. This is reminiscent of Werner Sombart's famous declaration that in the United States 'on the reefs of roast beef and apple pie socialistic Utopias ... are sent to their doom.' Quoted in I. Howe, *Socialism and America* (San Diego, CA: Harcourt Brace Jovanovich, 1985), p. 117.

7. *Marx Engels Collected Works*, vol. 27 (London: Lawrence and Wishart, 1990), p. 510.

8. Ibid., p. 517.

9. Ibid., pp. 521–2.

10. Ibid., p. 517.

11. M. Malia, *History's Locomotives: Revolutions and the Making of the Modern World* (New Haven: Yale University Press, 2006).

12. See F. Fukuyama, *The End of History and the Last Man* (Harmondsworth: Penguin Books, 1992).

Select Bibliography

Arendt, H., *On Revolution* [1963] (London: Penguin Books, 2006).

Avineri, S., *The Social and Political Thought of Karl Marx* (Cambridge: Cambridge University Press, 1971).

—— *Hegel's Theory of the Modern State* (Cambridge: Cambridge University Press, 1974).

Beiser, F.C., ed., *The Cambridge Companion to Hegel* (Cambridge: Cambridge University Press, 1993).

Bentham, J., *The Theory of Legislation* [1802], ed. C.K. Ogden (London: Kegan Paul, Trench, Trubner & Co., 1931).

—— *An Introduction to the Principles of Morals and Legislation* [1789] (New York: Hafner, 1965).

—— *The Correspondence of Jeremy Bentham*, 12 vols (London: Athlone Press and Clarendon Press, 1968–2005).

—— *The Collected Works of Jeremy Bentham*, 9 vols (Oxford: Athlone Press, Clarendon Press, Oxford University Press, 1970–2008).

—— *A Fragment on Government* [1776], intro. R. Harrison (Cambridge: Cambridge University Press, 1988).

Best, G., ed., *The Permanent Revolution: The French Revolution and its Legacy 1789–1989* (London: Fontana, 1988).

Boesche, R., ed., *Alexis de Tocqueville. Selected Letters on Politics and Society* (Berkeley, CA: University of California Press, 1985).

Brogan, H., *Alexis de Tocqueville, a Biography* (London: Profile Books, 2006).

Burke, E., *The Correspondence of Edmund Burke*, 10 vols (Cambridge: Cambridge University Press, 1958–78).

—— *Speeches and Letters on American Affairs* (London: Dent, 1961).

—— *The Writings and Speeches of Edmund Burke*, 9 vols (Oxford: Clarendon Press, 1981–2000).

—— *Reflections on the Revolution in France* (London: Dent, 1967. Also Harmondsworth: Penguin Books, 1986 and Stanford, CA: Stanford University Press, 2001).

Carver, T., *Friedrich Engels: His Life and Thought* (Basingstoke: Palgrave Macmillan, 1991).

Claeys, G., *Thomas Paine: Social and Political Thought* (Boston, MA: Unwin Hyman, 1989).

—— *The French Revolution Debate in Britain: The Origin of Modern Politics* (Harmondsworth: Palgrave Macmillan, 2007).

Cobb, R. and C. Jones, eds, *The French Revolution, Voices from a Momentous Epoch 1789–1795* (London: Simon and Schuster, 1988).

Furet, F., *Marx and the French Revolution* (Chicago, IL: University of Chicago Press, 1988).

Halévy, E., *The Growth of Philosophic Radicalism* (London: Faber & Faber, 1952).

Hampsher-Monk, I., *The Political Philosophy of Edmund Burke* (London: Longman, 1987).

—— *The Impact of the French Revolution: Texts from Britain in the 1790s* (Cambridge: Cambridge University Press, 2005).

Harrison, R., *Bentham* (London: Routledge and Kegan Paul, 1983).

Hegel, G.W.F., *The Philosophy of History*, intro. C.J. Friedrich (New York: Dover Publications, 1956).

—— *Hegel's Political Writings*, intro. Z.A. Pelcznski (Oxford: Clarendon Press, 1969).

—— *Lectures on the Philosophy of World History, Introduction* (Cambridge: Cambridge University Press, 1984).

—— *Introduction to the Lectures on the History of Philosophy* (Oxford: Clarendon Press, 1988).

—— *Elements of the Philosophy of Right*, ed., Allen W. Wood (Cambridge: Cambridge University Press, 1991).

—— *Hegel: Political Writings*, ed., L. Dickey and H.B. Nisbet (Cambridge: Cambridge University Press, 2007).

Hobsbawm, E.J., *The Age of Revolution 1789–1848* (New York: Mentor, 1964).

Hunt, R.N., *The Political Ideas of Marx and Engels*, vol.1. *Marxism and Totalitarian Democracy 1818–1850* (London: Palgrave Macmillan, 1978).

Kant, I., *An Answer to the Question: 'What is Enlightenment?'* (London: Penguin Books, 2009).

Keane, J., *Tom Paine: A Political Life* (London: Bloomsbury, 1995).

Kolakowski, L., *Main Currents of Marxism*, vol. 1, *The Founders* (Oxford: Oxford University Press, 1981).

Kuklick, B. ed., *Thomas Paine* (Aldershot: Ashgate, 2006).

Lock, F.P., *Burke's Reflections on the Revolution in France* (London: Allen and Unwin, 1985).

—— *Edmund Burke, vol.1: 1730–1784* (Oxford: Clarendon Press, 1999); *vol.2. 1784–1797* (Oxford: Oxford University Press, 2006).

Macpherson, C.B., *Burke* (Oxford: Oxford University Press, 1980).

Malia, M., *History's Locomotives: Revolutions and the Making of the Modern World* (New Haven, CT: Yale University Press, 2006).

Marx, K., *Capital, vol.1* [1867] (Oxford: Oxford University Press, 1995).
——— *Selected Writings*, ed., D. McLellan, 3rd edition (Oxford: Oxford University Press, 2001).
Marx, K. and F. Engels, *Karl Marx. Friedrich Engels. Collected Works*, 50 vols (London: Lawrence and Wishart, 1975–2005).
——— *Manifesto of the Communist Party* [1848] (Oxford: Oxford University Press, 1998).
McLellan, D., *Karl Marx: His Life and Thought*, 4th edition (London: Palgrave Macmillan, 2008).
Munck, T., *The Enlightenment: A Comparative Social History* (London: Arnold, 2000).

O'Brien, C.C., *The Great Melody: A Thematic Biography of Edmund Burke* (London: Sinclair-Stevenson, 1992). Abridged as *Edmund Burke* (Dublin: New Island Books, 1997).
Outram, D., *The Enlightenment* (Cambridge: Cambridge University Press, 2003).

Paine, T., *The Thomas Paine Reader*, ed., M. Foot and I. Kramnick (Harmondsworth: Penguin Books, 1987).
——— *Thomas Paine: Political Writings*, ed., B. Kuklick (Cambridge: Cambridge University Press, 1989).
——— *The Writings of Thomas Paine*, 4 vols, ed., M.D. Conway, New York [1894–6] (London: Routledge: Thoemmes, 1996).
Philp, M., *Paine* (Oxford: Oxford University Press, 1989).
Porter, R., *Enlightenment: Britain and the Creation of the Modern World* (London: Penguin Books, 2001).

Royle, E., *Revolutionary Britannia? Reflections on the threat of revolution in Britain, 1789–1848* (Manchester: Manchester University Press, 2000).
Rapport, M., *1848: Year of Revolution* (London: Abacus, 2009).
Ritter, J., *Hegel and the French Revolution: Essays on the Philosophy of Right* (Cambridge, MA: MIT Press, 1982).
Ryan, A., ed., *Utilitarianism and Other Essays: J.S. Mill and Jeremy Bentham* (London: Penguin Books, 1987).

Schofield, P., *Utility and Democracy: The Political Thought of Jeremy Bentham* (Oxford: Oxford University Press, 2006).
Stokes, E., *The English Utilitarians and India* (Delhi: Oxford University Press, 1959).

Taylor, C., *Hegel and Modern Society* (Cambridge: Cambridge University Press, 1980).
Tocqueville, A. de., *Democracy in America*, 2 vols (New York: Vintage Books, n.d).
———*The Old Régime and the French Revolution* (Garden City, NY: Doubleday Anchor, 1955).

———— 'The European Revolution' and Correspondence with Gobineau (Westport, CT: Greenwood Press, 1974).

———— Recollections (Garden City, NY: Anchor Books, 1975).

———— Alexis de Tocqueville: Journeys to England and Ireland, ed., J.P. Mayer (New Brunswick, NJ: Transaction Books, 1988).

Todorov, T., In Defence of the Enlightenment (London: Atlantic Books, 2009).

Toews, J.E., Hegelianism: The Path Towards Dialectical Humanism, 1805–1841 (Cambridge: Cambridge University Press, 1980).

Voltaire, F.M.A. de, Political Writings, ed., D. Williams (Cambridge: Cambridge University Press, 1994).

Waldron, J., 'Nonsense Upon Stilts': Bentham, Burke and Marx on the Rights of Man (London: Methuen, 1987).

Walker, A., Marx: His Theory and its Context (London: Longman, 1978).

Welch, C.B., De Tocqueville (Oxford: Oxford University Press, 2001).

Winik, J., The Great Upheaval: America and the Birth of the Modern World, 1778–1800 (New York: Harper Collins, 2007).

Index